Drugs and Security
in the
Caribbean

Ivelaw Lloyd Griffith

Drugs and Security in the Caribbean

Sovereignty Under Siege

Pennsylvania State University Press
University Park, Pennsylvania

Library of Congress Cataloging-in-Publication Data

Griffith, Ivelaw Lloyd.
    Drugs and security in the Caribbean : sovereignty under siege / Ivelaw
Lloyd Griffith.
        p.   cm.
    Includes bibliographical references and index.
    ISBN 0-271-01718-X (cloth : alk. paper)
    ISBN 0-271-01719-8 (pbk. : alk. paper)
    1. Narcotics, Control of—Caribbean Area.   2. Narcotics, Control
of—International cooperation.   3. National security—Caribbean
Area.   4. Sovereignty, Violation of—Caribbean Area.   I. Title.
HV5840.C315G75   1997
363.45′09729—dc21   96-40024
                                                                          CIP

It is the policy of The Pennsylvania State University Press to use acid-free
paper for the first printing of all clothbound books. Publications on uncoated
stock satisfy the minimum requirements of American National Standard for
Information Sciences—Permanence of Paper for Printed Library Materials,
ANSI Z39.48-1992.

This book is dedicated to
Richard L. Millett, Anthony P. Maingot, and Hal P. Klepak,
for friendship and in recognition of scholarship
that has influenced the contours of pedagogy
on the Caribbean and Central America,
and to
sufferers everywhere—those on drugs and those fighting drugs

Contents

List of Tables

List of Figures

Preface and Acknowledgments

This book is about drugs and security in the Caribbean. It does three things: examines the nature and scope of Caribbean drug operations; probes the security implications of those operations and the problems they precipitate; and assesses countermeasures adopted at the national, regional, and international levels to deal with the operations and resulting problems. The operations examined are drug production, consumption-abuse, trafficking, and money laundering. As to security, it is viewed in terms much broader than the traditional realist approach to the subject. By probing the various elements of the drugs-security matrix, this study is able to argue that the sovereignty of Caribbean countries is under siege. The siege is multidimensional, coming from domestic and international, and state and nonstate, sources, and it affects both formal-legal and positive sovereignty.

The analysis presented here, of the multifaceted nature of drug operations and of the scope and magnitude of their implications, should make this work valuable not only to Caribbean security specialists but to all serious Caribbeanists. Moreover, since the drug dilemma is an issue with numerous policy aspects, this study is policy relevant, although it is not intended to be policy prescriptive. Hence, it should be of interest to policy makers and analysts in government, nongovernmental organizations, and international governmental agencies, both within and outside the Caribbean. Further, this work should also be of value to scholars of international politics generally, since it provides a regional analysis of a transnational phenomenon that is of vital concern to the entire international community.

The two main subjects of this study—drugs and security—often present considerable challenges to researchers because of their sensitivity, and because of the dangers of "stepping on the wrong toes," as one interviewee put it. One of my challenges was that of securing data, even what should be public-domain data, from official sources. In one case, when I filed a Freedom of Information Act request with the U.S. Customs Service for data on seizures and fines, I was designated a "commercial requester" and stonewalled with a database search fee of $150.00 per minute. It took me fully one year working through alternative bureaucratic corridors to get some of the data desired. The challenge was undiminished when it came to nondocumentary data, for this involved securing access to, and exercising judgment on the credibility and reliability of, the source of the information.

Data for this work come from primary and secondary documentary sources, and from interviews. The latter took me to Antigua-Barbuda, Barbados, the Bahamas, Grenada, Guyana, Jamaica, Puerto Rico, and Trinidad and Tobago during 1994, 1995, and 1996 for discussions with officials from military, prison, police, customs, foreign-policy, and banking agencies as well as with people from nongovernmental organizations. Off-the-record interviews were also done in Miami, New York, and Washington with a variety of government and nongovernment officials from the Caribbean and the United States. Several days aboard U.S. Coast Guard cutter *Harriet Lane* during May 1996, as part of Operation Caribe Venture 3-96, also allowed me to gain some unique insights into narcotics countermeasures.

Beyond the data challenge was that of finding a theoretical framework to facilitate analysis of the myriad elements of the drugs-security matrix. To do this I designed a framework based on the notion of geonarcotics. That framework, which is outlined in the Introduction, is built on the interaction of four factors: drugs, geography, power, and politics. It recognizes that the geonarcotics milieu has both state and nonstate actors and that they interact in cooperative and conflictful ways. The interactions can be seen at all levels of analysis: individual, group, national, and systemic. The framework also posits that since the drug phenomenon is transnational and most states involved lack the assets to deal with it individually, the collective approach to countermeasures is necessary.

Little serious scholarship has been devoted to exploring conceptual linkages between drugs and security and to developing approaches suited to examining the domestic and international aspects of the drugs-security relationship. One reason for this has been the approach to the subject of security. Elite perceptions have also been a factor. Drugs were once not viewed by the political and bureaucratic elites of many countries as constituting a threat to security. Moreover, the preoccupation with Cold War security matters was such that for many scholars and policy makers the issue of drugs either was a low-agenda security matter or was entirely absent from the security agenda.

The circumstances in all three areas have changed over the last decade, dramatically in some cases. The reconceptualization of the term "security" is now largely a reality in both the scholarly and policy arenas. Drug operations have developed to such a magnitude that in many regions of the world the elites now affirm that drugs constitute a high-agenda national security item. In addition, the end of the Cold War has precipitated the displacement of once high-agenda items such as the global arms race, the Strategic Defense Initiative, and nuclear holocaust by such issues as AIDS, environmental concerns, and drug trafficking.

Completion of this study reflects a fairly successful engagement of the challenges noted above. But it also testifies to the existence of shared concerns about the issues held by several individuals and institutions, such that I was able to benefit from their assistance in many ways. I cannot name all the people who aided this work in some way, but I would like to acknowledge the assistance of many of those who helped with data, data sources, or otherwise facilitated the writing of this book. The list includes Brigadier David Granger of the Guyana Defense Force (ret.); Lancelot Selman, Director of the Strategic Services Agency, Trinidad and Tobago; Dave Alexander of the Ministry of Education, Grenada; Beverly Eighmy of the U.S. Department of State; Ricardo Mario Rodríguez of the Venezuelan Mission to the OAS; Captain Randy Beardsworth and Lieutenant Commander J. Chris Sinnett of the U.S. Coast Guard; Glen Andrade, Director of Public Prosecutions, Jamaica; Dion Phillips of the University of the Virgin Islands; and Michel Amiot, former Caribbean Director of the United Nations International Drug Control Program (UNDCP), now the European Union's Technical Advisor on drugs in the Caribbean.

Thanks also go to Muki Daniel of the UNDCP; Compton Hendy of the Barbados Agricultural Management Corporation; Godfrey

Springer of the Ministry of Agriculture, the Bahamas; Lionel Remy of the Trinidad and Tobago Petroleum Company; Beverly Steele of the University of the West Indies Center in Grenada; Wesley Kirton, Organization of American States (OAS) Director in the Bahamas; Jennifer Jackson of the University of the Virgin Islands; Colonel Allan Douglas and Commander Chris Annamunthodo of the Jamaican Defense Force; and Desmond Thomas of Trent University, Canada. I thank Sandy Thatcher for the invitation to have Penn State Press consider publishing the manuscript and for guiding it through the publication labyrinth. Thanks also go to the two manuscript reviewers for several helpful suggestions. Mention must also be made of four graduate students who worked with me during the four years of this study's gestation: Ainsworth James of John Jay College of Criminal Justice, who was helpful even after I left New York, and Patricia G. Lopez-Calleja, Dina Evans, and Ricky Perez of Florida International University.

This book is the final product of "Sovereignty Under Siege"—a project on drugs and security in the Caribbean. Gratitude must be expressed to the institutions that funded the project through grants: the John D. and Catherine T. MacArthur Foundation and the North-South Center of the University of Miami. I am also thankful for encouragement and assistance by friends and colleagues, notably Doris Dingle, Eduardo Gamarra, Joe Jackson, Donna Kirchheimer, Dario Moreno, Dorinda Mosby, Jorge Rodriguez Beruff, Mark Rosenberg, Cheryl Rubenberg, John Stack Jr., Mary Volcansek, Chris Warren, and W. Marvin Will. Special thanks also go to my wife, Francille, for preparing many of the tables. I also appreciate the support and tolerance by her, Shakina, and Ivelaw Jr., especially during stints away from the family as the work was undertaken.

I prefer not to end the Preface with the academically correct declaration that "all errors and shortcomings of this work are mine." Doing this study has led me to appreciate the depth of a statement made a quarter century ago by the late, noted Caribbean historian Walter Rodney: "Responsibility in matters of these sorts is always collective."

Ivelaw Lloyd Griffith
Miami, Florida
February 1997

Abbreviations

ABDF	Antigua-Barbuda Defense Force
ACCP	Association of Caribbean Commissioners of Police
ACS	Association of Caribbean States
CBRN	Caribbean Basin Radar Network
CFATF	Caribbean Financial Action Task Force
CCC	Caribbean Conference of Churches
CCLEC	Caribbean Customs Law Enforcement Council
CIA	Central Intelligence Agency
CICAD	Comisión Interamericana para el Control del Abuso de Drogas (Inter-American Drug Abuse Control Commission)
CLEIC	Caribbean Law Enforcement and Intelligence Committee
DEA	(U.S.) Drug Enforcement Administration
DOM	Départment d'Outre Mer
EU	European Union
FATF	Financial Action Task Force
EPIC	El Paso Intelligence Center
GAC	Guyana Airways Corporation
GANTSEC	(U.S. Coast Guard) Greater Antilles Section
GDF	Guyana Defense Force
HIDTA	high-intensity drug-trafficking area
HONLEA	Heads of National Law Enforcement Agencies
IADB	Inter-American Development Bank
IBC	international business corporation
IGO	international governmental organization
IMF	International Monetary Fund
INCB	International Narcotics Control Board

INCSR	*International Narcotics Control Strategy Report*
INGO	international nongovernmental organization
INL	(U.S.) Bureau for International Narcotics Control and Law Enforcement
INTERPOL	International Criminal Police Organization
JCF	Jamaica Constabulary Force
JDF	Jamaica Defense Force
JICC	Joint Information Coordination Center
MLAT	mutual-legal-assistance treaty
MNC	multinational corporation
MSC	Maritime Security Council
NACD	National Advisory Council on Drugs (Guyana)
NaCoDAP	National Council for Drug Abuse Prevention (Netherlands Antilles)
NDC	National Drug Council (Bahamas)
NCDA	National Council on Drug Abuse (Jamaica)
NGO	nongovernmental organization
OAS	Organization of American States
OECS	Organization of Eastern Caribbean States
OPBAT	Operation Bahamas and the Turks and Caicos
PROPUID	Programa Para la Prevención de Uso Indébido de Drogas (Program for the Prevention of the Illegal Use of Drugs)
PSC	(Jamaica) Port Security Corps
RABPF	Royal Antigua and Barbuda Police Force
ROTHR	Relocatable Over-the-Horizon Radar
RBDF	Royal Bahamas Defense Force
RBPF	Royal Bahamas Police Force
RGPF	Royal Grenada Police Force
ROCISS	Regional Organized Crime Intelligence Sharing System
RSKNPF	Royal St. Kitts–Nevis Police Force
RSLPF	Royal St. Lucia Police Force
RSVGPF	Royal St. Vincent and the Grenadines Police Force
RSC	regional security coordinator
RSS	Regional Security System
SEABAT	Sea Based Apprehension Tactics
SSU	Special Service Unit
TACADA	(Trinidad and Tobago) Technical Advisory Council on Alcohol and Drug Abuse

TCI	Turks and Caicos Islands
TTDF	Trinidad and Tobago Defense Force
TTPS	Trinidad and Tobago Police Service
UNDCP	United Nations International Drug Control Program
USCG	United States Coast Guard
UWI	University of the West Indies

Introduction:
The Siege in Conceptual Context

> Nothing poses greater threats to civil society in [Caribbean] countries than the drug problem, and nothing exemplifies the powerlessness of regional governments more. That is the magnitude of the damage that drug abuse and trafficking hold for our Community. It is a many-layered danger. At base is the human destruction implicit in drug addiction; but, implicit also, is the corruption of individuals and systems by the sheer enormity of the inducements of the illegal drug trade in relatively poor societies. On top of all this lie the implications for governance itself—at the hands of both external agencies engaged in international interdiction, and the drug barons themselves—the "dons" of the modern Caribbean—who threaten governance from within.
>
> —West Indian Commission

Drugs present a clear and present danger to the Caribbean. The epigraph above, which comes from *Time for Action,* the 1992 report by the West Indian Commission, captures the essence of the scope and gravity of this danger.[1] In many respects, the situation has worsened since 1992. Consider the following:

- Cocaine seizures in 1993 for just five Caribbean countries—the Bahamas, Belize, the Dominican Republic, Haiti, and Jamaica—

1. The fifteen-member commission was formed by Commonwealth Caribbean leaders in 1989 to help chart a course for the Commonwealth Caribbean into the twenty-first century. It was headed by former Guyana foreign minister and Commonwealth of Nations secretary-general Sir Shridat Ramphal, at the time chancellor of both the University of the West Indies and the University of Guyana.

totaled about 3,300 kilos. The 1995 seizures for those same nations amounted to almost 6,000 kilos—a 45 percent increase.

- In its Caribbean assessment for 1994, the U.S. State Department called St. Vincent and the Grenadines the Caribbean's second largest marijuana producer after Jamaica. Curiously, St. Vincent and the Grenadines is a thirtieth the size of Jamaica.
- Operation Dinero, an international money-laundering sting operation conducted out of Anguilla from January 1992 to December 1994, led to the seizure of nine tons of cocaine and U.S.$90 million worth of assets, including expensive paintings, one of which was Pablo Picasso's *Head of a Beggar*.

One also gets a sense of the magnitude of the drug problems when noting the following:

- The Port of Spain Prison in Trinidad and Tobago, built to hold 250 prisoners, had a daily average of 1,052 inmates in 1995 (compared to 916 in 1992), there mostly for drug-related crime.
- In 1995 Puerto Rico had the highest per capita murder rate in the United States, with 64 percent of the 680 murders committed related to drugs. Murders in 1996 totaled 868, and 80 percent of them were drug-related.
- On June 4, 1993, there was a strange shower over the Demerara River in Guyana. It "rained" 364 kilos of cocaine and U.S.$24,000. The shower came from a plane making an airdrop, part of a Colombia–Venezuela–Guyana–United States drug network.
- Between 1993 and 1996, more than 5,000 Jamaican deportees were returned to the island, most of them for drug-related crimes committed in the United States, Canada, and the United Kingdom. In 1993 the number was 923; in 1996 it was 1,158.
- A 1996 survey done by the General Directorate of Prisons in the Dominican Republic revealed that people convicted of drug crimes constituted the single largest group of prisoners in the country—30 percent of the 10,359 prisoners at the time of the study.

What is often called "the drug problem" is actually a multidimensional dilemma with four problem areas: production, consumption and abuse, trafficking, and money laundering. As later chapters show, these and their security consequences are not present uniformly in the Caribbean, or in any region for that matter. But they are sufficiently widespread in the Caribbean as to constitute a regional dilemma, and warrant analysis as such. This narcotics dilemma is also multifaceted: it has internal and external ramifications, involves state and nonstate actors, and affects all areas of social existence.

Although the literature on the Latin American drugs-security connection is large, the Caribbean connection has received relatively little scholarly attention. There are several reasons for this. First, in terms of scope and gravity, drug problems have been greater in Latin America. In addition, because Latin America has generated major national security/national interest concerns for the United States, media and academic attention has been focused there predominantly. Moreover, for some time within the Caribbean, drugs were problematic for only a few countries, notably the Bahamas and Jamaica. It has only been since the mid-1980s that drugs have become critical for all Caribbean countries.

Yet, while the situation was becoming progressively worse in most parts of the Caribbean after the mid-1980s, for many Caribbean leaders it was politically incorrect to acknowledge that their nations were more than just slightly implicated in the drugs business. They preferred to view the situation essentially as a South American problem or a U.S. problem. It has taken the cumulative effect of increased drug trafficking, production, abuse, and money laundering, dramatic drug-related crime and corruption, several drugs-driven or -related political crises, and disputes over narcotics countermeasures for *all* leaders to acknowledge that the drugs phenomenon is both critical to each of their individual nations and regionwide in scope and impact. For instance, at the end of the special December 16, 1996, drug summit, held primarily to discuss the maritime antidrug dispute involving the United States and Barbados and Jamaica, which is discussed further below, CARICOM leaders issued a statement indicating: "Heads of Government recognized that narco-trafficking and its associated evils of money laundering, gun smuggling, corruption of public officials, criminality, and drug abuse constitute the major security threat to the [entire] Caribbean today. They noted the vulnerability of the Region to the illicit drug trade through the destruction caused to civil societies and the possible use of the Region's territory for illegal narcotics transshipment to North America and Europe."[2]

Security Dimensions of Drugs

The drug dilemma is, thus, now a pernicious "equal opportunity" phenomenon in the Caribbean. But it is merely the regional manifestation of a truly international phenomenon. Presentation of this study's conceptual parameters here, therefore, demands that the discussion be framed in broad terms for appreciation of the global context and dimensions of the issue. The first task in this respect is to explain the meaning of the term "security."

Meaning of "Security"

"Security" has long been a concept with varying definitions and usages, mostly based on traditional realism. The realist approach to world politics focuses on the state as the unit of analysis and stresses the competitive character of relations among states, and the military and, to a lesser extent, the political aspects of security. It also views states as national actors rationally pursuing their interests, focuses mostly on external threats, and sees military and economic power capabilities as the critical ones. For the realist, security is "high politics."[3]

With the end of the Cold War there has been an increasing challenge to the traditional realist interpretation of world politics generally and of security in particular. This is due mainly to changes in world politics and in the nature, source, and severity of threats to actors in the international system. As part of this change, in many places the security agenda has been expanded to accommodate "new" threats and apprehensions. Scholars disagree about the na-

2. *Communiqué, Fifth Special Meeting of the Conference of Heads of Government of the Caribbean Community,* Barbados, December 16, 1996, 2.
3. For various definitions and usages of "security," see Buzan, *People, States, and Fear;* Romm, *Defining National Security;* and Fischer, *Nonmilitary Aspects of Security.*

ture of that broadened security agenda, but many of them place AIDS, the drug trade, destruction of the ozone layer, and global warming on the agenda. James Rosenau calls these interdependence issues: issues that are "distinguished from conventional issues by the fact that they span national boundaries and thus cannot be addressed, much less resolved, through actions undertaken only at the national or local level."[4]

The drug dilemma, then, is an interdependence issue, with multidimensional aspects. Studying its security implications therefore requires an approach to security that is itself multidimensional. In this context, for this study, "security" is defined as protection and preservation of a people's freedom from external military attack and coercion, from internal subversion, and from the erosion of cherished political, economic, and social values. Security is always relative—to problems, perceptions of the political and bureaucratic elites, capabilities, and often geopolitics, among other things. Hence, all states exist with a certain margin of insecurity. Caribbean states, and other small states elsewhere, however, have to accept an existence with a relatively wide margin of insecurity compared to, say, big powers, because of size, capability, geopolitics, and other factors. Moreover, when dealing with a region, it is important to view security as relational, since it is difficult to appreciate the national security dilemma(s) of any one state in a region without understanding security interdependence within the region as a whole.

This conception of security is multidimensional, with military, political, economic, and environmental aspects. Military security is concerned with violence and the instruments used to prosecute it, whether for offense or defense, and whether by states or subnational groups. Political security pertains to the stability of nations and the ideological and organizational elements that facilitate their maintenance. Economic security concerns the availability and access to economic capabilities, the economic equilibrium of states, and the economic welfare of individuals and groups within them. Environmental security pertains to the maintenance of the ecosystem, or at least to prevention of its deterioration. Security is not merely military hardware, although it may include this; it is not just

4. Rosenau, *Turbulence in World Politics*, 106.

military force, although it involves this; and it is not purely traditional military activity, although it encompasses military activity.[5] What, therefore, are some of the security implications of drugs?

Security Implications of Drugs

Military Security Concerns: Traffickers in some countries have often owned larger and more sophisticated military resources than the police or the military. In some parts of Latin America, they have relied on sophisticated communications systems, including digital encryption devices, to maintain secure communications within their organizations and to monitor law-enforcement countermeasures. According to one retired Colombian army general, traffickers track the movement of Colombian armed forces, aircraft, and ships better than do their respective commanders, and know more surely where they are and where they are going. During 1994 Colombian authorities discovered an advanced IBM computer used by traffickers in Cali to analyze calls to and from the police, counternarcotics agents, and the U.S. embassy in Bogotá. Moreover, not only are submersibles now used to make maritime deliveries, but by connecting to global-positioning-system satellites, pilots are able to locate drop sites accurately.[6]

In some countries efforts to deal with drug operations, especially production and trafficking, have taxed police forces beyond capacity, forcing some governments to commit and others to contemplate using military forces in antidrug measures. As many leaders around the world are learning, such measures are fraught with problems, including jurisdictional conflicts between military and police forces, resource (re)allocation, potential corruption (and in some cases increased corruption) of military personnel, training and technology adaptations, and the potential for (re)militarization. Some of these issues threaten fragile democracies under (re)con-

---

5. This definition was originally developed in Griffith, *The Quest for Security in the Caribbean,* chap. 1, and idem, "From Cold War Geopolitics."

6. Lee, *The White Labyrinth,* 104, and Sheridan and Marquis, "Cartel's High-Tech Tools."

struction in parts of Latin America and central and southwest Asia.[7]

In places where the military have never exercised direct political power, as in the Anglophone Caribbean, some leaders have worried that successful and prolonged use of the military in antidrug campaigns risks catapulting them into the countries' political power centers, with the potential for the development of a guardian mentality. If the military are seen—or worse, if they see themselves—as indispensable in this critical area, there is little to prevent them from intruding into the political arena, whether subtly or forcibly. Such a development in the Caribbean would jeopardize political stability and likely revive the militarization that a few countries experienced in the 1970s and 1980s, this time more pervasively.

Demands of drug operations have also led to increased arms trafficking. These operations often are not only truly international, but sometimes they implicate countries that are vulnerable by virtue of small size, openness, relative poverty, and corruptibility, as in the case of Antigua-Barbuda, which is discussed fully in Chapter 5. Also, some countries have the misfortune of not only one or more major drug operations but also insurgencies or guerrilla operations of one kind or another. Peru, Colombia, Myanmar (Burma), and Afghanistan are cases in point. Collaboration between drug operators and guerrillas has given rise to narcoterrorism. There is evidence that in parts of Latin America and southwest and central Asia guerrillas finance their activities by taxing the drug trade and by protecting traffickers' plantations, laboratories, and airstrips against raids by government forces. Moreover, drug traffickers in Latin America and Southeast Asia are said to finance guerrilla campaigns that serve their interests.

Some insurgents run their own drug outfits, as in Myanmar, where the Shan United Army is said to remain a powerful drug-trafficking and heroin-refining organization.[8] The drugs-arms-conflict connection is also present in the Balkans. It has been suggested that many traffickers in the former Yugoslavia, in providing

7. For more on these matters, see Lee, *The White Labyrinth*, chaps. 4 and 5; Bagley, "Myths of Militarization"; Schmitt, "Colorado Bunker"; and Lee and MacDonald, "Drugs in the East."

8. See U.S. Department of State, *International Narcotics Control Strategy Report* [hereafter *INCSR*] (1993), 258; and *INCSR* (1994), 256.

finance and equipment for the civil war in the region, are motivated by more than just profit. Evidence also indicates that Albanians have purchased weapons in Berne and Basel with the proceeds from the sale of heroin in Switzerland. Some of the weapons go to two insurgent groups: Kosovo's Front of Resistance and National Liberation of Albania.[9]

Political Security Concerns: Irrespective of the strength of the bonds between narcos and guerrillas, drug operations generate a significant amount of crime and violence around the world. The crimes include, among others, racketeering, kidnapping, bribery, tax evasion, theft, banking-law violations, import/export infractions, murder, burglary, illegal money transfer, and extortion. Because of the nature and dimensions of drug operations, these crimes are not all committed on an individual, random basis; they are mostly organized, well planned, and executed by national groups and international networks, often bound by national, ethnic, or racial ties. Examples are the Medellín, Tijuana, and Cali cartels, the Asian gangs, La Cosa Nostra, and the Jamaican posses.[10]

Drug operations also have generated increased violence, both political and nonpolitical. The violence has been unprecedented in the United States, Italy, and Latin America, especially in Colombia, Bolivia, Peru, and Mexico. Over the last decade thousands of ordinary citizens, businessmen, journalists, and political elites have been killed or maimed in drug-related violence. Violence undermines and wrecks the institutional basis for the maintenance of good government and public safety in many places in Latin America, Asia, Africa, and Europe. It seems to be systemic in some places, notably Italy, Jamaica, and Colombia.

Crime and violence have forward and backward, and vertical and horizontal, linkages with a major threat to political stability: corruption. Drug operators bribe the police and soldiers not to raid

9. Lee and MacDonald, "Drugs in the East," 100–101. For an excellent analysis of the financing of guerrilla operations worldwide, see Taylor, "The Insurgent Economy," esp. 35–44. For a February 1997 revelation about Colombia, see Johnson, "Scary Liaison in Colombia."

10. See Mills, *The Underground Empire;* Lyman, *Gangland;* Sterling, *Octopus;* idem, *Thieves' World;* Brana-Shute, "Jamaican Posse Gangs"; U.S. Senate, Committee on Foreign Relations, *Recent Developments in Transnational Crime Affecting U.S. Law Enforcement and Foreign Policy.*

laboratories or make arrests, and to drop investigations. They pay state prosecutors not to prosecute, judges not to convict, and prison officials to release colleagues. They bribe government ministers, journalists, political parties, banking officials, pilots and other airline workers, shippers, and others. It is not difficult to appreciate how drug operators can corrupt top officials in industry, business, and government: they have the money to do it and the means and will to make refusal an unpalatable alternative. In the latter regard, judges in some places are offered a choice between death if they convict or a reward if they dismiss charges.

In one recent Latin American case, investigations in Colombia during 1994 uncovered evidence of drug payoffs to a former president of the national congress, a former comptroller general, a then recently elected legislator, twelve retired army officers, over a hundred and fifty Cali police, almost all the Cali airport police, employees of El Valle telephone system, the Cali regional prosecutor, six of the twenty-two Cali city councillors, and the mayors of four Colombian cities, including Medellín. That same year, a scandal with greater political implications erupted when a taped telephone conversation leaked to the press showed drug kingpin Gilberto Rodríguez Orejuela and his brother Miguel discussing a U.S.$6 million contribution to President Ernesto Samper's election campaign. (The Rodríguez brothers were among six top Cali cartel leaders jailed in 1995 and 1996.) There was considerable political fallout—both within Colombia and between Colombia and the United States—as the matter snowballed in 1995 and 1996.[11]

Drug corruption is now a major threat to democratic (re)construction in many parts of the world, including Latin America, Africa, and central Asia.[12] Societies where corruption has long been part of the social-political culture are even more vulnerable. Corruption of police and military officials has distinct military security implications: it compromises agents of national security, such that (a) their capacity for effective action is undermined or destroyed and (b) indi-

11. See Lee, "Global Reach," 208–9; Sheridan, "The Samper Scandal"; and Chernick, "Colombia's Fault Lines."
12. See United Nations, *Report of the International Narcotics Control Board for 1992* [hereafter *UN Narcotics Report*]; Flynn, *The Transnational Drug Challenge*; Lee and MacDonald, "Drugs in the East"; Lorch, "In Zambia, a Legacy of Graft"; and Tanner, "Helped by New Freedoms, Russian Drug Trade Is Booming."

viduals and groups in the society become inclined to resort to vigilante tactics because of the perception or reality of a diminished official security capacity. Moreover, drug corruption not only undermines the credibility of governments, it also impairs the ability of officials to define and defend the "national interest" adequately. Hence, drug corruption subverts political security.

Economic Security Concerns: Drug abuse contributes to loss of productivity due to addiction, rehabilitation, and incarceration. It also increases health-care costs. For example, research done at the University of Southern California estimated the economic cost of drug abuse to the United States at $76 billion in 1991, a $32 billion increase over the 1985 estimate of $44 billion. That growth was attributed to four main factors: emergency room and other medical expenditures, the cost of treating an increased incidence of drug-related HIV/AIDS cases, increased criminal activity, and drug-related productivity loss.[13]

Drug operations also lead to distorted resource allocation by forcing governments to devote large proportions of their scarce resources to antidrug operations and to combating crime and violence. In addition, studies indicate that coca and cocaine not only cause inflation by introducing a huge monetary mass into the economy, they also raise the price of goods and services in coca-growing parts of the countries concerned. Drug operations may not *cause* distortions in social-economic growth, but they certainly *contribute to* them. Rensselaer Lee gives one Peruvian example: Tocache, a coca boomtown in Upper Huallaga Valley, with no paved streets, drinking water, or sewerage system for residents, but six banks, six telex machines, several stereo dealerships, and one of Peru's largest Nissan outlets.[14] Moreover, as Edwin Corr, former U.S. ambassador to El Salvador, has observed, "[T]he drug economy pays no [direct] taxes and increases the need for [generally] unpopular budget expenditures for the police and the military."[15]

---

13. U.S. Office of the President, *National Drug Control Strategy* (1994), 10. See also idem, *National Drug Control Strategy: 1996*, 12, and Godson and Olson, *International Organized Crime*, 35–44, for other extensive estimates of the economic costs of drugs.

14. Lee, *The White Labyrinth*, 43.

15. Corr, "Rubik's Cube, Manwaring's Paradigm," 186.

Drug operations, especially production and trafficking, have a strong impact on some economies, generating a high percentage of their gross domestic product (GDP). In Jamaica, for example, marijuana operations are said to have contributed between U.S.$1 billion and $2 billion to the island's foreign-exchange earnings during the 1980s, more than all other exports combined. Bolivia's 1986 coca production, estimated at $600 million, was nearly twice the $345 million from natural gas sales and amounted to 15 percent of Bolivia's GDP.[16] Indications are that in Russia annual sales of drugs amount to some $800 million, and criminal-justice officials there contend that much of the start-up capital for small legitimate businesses, such as stores, fruit stands, and restaurants, comes from those takings.[17]

Part of the economic dilemma is that drug operations do have positive-sum aspects. Lee shows that the Latin American cocaine business has beneficial economic multiplier effects, since local businessmen have expanded production to meet drug-industry demands for farm equipment, simple chemicals, filters, and other items, and many banks and legal and accounting firms specialize in services for the drug industry. Further, traffickers' demands for luxury housing boost the construction industry, generating work for contractors and local producers of materials such as cement, bricks, and glass. In addressing the issue, former Bolivian finance minister Flavio Machicado estimated that coca dollars have allowed for the creation of some 300,000 jobs with no direct connection to drugs.[18] Many analysts agree that drug operations provide an economic safety valve by providing jobs and generating income and foreign exchange when the formal economy falters.

Environmental Security Concerns: Most of the environmental concerns pertaining to drugs relate to cocaine and heroin production. Cocaine production, for example, gives rise to deforestation, pollution, species destruction, and soil erosion, and presents a danger to human health. A look at operations in Peru, the world's greatest coca producer, provides an appreciation of some of the problems

16. Griffith, "Some Security Implications," 28, and Kawell, "The Addict Economies," 36.
17. Lee, "Global Reach," 208.
18. Kawell, "The Addict Economies," 37.

involved. Experts at Peru's National Agrarian University estimated that in 1986 the 160,000 hectares of coca cultivated produced 6,000 metric tons of basic paste, requiring 57 million liters of kerosene, 32 million liters of sulfuric acid, 16,000 metric tons of toilet paper, 6.4 million liters of acetone, and 6.4 million liters of toluene.[19]

The considerable waste involved is dumped and flushed into rivers and streams, with adverse consequences. Whereas kerosene, for instance, is said to have only a moderately toxic effect on humans, the effects of its ingestion and inhalation by fish and amphibians are chronic, and its long-term presence in water reduces dissolved-oxygen levels. Sulfuric acid is highly corrosive and toxic and dissolves easily in water. The fish, amphibians, and flora in the rivers running through drug-producing areas are unable to escape acute or chronic sulfuric acid poisoning. Toxins like acetone and toluene, which are highly soluble in water and extremely toxic, are particularly harmful to fish and amphibians if they are ingested, inhaled, or absorbed cutaneously.[20]

There are indications that several species of fish, amphibians, aquatic reptiles, and crustaceans have already disappeared completely from rivers and streams in areas where maceration pits are located. These include the caracha, the bagres, and the carachama fish. It must be noted, however, that the pollution has consequences not only for plants and animals but also for humans, since the lack of adequate supplies of potable water in some places forces residents to use the contaminated water, thereby contracting various diseases. According to one source, over 150 streams and small to medium-sized rivers have been polluted in Peru alone.[21]

Deforestation also results from cocaine production. Marc Dourojeanni asserts that since the coca boom began in the early 1970s, coca production has directly caused the deforestation of 700,000 hectares of jungle in the Amazon region. "One can go on to say that coca is the direct cause of 10 percent of the total deforestation in the Peruvian Amazon Region this century."[22] A look at Southeast

19. U.S. Senate, Committee on Governmental Affairs, *Cocaine Production, Eradication, and the Environment*, 143.

20. Ibid., 144–46.

21. Ibid., 148.

22. Ibid., 85.

Asia reveals that because of shifting opium poppy cultivation, forests in Thailand are being destroyed at the estimated rate of
280,000–300,000 hectares per year. The total area affected
amounts to some 2.8 million hectares—70 percent of the country's
northern forest areas.[23] Deforestation has several consequences:
the loss of soils through erosion, extinction of genetic resources,
alteration of hydrological balance, reduction of hydroelectric potential, increased difficulties in river navigation, shortage of wood and
lumber, and reduction in wildlife, among other things.[24]

Framework for Analysis

Considering the discussion above, the nexus between drugs and
security lies in the several consequences and implications of drug
operations for the protection and development of individuals and of
state and nonstate entities. The growing significance of drugs as
a security matter is evidenced in the development of geonarcotics:
relations of conflict and cooperation among national and international actors that are driven by drugs. Geonarcotics itself is built on
the interrelationship of four factors: drugs, geography, power, and
politics.

Four Factors

Geography is a factor because of the global dispersion of drug operations and because certain geographical features facilitate some operations. For example, the terrain in parts of South America and
central and south Asia enhance the prospects and potential for cocaine and heroin production. Moreover, the Bahamian archipelago
and other topographical features of Latin America and the Caribbean, and of central, west, and Southeast Asia, facilitate trafficking.
One official in Italy's Central Directorate for Anti-Drug Services has

23. La-Ongsri, "Drug Abuse Control and the Environment in Northern Thailand,"
33.
24. For a useful examination of the environmental impact of heroin and marijuana production outside Latin America, see Armstead, "Illicit Narcotics Cultivation
and Processing."

noted: "The geographical location of Italy, its 8,000 kilometers of coastline and the operation of tough criminal organizations such as the Mafia have all contributed to the country becoming one of the focal points of the world's drug trade."[25]

Power in the geonarcotics milieu involves the ability of an individual or a group to secure compliant action. This power is both state and nonstate in source and origin. In some cases, nonstate sources—for example, drug barons and cartels—can exercise relatively more power than state entities. And politics, the fourth factor, is, in this context, another name for control of resource allocation, in the Lasswellian sense of the ability of power brokers to determine who gets what, how, and when. Since power in this milieu is not only state power, resource allocation is not exclusively a function of state power brokers. Moreover, politics becomes perverted, and all the more so in places where it already was perverted.

Figure 1 shows the components of the geonarcotics framework, identifying the main problems, the security dimensions, some of the threat areas involved, some of the countermeasures used, and the actors involved. The framework pays attention to both internal and external security because the distinction between the two is often blurred. Since security does not revolve only around a military axis, attention is paid to both military and nonmilitary countermeasures.

There is no uniformity in drug operations or in their impact on individuals and societies around the world. Some countries are affected by several or all operations; others by just one or a few. However, because the narcotics phenomenon is multidimensional, a meaningful understanding of any single drug operation or security implication requires an appreciation of the complete narcotics package. A comprehensive approach offers the best possible prospect for meaningful understanding of both the phenomenon as a whole and the dynamics of its individual parts. This is not to suggest that comprehensive analysis is either absolutely necessary or the only credible approach.

The geonarcotics milieu involves a variety of actors, state as well as nonstate, as Figure 1 shows. The variety is understandable given the multidimensional and transnational character of the drug phenomenon. Actors vary in the way they are affected by the various

25. Marotta, "Drug Abuse and Illicit Trafficking in Italy," 15.

Fig. 1 Geonarcotics: A Framework

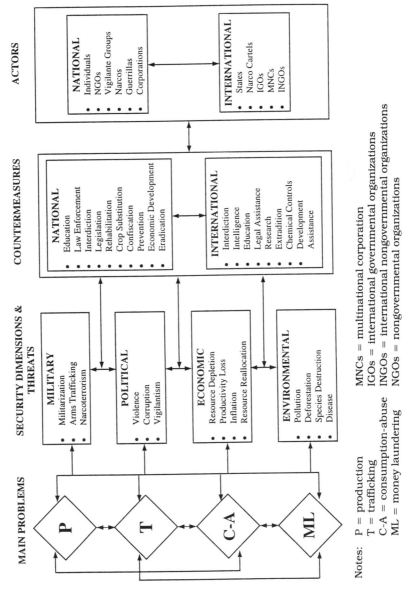

Notes: P = production   MNCs = multinational corporation
        T = trafficking   IGOs = international governmental organizations
        C-A = consumption-abuse   INGOs = international nongovernmental organizations
        ML = money laundering   NGOs = nongovernmental organizations

problem areas, and their countermeasures also vary. Some initiate and maintain counternarcotics regimes; others strive to circumvent or eliminate them. Actors are proactive as well as reactive, and both proactive and reactive behaviors are possible from the same actor. For example, cartels are proactive in relation to production and trafficking, but reactive when states, INGOs, and NGOs introduce countermeasures.

Drug operations generate two basic kinds of interactions—conflict and cooperation—among different actors and at different levels. Relationships are bilateral and multilateral, symmetrical and asymmetrical, and involve both vertical and horizontal flows. Not all interactions involve force or military capabilities. Some involve nonmilitary pressures, such as the application of economic and political sanctions by the United States against countries that, in its estimation, are not proactive enough in fighting drugs. The range of sanctions includes loss of tariff benefits, a 50 percent withholding of bilateral aid, suspension of air services, cancellation of visas, and the denial of support for aid requested from multilateral funding institutions.[26] In 1996, several of these sanctions were imposed against Afghanistan, Colombia, Iran, Myanmar, Nigeria, and Syria following their "decertification"—a declaration that they had failed to adopt effective narcotics countermeasures or to show good-faith efforts in that regard.

Conflict interactions include protests, complaints, warnings, and threats. They can also include a range of physical actions, such as seizures, blockades, and armed attacks.[27] Many of these conflict types exist in the geonarcotics milieu. Figure 2 shows some of the actor relationships involved. Some actors are engaged simultaneously in both cooperation and conflict. An example of this is the United States–Colombia relationship over the past decade, but especially after the inauguration in 1994 of President Ernesto Samper. Both conflict and cooperation were heightened after the March 1996 decertification. U.S. action was declared by Colombia as unacceptable interference in its internal affairs, but Colombia

26. See U.S. Senate, Committee on Foreign Relations, *International Narcotics Control and Foreign Affairs Certification*, and Perl, "International Narcopolicy and the Role of the U.S. Congress," 91–95.

27. See McClelland and Hoggard, "Conflict Patterns in the Interactions Among Nations," 711–24.

Fig. 2 Conflict Interactions in the Geonarcotics Milieu

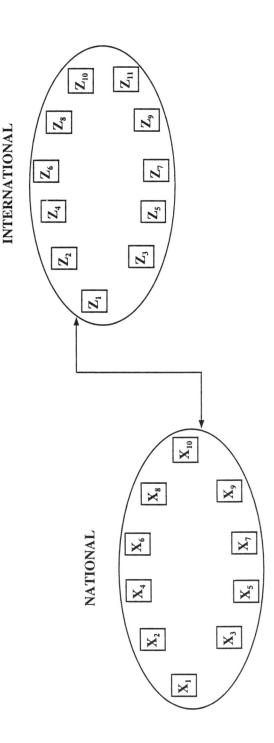

X_1 = State vs Narcos
X_2 = Narcos vs Narcos
X_3 = Narcos vs Guerrillas
X_4 = Vigilantes vs Narcos
X_5 = Vigilantes vs State

X_6 = NGOs vs Narcos
X_7 = NGOs vs State
X_8 = States vs Corporations
X_9 = Narcos vs Corporations
X_{10} = Interactions Involving
       Individuals

Z_1 = Consuming States vs
     Supplying States
Z_2 = Narcos vs Supplying States
Z_3 = Narcos vs Consuming States
Z_4 = IGOs vs Supplying States
Z_5 = IGOs vs Consuming States

Z_6 = INGOs vs Supplying States
Z_7 = INGOs vs Consuming States
Z_8 = States vs MNCs
Z_9 = IGOs vs MNCs
Z_{10} = INGOs vs MNCs
Z_{11} = Narcos vs MNCs

offered to review antidrug plans with the United States, with a view to improving cooperation.[28] Indeed, in February 1997, the United States and Colombia signed a maritime cooperation treaty aimed at boosting drug interdiction.

As Figure 2 indicates, conflict interactions exist both nationally and internationally. Figure 2, however, does not show another reality: conflict interactions can involve more than two actors at any one time. One example of this would be conflict relations of one state with others, as well as with guerrillas and narcos, as in Mexico, Myanmar, Peru, and elsewhere. Regarding nonstate conflict, Rosenau rightly states that NGOs and INGOs have emerged as prime movers on several interdependence issues, mobilizing constituencies, framing agendas, and monitoring compliance like a world police force. Since the NGO community is not united around a common core of beliefs, these issues constitute an arena for cooperation as well as conflict, as different groups compete for scarce resources and access to states.[29]

While turf and market interests often lead to conflict among cartels and other drug actors, these actors also engage in cooperation. There is evidence of cooperation involving Colombian cartels, Mexican organizations, Japanese *yakuza*, Chinese syndicates, Nigerian networks, and Sicilian and Russian organizations. Their cooperation usually involves market rationalization, trafficking logistics, money laundering, and drugs-weapons, drugs-cash, and drugs-drugs exchanges. Consequently, as one analyst notes, "in general, international narco-cooperation opens new markets for narcotics and other illegal products, exploits economies of scale for selling in those markets, enhances organized crime's penetration of legal economic and financial systems, and generally increases the power of criminal formations relative to national governments."[30]

The nature and source of drug threats could be external, internal, or both, depending on the actors and problem areas involved. For states, while some problems create threats within one area, the multidimensional and transnational nature of drug operations precludes strict internal-external distinctions between threats or implications. Whether the state faces one problem (say, production) or

28. See Schemo, "A U.S. Slap in the Hand Brings Colombia Out Punching."
29. Rosenau, *Multilateral Governance and the Nation-State System*, 20.
30. Lee, "Global Reach," 210.

several (such as production, abuse, and trafficking), the security implications tend to have both internal and external ramifications. Hence, the real issue is not whether there are internal *or* external implications, but the nature and extent of *both* sets of implications.

Contrary to the impression created by some media, the "war on drugs" is not purely a military matter. Hence, the application of military countermeasures alone would be futile. Indeed, some of the most sophisticated weapons have zero or near-zero utility in efforts at combating drugs. Attempts by U.S. officials to commit resources of the North American Aerospace Defense Command (NORAD) to the "drug war" demonstrate this stark reality. The NORAD surveillance system, which was designed to identify high-flying Soviet bombers and nuclear-tipped missiles, is blind to aircraft flying below ten thousand feet, the altitude range of most aircraft on drug-trafficking missions.[31] This is not to suggest, however, that there is no need or room for military capabilities in fighting drugs. Such are appropriate, for example, in operations against drug production and drug and arms trafficking.

International countermeasures offer the best prospect for dealing with the transnational drug phenomenon, especially since all state and nonstate actors battling the dilemma face resource limitations. Yet, collaboration among states also results in conflict, often because of domestic factors, including party rivalry, leadership changes, composition and control of the military, and budgetary and economic conditions. Some of these factors help explain a second reason for conflict: perceptual differences among ruling elites, which cause disparate definitions of the nature and severity of threats and, therefore, varied policies and measures to deal with them.

State and nonstate actors have been collaborating to create and maintain various counternarcotics regimes.[32] For reasons not appropriate to pursue here, such regimes have been having varying degrees of support and success. In the Americas, for example, the Inter-American Drug Abuse Control Commission (CICAD) lamented in March 1994 that "[d]espite all the efforts undertaken to date at

31. Schmitt, "Colorado Bunker."

32. For various regimes, see Rolley, "United Nations' Activities in International Drug Control"; *INCSR* (1996); *UN Narcotics Report;* Donnelly, "The United Nations and the Global Drug Control Regime"; and Bagley and Walker, *Drug Trafficking in the Americas,* 513–34.

the national and regional level, the problems related to the production, processing, trafficking, and use of narcotics and psychotropic substances have not only persisted, but spread dangerously."[33]

Sovereignty

The multiple dynamics of the geonarcotics milieu presented above have considerable implications for the issue of sovereignty. No study dealing with sovereignty, especially when small states are involved, can afford to overlook its formal-legal aspect: freedom from outside interference—that no authority is legally above the state except that which the state voluntarily confers on international bodies it joins. This is a central principle of international law, but also a sensitive issue for societies whose experience with colonization is still fresh in the national memory, and for those which have been victims of intervention.

But while looking at formal-legal sovereignty is necessary, it is not sufficient. The dynamics of drugs, geography, power, and politics oblige us to consider sovereignty in its political aspect, what is often called "positive sovereignty." As Robert Jackson argues, positive sovereignty enables states to take advantage of their independence. A government that is positively sovereign not only is able to enjoy rights of nonintervention, but has the ability to provide "political goods" for the society over which it exercises governance. Positive sovereignty includes having the economic, technical, military, psychological, and other capabilities to declare, implement, and enforce public policy, both domestic and foreign.[34]

Subsequent chapters show that both formal-legal and positive sovereignty are compromised in the Caribbean. And this is so whether you take what Innis Claude Jr. called the "chunk" or the "basket" approach to sovereignty.[35] The challenge to Caribbean political elites has two main elements. One is the actual and potential

33. Organization of American States, *Addendum to the Report of the Drafting Group to the Fifteenth Regular Session of CICAD,* 3.

34. Jackson, *Quasi-States: Sovereignty, International Relations, and the Third World,* 29.

35. The chunk approach sees sovereignty as monolithic and indivisible. The basket approach views it in variable terms, as a basket of attributes and corresponding rights and duties. See Fowler and Bunck, *Law, Power, and the Sovereign State,* 64–80, for a discussion of these two approaches.

challenge to governability presented by drug actors—in essence a challenge to positive sovereignty. These actors do not seek to command the institutions of state power directly, but through corruption and other direct and indirect methods, they aim at altering the political and socioeconomic dynamics of society in ways that are (a) conducive to their own pursuits and (b) generally not in the best interest of national security and good governance. In some respects they are analogous to interest groups, which aim not to exercise direct power but to influence the gaining of power and the making and execution of policy.

The other main sovereignty challenge has an international dimension, falling within the formal-legal realm. Often, the sovereign authority of the leaders of small states is challenged by other states. Some powerful states, in pursuing their own agendas vis-à-vis drug trafficking, find the actions of others inimical to their interests. Consequently, they adopt the kind of economic, political, and sometimes military measures that infringe on the sovereignty of small states. In the case of the Caribbean, the geonarcotics milieu is such that geography, power asymmetries, and the existence of the United States as the world's largest drug consumer all combine to heighten the region's vulnerability. This makes countries subject to sovereignty infringement, something that countries often have protested loudly.[36]

However, the challenge to sovereignty at the international level is not restricted to relationships among states. It is also a function of interaction between states and narcos, between states and IGOs, and between states and INGOs. Some IGOs are able to challenge and often subordinate small states to their interests because they possess relatively greater economic, political, or other resources than the small states, or otherwise are able to mobilize such resources. Further, the sovereignty challenge does not arise only from conflict relations; it also results from efforts at cooperation.

An example of this is the controversy between the United States and Jamaica and Barbados that surfaced in 1996 over maritime and air "hot pursuit," which all parties involved agree is vital to

---

36. See, for example, West Indian Commission, *Time For Action*, 348–49; Sanders, "The Drug Problem," 232; and Jamaica, Office of the Prime Minister, *Speaking Notes for the Hon. P. J. Patterson.*

dealing with drug trafficking.[37] The essence of the controversy is, on the one hand, the insistence by Barbados and Jamaica that "hot pursuit" by the United States not be extended into their twelve-mile territorial waters, and, on the other hand, the desire of the United States for the right to full "hot pursuit" to maximize the operational efficiency of that interdiction measure. The dispute developed added dimensions as Barbados and Jamaica called for "linkage" between shiprider agreements and other matters, including arms trafficking, deportees, and banana-market guarantees, and as the United States accused Jamaica of foot-dragging in fighting drugs.

Conclusion

Of all the countries in the Americas, those in the Caribbean are least able to cushion the impact of domestic and international sovereignty challenges presented by drugs. This study explains why this is so. Important work has been done on the security aspects of the Caribbean drug dilemma, but these have focused mostly on two or three countries, a couple of problems, a few countermeasures, or one or two security considerations.[38] I also have examined some of the security aspects of regional drug operations.[39] However, although I have explored many of the problems and security implications, those evaluations lack both comprehensiveness and adequate attention to a wide range of countermeasures. There is, thus, need for a comprehensive study of drug operations, their security implications, and efforts to combat them. The first task in this endeavor is to understand the nature of the problems that place the sovereignty of states in the Caribbean under siege.

37. See Becker, "Sovereignty or Survival"; Cox, "Patterson Against Drugs, for Sovereignty"; Sealey, " 'No' to Drugs Agreement"; and Bohning, "Anti-Drug Pacts Founder Between U.S., Caribbean."

38. See Pollard, *The Problems of Drug Abuse in Commonwealth Caribbean Countries;* Cumberbatch and Duncan, "Illegal Drugs"; MacDonald, *Dancing on a Volcano,* chaps. 6–8; Maingot, *The United States and the Caribbean,* 142–82; Meason, "War at Sea"; Sanders, "Narcotics, Corruption, and Development"; idem, "The Drug Problem"; Morris, *Caribbean Maritime Security,* 132–65; and Bagley and Walker, *Drug Trafficking in the Americas,* chaps. 24 and 25.

39. See *The Quest for Security in the Caribbean,* 243–75, "Some Security Implications," "Drugs and Security in the Commonwealth Caribbean," "Drugs in the Caribbean: An Economic Balance Sheet," and "Caribbean Manifestations."

PART I

PROBLEMS
AND
ACTORS

1
Narcotics Production and Consumption-Abuse

The fundamental source of the drug problem, of *narco-tráfico* in the Americas, is the presence and power of consumer demand. . . . So long as demand continues, there will be people engaged in supply.   —Peter Smith

The drugs that feature in the Caribbean are mainly marijuana, cocaine, and heroin, and their derivatives, such as crack, which comes from cocaine. However, as far as production is concerned, only marijuana is produced in the region. The consumption-abuse situation is different, however, since all the drugs are involved. Hence there is variability in both production and consumption-abuse. This chapter examines this variability, noting national and international, and political and economic, aspects of the contemporary production problem, and sociological and economic elements of the consumption-abuse challenge. It also highlights some of the dynamics of the geography and politics factors involved in the region's geonarcotics milieu.

Drugs and Geography

Marijuana: An Appreciation

Marijuana is a tobacco-like substance produced by drying the leaves and flowering tops of the Indian hemp plant. The plant's scientific name, *Cannabis sativa* (Latin for "cultivated hemp"), was given in 1753 by Carl Linnaeus, a Swedish naturalist. (It is sometimes called *Cannabis sativa L* out of respect for Linnaeus.) The potency of marijuana varies, depending on the soil used, climate involved, cultivation techniques, and the mixture of plants. For example, while most varieties in the United States have a THC (tetrahydrocannabinol) concentration of less than 0.5 percent, those in Jamaica, Colombia, and Mexico have between 0.3 and 7 percent. Sinsemilla (from the Spanish *sin semilla*—without seed) has been known to have as much as 20 percent THC.

Contrary to popular belief in parts of the Caribbean, sinsemilla itself is not a distinct variety of marijuana. It is derived from the same plant through a particular method of cultivation. During flowering, the buds of female plants become sticky with resin, which is generally saturated with THC. If the female flowering plants are not pollinated, these tops continue to produce both flowers and resin, becoming increasingly potent. The cultivators of the plant who are interested in sinsemilla will kill the male plants as soon as they are old enough to have their sex determined—about two or three months after pollination.[1]

Marijuana is relatively easy to breed. It can grow in a variety of temperate and moisture conditions, but it grows best in hot areas. It prefers open spaces and needs very little water, except during germination and the establishment of the main root. *Cannabis sativa* generally grows between five and eighteen feet, with long, narrow leaves. On the other hand, *Cannabis indica*, the other variety that is popular in the Caribbean, is short, growing four feet or less. It is also more densely branched. Marijuana has several folk and street names, including pot, weed, herb, reefer, grass, and sinsem-

---

1. U.S. Department of Justice, Drug Enforcement Administration, *Drugs of Abuse* [hereafter *Drugs of Abuse*], 45; Murray, "Marijuana's Effects on Human Cognitive Functions," 24–27; and Weisheit, *Domestic Marijuana*, 53–60.

illa. However, in the Caribbean, it is known most popularly as ganja.

The presence of marijuana in the Caribbean dates to the nineteenth century. The indenture labor system was introduced in the 1830s after slave emancipation in the British empire and the consequent loss of black slave labor for the sugar plantations. Under that system, indentured workers were brought from Africa, Asia, and Europe to compensate for the labor displacement. The workers who came to the Caribbean were brought mainly from India, the first set arriving in 1834 in Guyana, then called British Guiana. (Jamaica observed the 150th anniversary of the arrival of East Indians on May 10, 1995. May 30, 1995, marked the 150th anniversary of the arrivals in Trinidad. The Trinidad government decided in 1995 that from 1996, May 30 will be designated Arrival Day and celebrated annually as a national holiday.) It was the Indians who brought cannabis to the Caribbean. Indeed, the term by which marijuana is most popularly known in the Caribbean—"ganja"—is itself the Hindi word for cannabis.[2] Yet, while this historical context is important, it does not by itself explain Caribbean marijuana production. Also needed is an appreciation of the role of geography.

Geographic Profile of the Caribbean

The region gets its name from the Carib, American Indians who originally inhabited some of the islands and part of the neighboring South American coast, and is dominated geographically by the Caribbean Sea. As Table 1 shows, Caribbean territories vary greatly in size, ranging from uninhabitable rocks and cays to island Cuba (110,860 km^2) and mainland Guyana (214,970 km^2).

The Caribbean islands fall into four major groupings: the Greater Antilles (Cuba, Jamaica, Hispaniola [Dominican Republic and Haiti], and Puerto Rico); the Lesser Antilles, which lie to the east of Puerto Rico, forming an arc that runs from the Virgin Islands in the north to Grenada in the south; the southern islands along the South American coast—Trinidad and Tobago, Aruba, Bonaire, and Curaçao—and the Bahamian archipelago. The Bahamas, comprising some seven hundred islands and two thousand rocks and cays,

---

2. Rubin and Comitas, *Ganja in Jamaica*, 16–20.

Table 1   Geographical Features of Caribbean Countries

Country	Total Area (km²)	Coastline (km)	Terrain
Anguilla	91	61	Flat and low-lying; coral and limestone
Antigua-Barbuda	440	153	Mostly low-lying; limestone; some higher volcanic areas; 16% coral and woodlands
Aruba	193	69	Flat with a few hills; scant vegetation
Bahamas	13,942	3,542	Long, flat coral formations with some rounded hills; 32% forest and woodlands
Barbados	432	97	Relatively flat; rises gently to central highland region; 77% arable land
Belize	22,960	386	Flat, swampy coastal plain; low mountains in South; 44% arable land
British Virgin Islands	150	80	Coral islands, relatively flat; volcanic islands, hilly; 33% meadows and pastures
Cayman Islands	264	160	Low-lying limestone base surrounded by coral reefs; 23% forest and woodlands
Cuba	110,860	3,735	Mostly flat to rolling plains with rugged hills and mountains in the southeast; 23% pastures and meadows; 17% forest and woodlands
Curaçao	444	—	Level with hilly region
Dominica	750	148	Rugged mountains of volcanic origin; 41% forest and woodlands
Dominican Republic	48,442	1,288	Rugged highlands and mountains with fertile valleys interspersed; 43% meadows and pastures; 13% forest and woodlands
French Guiana	90,909	378	Low-lying coastal plains rising to hills; small mountains; 82% forest and woodlands

Table 1   (continued)

Country	Total Area (km²)	Coastline (km)	Terrain
Grenada	345	121	Volcanic in origin with central mountains; 15% arable land
Guadeloupe	1,780	306	Basse-Terre is volcanic in origin; interior mountains; 40% forest and woodlands
Guyana	214,970	459	Mostly rolling highlands; low coastal plain; savanna in South; 83% forest and woodlands
Haiti	27,750	1,771	Mostly rough and mountainous; 26% arable land
Jamaica	11,424	1,072	Mostly mountainous with narrow discontinuous coastal plain
Martinique	1,100	290	Mountains with indented coastline; dormant volcano; 20% forest and woodland
Montserrat	102	40	Volcanic; mostly mountainous; small coastal lowland; 40% forest and woodlands
Puerto Rico	9,104	501	Mostly mountains with coastal-plain belt in north; mountains precipitious to sea on west coast; 41% meadows and pastures
St. Kitts–Nevis	269	135	Volcanic with mountainous interior; 22% arable land
St. Lucia	616	158	Volcanic; mountainous with broad fertile valleys, 13% forest and woodlands
St. Vincent & the Grenadines	388	84	Volcanic; mountainous; 41% forest and woodlands
Suriname	163,270	386	Mostly rolling hills; narrow coastal plains with swamps; 97% forest and woodlands
Trinidad & Tobago	5,128	362	Mostly plains with some hills and low mountains; 44% forest and woodlands

Table 1   (continued)

Country	Total Area (km²)	Coastline (km)	Terrain
Turks & Caicos	417	389	Low, flat, limestone; extensive marshes and mangrove swamps; 2% arable land
U.S. Virgin Islands	352	188	Hilly to rugged and mountainous with little level land; 26% meadows and pastures

SOURCES: *The World Factbook, 1995; Caribbean Development Bank Annual Report, 1995; 1996 Caribbean Basin Commercial Profile.*

is not really in the Caribbean Sea, but in the western Atlantic Ocean. Many of the Bahamian islands are only a few feet above water, and only twenty-two are inhabited. The largest island is Andros.

Yet, neither geography generally nor the Caribbean Sea specifically is the sole defining feature of the Caribbean region. Indeed, there is no single definition of the Caribbean; there are three, and they are guided by factors of geography, ethnohistory, politics, and economics. By one definition, the Caribbean comprises the islands in the Caribbean Sea along with the Guianas. This is essentially a geopolitical definition. A second definition is influenced by ethnohistory, politics, and geography, and it focuses on the English-speaking Caribbean. The third definition, featuring all the factors mentioned above, refers to the Caribbean Basin: the island nations in the Caribbean Sea, the countries in Central America, those in northern South America, and Mexico.

This study deals mainly with the Caribbean as defined in the first sense. However, reference is made often to developments in the Caribbean Basin. This makes it important to offer a comment on the geography of a few basin countries that have had long and strong ties to the island nations and that are deeply implicated in the Caribbean narcotics phenomenon. Belize and Guyana are two such countries.

Belize is located in northern Central America. It has the second largest barrier reef in the world (after Australia), flanking the entirety of its coastline, with small cays dotting the reef. As Table 1 shows, Belize has a total area of 22,960 km². The northern half of the country consists of lowlands, large areas of which are swampy. The south is dominated by mountain ranges, notably the Maya mountains, which rise about 1,122 meters (3,681 feet). Slightly less than half of Belize is covered with forests. There are numerous mangrove swamps and lagoons along the coast. The climate is subtropical.

Like Belize, Guyana is mainland territory, but on the South American continent. It has three geographical zones: the coastal plain, comprising about 5 percent of the country's area but home to some 90 percent of the population; the white sand belt, which is about 150 to 250 km wide, contains most of the country's bauxite, gold, and diamonds, and supports a dense hardwood forest; and the interior highland, the largest of the three, comprising a series of plateaus, flat-topped mountains, and savannas. Four-fifths of the country is covered with forests. Guyana has a tropical climate and is a water-rich country with numerous water falls, one of which—Kaieteur Falls—has a drop of 226 meters (741 feet), four times that of Niagara Falls.[3] Quite appropriately, the word "Guyana" is derived from an Amerindian term meaning "land of many waters."

In climatic terms, the Caribbean is uniformly warm and humid, and all the territories, except the northern Bahamas, are south of the Tropic of Cancer. Generally, the mountainous islands receive more rain than the flat ones, and the smaller ones receive less than the larger ones. In terms of natural environment, there are six main types: tropical rain forests, seasonal rain forests, dry forests, savanna, woodlands and cactus scrub, and mangrove swamps.[4] And, as Table 1 indicates, most Caribbean countries have high proportions of their territories either in forests and woodland or in meadows and pastures, a feature that provides the clandestinity needed for marijuana cultivation.

Hurricanes are the region's most feared climatic hazard. They occur annually between June and November, often starting as tropical storms. The 1995 hurricane season brought several destructive storms. Two of them, Hurricane Luis and Hurricane Marilyn, both

3. Merrill, *Guyana and Belize*, 31–35, 189–93.
4. Rogozinski, *A Brief History of the Caribbean*, 3–12.

of which occurred during September, killed nineteen people and destroyed millions of dollars worth of property, especially in Antigua-Barbuda, the U.S. Virgin Islands, St. Martin, and Puerto Rico. In Antigua alone, Luis killed three people and destroyed 65 percent of the buildings. And according to the Caribbean Disaster Emergency Relief Agency (CDERA), it caused U.S.$765 million worth of damage in Antigua-Barbuda, St. Kitts–Nevis, and Dominica. Marilyn killed eleven people and damaged 70 percent of the buildings in St. Thomas, U.S. Virgin Islands.[5] Thankfully, the 1996 hurricane season was not as destructive as that of 1995. The worse storms were hurricanes Edouard and Fran, but they did not take many lives, although there was a fair amount of property damage.

Drug Production

Because of its physical geography, especially its climate and soil, the entire Caribbean is hospitable to the cultivation of marijuana. Moreover, the numerous forest areas provide excellent cover for clandestine production. However, until the mid-1980s, the only significant cultivation was in Belize and Jamaica. Although in Jamaica there was a significant local use, the high production levels in both places were driven by the availability of an export market, primarily in the United States. As a matter of fact, in 1984 these two countries ranked among the top five foreign sources of marijuana for the United States. In both countries marijuana has at times been the largest cash crop, once producing some U.S.$350 million annually in Belize and an estimated U.S.$1 billion to $2 billion in Jamaica.[6]

Marijuana is cultivated mostly in the North and West of Belize, in small plots of one acre or less. Significant cultivation began in the 1960s, and by the early 1980s Belize was the fourth largest supplier of the crop to the United States, after Colombia, Mexico, and Jamaica. However, production has plummeted since 1985, largely due to eradication countermeasures by the Belize government, often under pressure from the United Sates. Table 2 shows both a fairly progressive decline in the areas cultivated and an increase in crop destruction between 1987 and 1991.

5. For a 1995 end-of-season hurricane review, see Markowitz, "At Last, a Mean Season Ends."

6. MacDonald, *Dancing on a Volcano*, 89.

Table 2   Marijuana Civilization in Belize and Jamaica (hectares)

	1987	1988	1989	1990	1991	1992	1993	1994	1995
Belize									
Cultivation	1,088	660	436	400	320	NA	49	NA	NA
Eradication	870	528	363	333	266	51	89	10,751 plants	135,216 plants
Jamaica									
Cultivation	1,330	1,257	1,790	2,250	1,783	1,200	1,200	1,000	1,000
Eradication	650	650	1,510	1,030	833	811	456	692	695

SOURCE: *International Narcotics Control Strategy Report* (various years)

NA = Not available.

The most dramatic eradication countermeasure was aerial spraying, which began in 1982, with help from Mexico and the United States. George Price, then the prime minister, found it politically expedient to discontinue spraying in 1984, given the impending general elections and the fact that spraying operations generated a storm of protest from environmentalists and farmers. Belize specialists believe that the loss of the 1985 elections by Price and the People's United Party (PUP) was due partly to anger generated by farmers. Spraying was, however, resumed in 1986 by the new government. The victorious Manuel Esquivel defined the drug problem as a serious national security threat, justifying an "all-out war." In fact, he perceived the drug trade as a greater threat to the country's sovereignty and democracy than the long-standing territorial claim by Guatemala.[7]

The manual and aerial crop destruction was so successful that in 1994 the U.S. Department of State boasted: "Belize, once the fourth largest producer of marijuana in the world, has reduced production to negligible levels through an aggressive aerial eradication campaign using USG [United States Government] spray aircraft and GOB [Government of Belize] manual eradication operations."[8] However, the success of this eradication onslaught was jeopardized by three developments: the cultivation of the *indica* variety of canna-

7. See Young, "The Territorial Dimension of Caribbean Security," 142–43, and *INCSR* (1991), 135.
8. *INCSR* (1994), 137.

bis, which matures in three to four months; the withdrawal in 1993 of Department of State spray aircraft due to budget cuts; and the completion in October 1994 of the phased withdrawal of British Forces Belize, the garrison that Britain had maintained in Belize since 1981 because of the military threat from Guatemala. To aggravate the situation further, in January 1995 the Belize government completely halted aerial eradication because of environmental concerns.

In Jamaica, marijuana grows year-round and is traditionally harvested in two main annual seasons of five- to six-month cycles. But the *indica* variety mentioned above makes four harvests possible per year. Large-scale cultivation of five- to fifty-acre plots was once common, but because of eradication measures, most cultivation is now done in plots of one acre or less, with yields of about 1,485 pounds per hectare. Cultivation was once highly concentrated in the wetlands of western and central Jamaica, but production countermeasures have resulted in shifts to remote highland areas, including the Blue Mountains in the eastern part of the country.

Most of the cultivation is now done on inaccessible ridges, valleys, and mountainsides, where, in some places, elevations are as high as 2,500 feet. As Figure 3 shows, marijuana cultivation takes places virtually everywhere in Jamaica, but significantly in the parishes of St. Catherine, St. Ann, Westmoreland, Hanover, St. Elizabeth, and St. James. There are twenty-three major cultivation areas: Sligoville, Ewarton, Lluidas Vale, Kitson Town, and Worthy Park in St. Catherine; Alderton, Higgins Land, Stephney, Abouker, Murray Mountain, Bethany, and Alexandria in St. Ann; Bogues, Elim, and Georges Valley in St. Elizabeth; Orange Hill, Revival, Sheffield, New Hope, and Brighton in Westmoreland; and Mafoota, Roehampton, and Catadupa in St. James.[9]

As in Belize, the marijuana eradication agenda has been driven largely by the United States in its efforts to deal with drug-source countries, part of its supply-side strategy. Most of the eradication has been done under a program called Operation Buccaneer, which is explained fully in Chapter 7. But unlike Belize, the results have been quite uneven, as Table 2 indicates. The years 1989 and 1990,

9. Jamaica, Ministry of Agriculture, *Alternative Systems for an Illegal Crop*, 14–20.

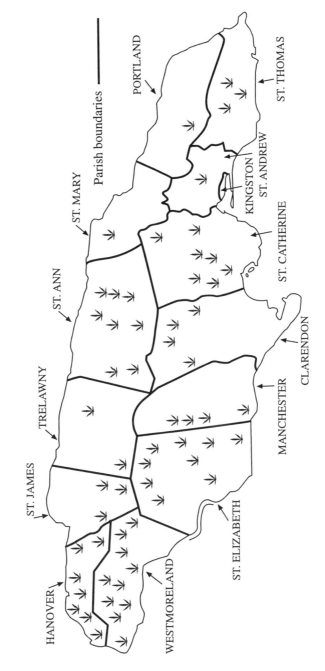

Fig. 3 Main Ganja Cultivation Areas in Jamaica

for example, saw dramatic successes in eradication. But there has been an equally dramatic decline in quantities destroyed thereafter. This is due to several factors: domestic politics, shifts in cultivation cites, changes in variety, reduced resources for eradication, and resistance to aerial spraying.

On the last issue, the United States complained in 1994 that "for environmental reasons and because of political opposition, the GOJ [Government of Jamaica] has failed to accept the alternative suggested by the USG [United States Government] of eradication by aerial spraying."[10] In response, one Jamaican official indicated that Jamaica uses the "backpack" method of spraying that targets only young plants and nurseries. Jamaica rejects other methods because they risk contaminating legitimate produce and groundwater supply.[11]

Table 2 shows a significant decline in acreage eradication since 1993, where the eradication target has been 1,000 hectares annually. The eradication shortfall is partly the result of new strategies adopted by cultivators. Jamaica's national security minister reported to Parliament in 1993 that "[t]he [eradication] program has driven ganja farmers to new tactics: they now interplant ganja with other crops and grow the herb in almost inaccessible places."[12] Aerial spraying of cannabis in Jamaica is more controversial than in Belize partly because marijuana is an even larger source of income there. One estimate for the 1980s placed the number of farmers cultivating the crop at six thousand. During that same decade, ganja was once said to have contributed between U.S.$1 billion and $2 billion to Jamaica's foreign-exchange earnings, surpassing all other exports, including bauxite, sugar, and tourism.[13] However, the pressure to eradicate has continued.

Economic pressures, the lucrativeness of the drug market, and the balloon effect of countermeasures in Belize, Jamaica, and Latin America are among the reasons other Caribbean countries have taken to significant marijuana production (and export). The Bahamas, for example, which, as will be seen in Chapter 2, features prominently in drug trafficking, has traditionally been neither a

---

10. *INCSR* (1994), 197.
11. Interview with Captain Edwards, December 1994.
12. Jamaica, Parliament, *Presentation of the Hon. K. D. Knight* (1993), 19.
13. MacDonald, *Dancing on a Volcano*, 90.

drug-producing nor drug-refining country. However, the production alarm was sounded in 1991 following the discovery and destruction of forty thousand cannabis seedlings and one thousand medium-sized plants, and the seizure of twenty-two kilos of prepared marijuana, all in one part of the archipelago: Andros Island. Plots were also discovered and destroyed at New Providence and Eleuthera.[14] Moreover, in October 1996, police raids on Grand Bahama Island led to the confiscation of some eight thousand marijuana plants, worth about $7 million.[15]

The size of plots destroyed elsewhere in the region, as well as the frequency with which they are destroyed, is evidence of increased production. In Grenada, for example, 10,862 plants were uprooted in 1992, 9,323 in 1993, and some 20,000 in 1994. Police officials there indicated that the high-cultivation areas are Grand Etang, St. Andrew, St. David, St. Patrick, and Upper Homitage. These are in the central part of the island, which has mountainous terrain. They are also in rural Grenada, where there is high unemployment and many abandoned sections of land, all of which drug operators exploit.[16]

In Dominica, 11,880 plants were burned in 1992, and 11,140 were burned in 1993. The figure for 1994 was higher: 48,855; for 1995 it was 126,000. In St. Lucia, 87,760 plants were reportedly destroyed in 1992, but the number destroyed in 1993 increased dramatically: 181,500. For 1994 the figure was 81,923, and for 1995 it was almost three times higher than 1994: 235,000 plants. A spirited U.S.-sponsored eradication program in St. Vincent and the Grenadines between October 1991 and February 1992 eliminated some 2 million ganja plants. The figure for 1993 was a mere 12,000, however, reflecting not only reduced British and American counternarcotics assistance but also factors related to elections there, which were held in February 1994.[17] With the seizure of 881 kilos of marijuana in 1994, the U.S. Bureau for International Nar-

14. *INCSR* (1992), 193, and Bahamas, Ministry of Foreign Affairs, *Bahamas Narcotics Control Report, 1991*, 9.

15. *Caribbean Today*, "Bahamas."

16. Interviews with Assistant Commissioner Darius, Superintendent Raymond, Assistant Commissioner Cadore, Assistant Superintendent Charles, Assistant Superintendent Antoinne, and Superintendent Clarkson, Grenada, July 1994.

17. *INCSR* (1994), 211–14; *INCSR* (1995), 194–98; and *INCSR* (1996), 198–206.

cotics Control and Law Enforcement Affairs (INL) reported: "Among Caribbean islands St. Vincent is second only to Jamaica in marijuana production. Marijuana is probably St. Vincent's largest export earner."[18] According to the 1996 *INCSR* a combined eradication mission in February and March 1995 undertaken with U.S. air support resulted in the eradication of 7 million marijuana plants and the destruction of some 8,000 pounds of processed marijuana.

There are two features about Guyana that are conducive to all sorts of clandestine activities. The first is its physical geography, which was described briefly above. The second is an aspect of its social geography: it has one of the lowest population densities in the world, with 214,970 km² of territory and a population of about three-quarters of a million. Moreover, most of the population lives along the Atlantic coast, leaving vast expanses of territory underpopulated and underpoliced. It is therefore surprising that major marijuana cultivation did not begin there before the late 1980s. The marijuana seizures are reported mostly in the Demerara-Mahaica, Mahaica-Berbice, and East Berbice–Corentyne regions, in the northeastern and eastern parts of the country. This is not because cultivation takes place only there, but because the capability limitations of military and police agencies restrict their effective responses to these and a few other areas. Military intelligence sources indicate that marijuana cultivation is also undertaken in the Cuyuni-Mazaruni, Upper Demerara–Berbice, Essequibo Islands–West Demerara, and the Upper Takatu–Upper Mazaruni regions, in west-central, east-central, northern, and southwestern Guyana, respectively.[19]

Given what one law-enforcement official called "the almost overnight development of a drug monster" and serious resource constraints on all law-enforcement and military entities in the country, the strategy for eradication that has been adopted involves joint operations with detachments from the army, the police, and the coast guard. Joint operations, for example, led to the discovery in March 1992 of 60,000 pounds of marijuana in the Mahaica River area, and ten fields with an estimated 160,000 marijuana plants along the

18. *INCSR* (1995), 197.
19. Interviews with Assistant Commissioner Felix and Lieutenant Colonel Collins, June 1994.

Maduni Creek, all in the Demerara-Mahaica administrative region. Two months later, similar operations uncovered 79,700 pounds of marijuana, this time in the Berbice River area, in eastern Guyana. That find had an estimated street value of G$1 billion (about U.S.$14.2 million). In July 1994 the Mahaica area was also the scene of joint operations in which ninety-four acres of the crop were destroyed. The next month the same area was raided, and over fifty acres of ganja were burned. During 1995 about a hundred hectares of marijuana were eradicated, and eleven metric tons of the product were destroyed.[20] Toward the end of 1996—on December 11 and 17 to be exact—two raids by narcotics police in Upper Demerara River led to the eradication of 48,700 kilos of marijuana.

In the case of Trinidad and Tobago, there are no accurate estimates of cannabis cultivation, but police officials indicated that most of the country's cultivation is done in the forested northern and central ranges and along the coast.[21] As in Guyana and elsewhere in the Caribbean, joint police-army operations have been the center of eradication and confiscation countermeasures, eradicating 783,024 marijuana plants and destroying 2.1 metric tons of cured marijuana during 1994, according to the 1995 *INCSR*. During 1995 over 5.4 million metric tons of mature plants were eradicated and 1,634 kilos of cured leaves were destroyed.[22] However, unlike those in Guyana, crop eradication measures in Trinidad and Tobago have been subject to criticism from both local and international sources. This is not because Trinidad and Tobago has an abundance of resources and is not using them, but because of the (not incorrect) perception that corruption and inefficiency are widespread. The U.S. Department of State, for example, has lamented that "[c]oordination is lacking . . . [and] drug-related corruption is a continuing problem."[23]

Elsewhere in the Caribbean, ganja cultivation takes place in the

20. Persaud, "Police, Army Uncover Biggest Ganja Plot Yet"; Gilbert, "Police Discover G$1 Billion of Ganja in Berbice"; Khan, "Four Held in $720M Mahaica Marijuana Bust"; *Stabroek News*, "Cops Raid Mahaica Marijuana Fields"; and *INCSR* (1996), 175.
21. Interview with Commissioner Bernard, July 1994.
22. *INCSR* (1996), 195.
23. *INCSR* (1994), 206. See also Marajh, "Police 'Drug Cartel' Charges Made in 1991—Murray Told NAR Government," and *Trinidad Guardian*, "Nation's Laws Must Be Enforced—Panday."

Dominican Republic, Puerto Rico, Suriname, French Guiana, St. Kitts–Nevis, Montserrat, and Haiti, especially in the Moron section of the Grand Anse region. There is variation in the size of plots cultivated. In some places, ganja production is primarily for domestic use, but in most of them the product is also exported. In St. Kitts–Nevis, for example, about 25,000 marijuana plants were destroyed during 1994; and 240,600 were destroyed in tiny Montserrat that year.

Drug Consumption and Abuse: A Portrait

The Danger Drugs

As noted earlier, the consumption-abuse problem in the Caribbean involves three main drugs: marijuana, cocaine and its derivative crack, and, to a lesser extent, heroin. However, there are also "designer drugs," concocted by combining these substances. For example, in 1993 a product called "seasoned spliff," a ganja cigarette laced with cocaine, first appeared in the Bahamas, Jamaica, and elsewhere. It was found that many people became cocaine addicts unwittingly because they were unaware of the presence of cocaine in the "normal" ganja cigarette.[24] Like production, drug use differs from place to place and in quantity and type.

Marijuana is generally smoked or chewed. Smoking is done in either of two main ways. The first and more popular form is that in which the marijuana is rolled up to form a cigarette; it is called a *spliff* or *sklif*. The second smoking method involves the use of a *chillum*, a pipe bowl made of wood, coconut shell, or horn, and fitted with a stem of wood or rubber tubing. The *chillum* is used at gatherings and is passed from user to user. It is important to note here that in the Caribbean, as in many other places, marijuana is not only used as a "drug," in the sense of a narcotic, intoxicant, depressant, or hallucinogen, but also for medicinal purposes. In that respect, it is brewed as a tea and tonic, cooked in food, and applied as a poultice or a liniment. It is also cooked as a vegetable and used

24. Browne, "Drug Abuse Still a Major Problem Here."

to protect babies and infants from evil spirits.[25] One writer, for example, reported the following based on field research among (Oriental) Indians in Trinidad and Tobago in 1990: green leaves, shoots, and roots of marijuana are boiled and taken with milk for asthma and chest colds; dried leaves, shoots, and seeds are soaked in rain water and white rum for one month and taken one teaspoon at a time for diabetes, bronchitis, and high blood pressure.[26]

Interestingly, the "marijuana as medicine" issue in the United States resurfaced with drama in 1996 after voters in the November elections in Arizona and California approved propositions allowing physicians in their states to prescribe marijuana for medical use. Federal officials, including President Bill Clinton, reacted swiftly and sharply to what they perceived as a subterfuge for the legalization of marijuana. Attorney General Janet Reno, for example, announced that physicians in any state who prescribed marijuana could lose the privilege of prescriptions, be excluded from Medicare and Medicaid reimbursements, and even be prosecuted for a federal crime. The respected *New England Journal of Medicine*, however, offered a spirited response to the threats from the federal officials. In its January 30, 1997, editorial, Dr. Jerome Kassirer charged: "It is a hypocritical to forbid physicians to prescribe marijuana while permitting them to use morphine and meperidine to relieve extreme dyspnea and pain." The editorial counseled: "Federal authorities should rescind their prohibition of the medicinal use of marijuana and allow physicians to decide which patients to treat. The government should change marijuana's status from that of a Schedule 1 drug (considered to be potentially addictive and with no current medical use) to that of a Schedule 2 drug (potentially addictive, but with some accepted medical use) and regulate it accordingly. To ensure its proper distribution and use, the government should declare itself the only agency sanctioned to provide the marijuana."[27]

While marijuana is abused in many places in the Caribbean, it has had a long history of socioreligious use, dating from the intro-

---

25. Rubin and Comitas, *Ganja in Jamaica*, 48–53; Dreher, *Working Men and Ganja*, 173–74; and Chevannes, *Background to Drug Use in Jamaica*, 12.
26. Mahabir, "Marijuana in the Caribbean," 36.
27. Kassirer, "Federal Foolishness and Marijuana."

duction of Indian indentured workers. Consider this observation, the relevance of which goes beyond Jamaica:

> Most significantly, the complex of cultural beliefs that is linked with cannabis among working-class users in Jamaica parallels that of India. This includes the methods of preparation and use, the role of ganja in folk medicine, in divine mythology, in pragmatic and ritual uses, and the social class framework of use and attitudes towards ganja. The ganja complex is a cultural innovation from the period of East Indian indenture, diffused to the black cane cutters through association with indentured workers on the sugar plantations and incorporated into working-class life styles.[28]

Marijuana's socioreligious use pattern has changed over the years, and it is now associated primarily with the Rastafarians, Afrocentric social-religious sects that identify with the late emperor Haile Selassie of Ethiopia. In one study, Horace Campbell notes that "those who lived close to the [Rastafarian] settlements would notice from time to time a familiar billowing of smoke and hear the 'puck, puck' of the chillum pipe."[29] Rastafarianism, which originated in Jamaica in the 1930s, has since spread to other parts of the Caribbean and, through Caribbean migration, to Europe and North America. Hence, in the Caribbean, this Rastafarian-linked socioreligious use of marijuana is found in places with large numbers of Rastafarians, including Jamaica, Guyana, Grenada, and Trinidad and Tobago. As Scott MacDonald indicates, for the Rastafarians ganja is not a drug but an herb. And they cite Gen. 1:12 and 3:8, Exod. 10:12, and Ps. 104:14 as biblical justification for its use.[30]

Although there is no consensus within the scientific community about the consequences of marijuana use, evidence suggests that it can lead to euphoria, disorientation, and increased appetite, the last condition itself being a desired effect from a medicinal stand-

28. Rubin and Comitas, *Ganja in Jamaica,* 17.
29. Campbell, *Rasta and Resistance,* 107.
30. MacDonald, *Dancing on a Volcano,* 91. For a description of the ritual smoking of ganja by Rastafarians, see Chevannes, *Background to Drug Use in Jamaica,* 11–12.

point. Marijuana use is known to relax many inhibitions, and over-use is said to cause fatigue, paranoia, and possibly psychosis. Marijuana use is also credited with impairing intellectual judgment and short-term memory as well as human psychomotor functions, evident especially in subjects' operation of automobiles.[31] It is useful to note, however, that one study found that claims about the consequences of routine ganja consumption—impairment of the ability to work, apathy, lethargy, unsound judgment, detachment from reality—are not supported by evidence from rural Jamaica. In fact, the exact opposite seemed true.[32]

Cocaine is the most potent stimulant of natural origin. It is extracted from the coca plant, *Erythroxylon coca*, which has been grown in South America's Andean region since prehistoric times. Illicit cocaine is usually distributed as a white crystalline power, often diluted by a variety of ingredients, including lactose and mannitol. It is the adulteration of cocaine that increases its volume, thereby increasing its profitability. The substance is peddled under numerous names, among them coke, flake, snow, superblow, and crack.

Crack itself delivers ten times the impact of powered cocaine, with, of course, ten times the danger. It is made by mixing cocaine with bicarbonate of soda and water, baking to a paste, and allowing the mixture to harden. The mixture makes a crackling sound while being boiled—hence the name of the product. And because it can be easily concocted and is cheap, crack use has grown rapidly in parts of the Caribbean and elsewhere. According to the United Nations International Drug Control Program (UNDCP), crack production in the Caribbean began in Trinidad.

Cocaine is a stimulant with powerful psychotropic impact. The intensity of its effects depends on the rate of entry into the blood stream. Intravenous injection or smoking produces an almost immediate experience. Inhalation, via the smoking of crack, for instance, also produces a fast effect. However, the cocaine "high" is over very quickly. Indeed, with a one- to two-hour duration, cocaine has the shortest "high" of all dangerous drugs. By comparison,

31. See *Drugs of Abuse*, 31, and Kleiman, *Marijuana*, 4–14.
32. Dreher, *Working Men and Ganja*, 197.

opium, morphine, and heroin have a three- to six-hour "high," and that of angel dust, PCP, and TCP lasts for several days.[33] Because of cocaine's short "high" and the intensity of its pleasurable effect, there is an extraordinary dependency factor. Addicts need to resort to larger doses at shorter intervals, and addiction has serious psychological consequences. There is often a toxic psychosis similar to paranoid schizophrenia, reflected by anxiety, restlessness, and extreme irritability. Tactile hallucinations develop in some cases, to the point where addicts injure themselves trying to remove imaginary insects from under their skin. Others feel persecuted and fear that people are watching and following them. Cocaine overdose can also be fatal. Death can result from seizures, respiratory failure, strokes, and cerebral hemorrhage.[34]

Unlike marijuana and cocaine, heroin is a semisynthetic narcotic, derived from morphine, which itself is obtained from the opium poppy, *Papever somnifernum*. It was first synthesized in 1874, and the German company Bayer started producing it commercially as a pain remedy in 1898. Pure heroin is a white, bitter-tasting power, but illicit heroin varies in color and form. The color variation—from white to dark brown—results from manufacturing impurities or from additives. Pure heroin is rarely peddled on the street. Street heroin often has a mere 5 percent of the pure matter, with diluents such as sugar, powered milk, or quinine, in ratios ranging from 9:1 to as much as 99:1. Heroin use creates high physical and psychological dependency. It causes drowsiness, respiratory depression, constricted pupils, and nausea, and overdose can be fatal.[35] Known also as horse, smack, dope, snow and by other names, heroin is administered through injection, sniffing, or smoking.

The AIDS epidemic in many parts of the world has caused many heroin users to alter their pattern of administering the drug. Addicts in the United States and elsewhere have been resorting to more sniffing and less injecting.[36] However, heroin is not the only

---

33. Scherer, *Crack Cocaine*, 4–12; Massing, "Crack's Destructive Sprint Across America"; and *Drugs of Abuse*, 30–31.

34. *Drugs of Abuse*, 40. I am also grateful to Francille Griffith, R.N., for explaining the fatal consequences of the abuse of cocaine and other substances.

35. *Drugs of Abuse*, 14–15, 30–31.

36. See Treaster, "Fearing AIDS, Users of Heroin Shift to Inhaling Drugs."

drug linked to the spread of AIDS. One study in the United States found that 32 percent of the 182,834 AIDS cases reported to the Center for Disease Control up to June 1991 were associated with illicit drug use. Moreover, it was found that a link exists between AIDS and crack, in that crack addicts desperate for a new "hit" exchange sex for drugs or money to buy them, thereby contributing to the spread of AIDS.[37] This phenomenon also exists in the Caribbean.[38]

Patterns of Consumption and Abuse

The progression of drug use in the Caribbean usually involves alcohol and tobacco as the "gateway drugs," followed by marijuana and then cocaine. Interestingly, however, cocaine addicts often will have begun their drugs experience with ganja use, but not all ganja users progress to cocaine.

Drug consumption and abuse are not limited to any single social class or economic or ethnic group, although the consumption of certain drugs is higher in certain groups. Marijuana, for example, is predominantly a working-class drug of choice. Crack cocaine is widespread among lower- and middle-class people because it is considered "hard" and a "status" drug, but yet is cheap. Heroin, on the other hand, is a rich man's drug. Hence, partly because of cost, it is not widely available in the Caribbean, except in Puerto Rico and the U.S. Virgin Islands. Apart from the cost factor, the impact of heroin abuse in the region has been mitigated by what one Bahamian psychiatrist called a Caribbean "needle phobia."[39] But there is concern in many parts of the region that the liquid and smokable heroin now available in parts of Latin America will spread to the Caribbean. And given the increased heroin trafficking, it is realistic to expect a spillover, as happened with cocaine. The result would be a larger number of heroin addicts.

Cocaine and heroin consumption and abuse are primarily the results of a spillover from trafficking operations. Hence, they are most

37. See Nwanyanwu et al., "Acquired Immune Deficiency Syndrome," 399–408, and *Miami Herald*, "Crack Cocaine Speeds Spread of AIDS."
38. See United Nations International Drug Control Program, *Subregional Program Framework for the Caribbean, 1994–1995*, 11, 12.
39. Interview with Dr. Clark, December 1994.

significant in the major transit states, notably the Bahamas, Puerto Rico, Jamaica, Belize, the Dominican Republic, Trinidad and To-bago, and, to a lesser extent, Guyana. In the case of the Bahamas, not too long ago—in 1991—the INL reported: "The Bahamas suffers from a serious drug abuse and addiction problem brought about by the ready availability of drugs as they transit the country. Cocaine is the drug of choice for addicts."[40] The problem in Belize was dram-atized during the September 1991 Belize Games when close to 25 percent of the 180 winning athletes tested positive for illegal drug use. And in St. Vincent and the Grenadines, in 1993, over 60 per-cent of all mental-hospital admissions had a history of drug abuse, usually multiple use.[41]

The late Carl Stone's 1990 study of drug abuse in Jamaica con-cluded that the pattern of cocaine confiscation suggested that the country had become a cocaine and crack market for both locals and tourists. Stone considered the use of these drugs, combined with the long tradition of ganja use, to have created a serious drug-abuse problem in the country. Not surprisingly, it was found that Jamai-can public opinion has a favorable view of ganja, alcohol, and to-bacco use, and reserves most of its concern for cocaine use. Drugs were found to be used increasingly by the urban youth in areas such as Kingston, St. Andrew, and Spanish Town, and in tourist centers such as Ocho Rios, Negril, and Montego Bay. The study also found that crack and cocaine were used mostly by people in the country's highest and lowest socioeconomic groups. Moreover, it detected that ganja, once used mainly by the lower class and the Rastafarians, had become part of the lifestyle of the "fast-moving uptown yuppies."

Stone also indicated a sharp contrast between the frequency of cocaine and crack use and that of marijuana. Among users of the former drug there was a greater concentration of daily and weekly users, reflecting the compulsive nature of cocaine use. For cocaine, there was a 2 percent occasional use, a 21 percent monthly use, a 37 percent weekly use, and a 40 percent daily use. For marijuana, the results were as follows: occasional use, 38 percent; monthly

40. *INCSR* (1991), 192.
41. See *INCSR* (1992), 142, on Belize, and United Nations International Drug Con-trol Program, *Subregional Program Framework for the Caribbean, 1994–95*, 10, on St. Vincent.

use, 14 percent; weekly use, 27 percent; and daily use, 21 percent.[42] The study also showed "a close relationship between the use of various drugs to a degree that one can define a syndrome of multiple drug use as a central feature of Jamaica's drug culture."[43] Stone's findings contradicted analysts who had argued previously that marijuana use in Jamaica was resistant to the use of "hard drugs." Stone contended that the previous approach to drug abuse in Jamaica was flawed in examining the use of each different substance as a separate and distinct phenomenon.

Studies more recent than Stone's, commissioned by the Jamaica National Council on Drug Abuse, have found that the peak incidence of crack cocaine abuse is among people between ages fifteen and thirty, with twenty-five- and twenty-six-year-olds being the biggest users. However, crack addicts as young as eleven years of age have been admitted to the Detoxification Unit of the University of the West Indies Hospital in Mona, Jamaica.[44] There have been even younger addicts—nine-year-olds—in the Bahamas, where forty years is the prevalent outer age.[45] Given the long-time high incidence of trafficking there, it is understandable that the Bahamas was one of the first Caribbean societies to experience cocaine addiction. The problem was said to have started in 1983. That year 69 addicts were admitted to the Sandilands Rehabilitation Center for treatment, but the next year there were 220 admissions. Indeed, some researchers contend that the crack epidemic began in the Bahamas two to three years before it did in the United States.[46]

An assessment of the situation in Trinidad and Tobago reveals that marijuana use increased significantly during the 1970s. This was followed in the 1980s by "an escalation in overall drug usage, particularly that of cocaine," resulting mainly from the significant increase in the production of cocaine in South America and a shift in trafficking routes to and through the southern Caribbean.[47] Al-

42. Stone, "National Survey on the Use of Drugs in Jamaica," 35.
43. Ibid., 40.
44. Browne, "Drug Abuse Still a Major Problem Here," and Fox, "Situation Analysis of Drug Abuse in Jamaica."
45. Neville and Clarke, "Drug Abuse in the Bahamas," 196.
46. Jekel et al., "Nine Years of the Freebase Cocaine Epidemic in the Bahamas," 23.
47. Trinidad and Tobago, Ministry of Consumer Affairs and Social Services, *Strategic Plan, 1992–97,* 7.

though only a minority of all drug users in Trinidad and Tobago (and elsewhere) ever seek treatment, admissions to treatment facilities is one way of appreciating the extent of the problem. According to the National Alcohol and Drug Abuse Prevention Program (NADAPP), with the exception of 1987, the number of cocaine, marijuana, and heroin addicts admitted to treatment centers in Trinidad and Tobago increased progressively between 1983 and 1988: 376 in 1983, 602 in 1984, 785 in 1985, 877 in 1986, 1,055 in 1987, and 1,061 in 1988.

There is a certain correlation between drug use and race in Trinidad that may well exist in Guyana, because the racial pluralism and the socioeconomic profiles of the people of African and Indian descent are similar in Guyana and Trinidad and Tobago. One Jamaican psychiatrist with long treatment and research experience in Trinidad and Tobago has noted: "Trinidad and Tobago is almost equally divided into populations of people of East Indian and African descent. Yet admissions for alcoholism have consistently reflected a ratio of two to three East Indians to every one person of African descent admitted." However, "with the advent of the cocaine epidemic we saw a mirror opposite of the situation developing with respect to the drug abuse population. Data from Caura hospital demonstrated that 60 percent of admissions for [cocaine] drug dependence were people of African descent whereas only 30 percent were East Indians."[48]

Motivation for Consumption

The consumption-abuse profile presented above begs the question, Why do people in the Caribbean consume drugs, especially considering the prices for some of the substances involved?[49]

There is, of course, no single reason for this. Like people in other

48. Lewis, "Overview of Cocaine Abuse in Trinidad and Tobago," 3.
49. Fall 1995 DEA estimates of the cost of cocaine, for example, were as follows (per kilo, in U.S. dollars): Antigua-Barbuda, $5,000–$7,000; Bahamas, $10,000–$12,000; Dominican Republic, $6,000–$8,000; Jamaica, $6,000–$7,000; Puerto Rico, $12,000–$14,000; St. Martin, $11,000–$13,000; Trinidad and Tobago, $3,000–$4,000. For comparative purposes, consider the prices in three major U.S. cities: Los Angeles, $15,000–$20,000; Miami, $15,000–$19,000; New York, $17,000–$23,000. These price estimates reflect a general pattern in relation to cocaine prices: the further from South America you go, the higher the prices become.

regions of the world, people in the Caribbean take drugs mainly because of the effects they produce: mood change, excitement, relaxation, pleasure, stimulation, and sedation. Illegal drug consumption is also predicated on the belief that drugs enhance physical and mental performance. In addition, drug use and abuse are influenced by the availability of drugs, the personality and disposition of individuals, religion, peer pressure and peer usage, and perceptions of the drugs' effectiveness in rendering the desired results. Some people also take drugs because the practice is proscribed; others see it as a way to demonstrate rebelliousness.[50] Thus, at any one time and in any one country in the region a variety of socioeconomic, social-psychological, and political factors would be part of the motivational matrix for drug consumption and abuse.

It is apposite here to relate a personal encounter with some of the socioeconomic dynamics involved. In July 1994, while on a research trip in Grenada, I met a woman in the Belmont section of the island, close to the capital, St. George's. This woman—Ms. G. for purposes of reference here—was in her mid-thirties and had grown up with a friend of mine then resident in New York, now living in Washington, D.C. She was unaware of my research agenda, but I was introduced to her as "Doc from New York" (where I then resided). During the course of a few hours of conversation over beer, I was taken into a great deal of confidence by Ms. G. and her cousin, the woman who had made the introduction.

Ms. G. was not only a drug user—not too difficult to tell from her deportment (or lack of it)—but she was also a ganja cultivator, a crack dealer, and, allegedly, a prostitute and a thief. She herself told me about the drug-related part of her life, complaining that her reputed husband, "Rastaman," often stole from her ganja plot, "even when his was in a giving state." She also complained about Rastaman's physical abuse, showing me (with a certain perverted pride) a large scar on her left leg, the result of a wound inflicted from one of Rastaman's frequent "beatings." Indeed, the practice was so regular that she vowed to leave him, to which her cousin retorted "Again?! I tired hearing you sa' you leavin' Rastaman." The highlight

---

50. U.S. Department of Justice, National Drug Intelligence Center, *Drugs, Crime, and the Justice System,* 20–22, and Wray and Young, "Consequences of Substance Abuse," 47–48.

of the conversation was when Ms. G. indicated a "good way to use coke," one that Rastaman often used with her: rubbing wet cocaine on the male genitals to "have sex for three to four hours." Never did I expect to hear this from someone in the Caribbean, least of all in Grenada. This gave a whole new meaning to the term "Isle of Spice," by which Granada is affectionately known. I learned of Ms. G.'s prostitution and robbery activity from her cousin after she had left. According to the cousin, she sold her body to get crack when neither she nor Rastaman had any. In addition, the two of them often colluded to rob tourists; she would present herself as a "good night prospect," after which, either on the way to the intended victim's hotel or when there, Rastaman would perpetrate the robbery.

That Sunday afternoon in Belmont was quite a revealing experience, allowing me to get a close encounter with some of the social dynamics of drugs in the region. If nothing else—and there is much else, as later chapters will show—that encounter was one of the stark confirmations of what has become increasingly obvious to me: the Caribbean has truly lost its innocence with the spread of drugs.

In giving his explanation of drug abuse generally, Winston Davidson, a Jamaican medical doctor, offered a "model of causation" purported to have universal applicability. It is a comprehensive schema involving four main elements: the environment, the host (human), the agent (drug), and the natural history of drug addiction. Environment factors include economic, social, cultural, and other influences, while host factors are psychobiological, with genetic, stress, personality, and hedonistic elements. Availability, production, and addictive property are some of the aspects of the agent that Davidson factors into the matrix.[51] In the Jamaican study mentioned earlier, Carl Stone suggested that all classes and levels of Jamaican society are "highly disposed" to consuming drugs that relax tensions, suppress worries, manage stress, and "give a feeling of overcoming problems and being on top of the world." Such a rationalization of drug use involves short-term pleasure and long-term pain, for both individual users and the society as a whole. Nevertheless, it is a rationalization used elsewhere in the Caribbean.

Curiously enough, the geography factor discussed earlier in rela-

51. Davidson, "Integrated Demand Reduction Strategy," esp. 5–7.

tion to production is also at play in the consumption-abuse area. The geographic proximity of the United States to the Caribbean, which is detailed in the next chapter, is an important consideration here. For one thing, it permits frequent commercial contact between the two areas, facilitating drug-use interaction involving business-persons and tourists, apart from general social interaction. Harsh evidence of this exists. During the early 1990s reports indicated that about 25 percent of the visitors to Jamaica flocked the major tourist resorts—Montego Bay and Ocho Rios—in search of drugs.[52] Between January and March 1994 alone, thirteen tourists died from cocaine overdose in two tourist areas: Montego Bay, in north-western Jamaica, and Westmoreland, in the West. They were not only users but also traffickers. In one dramatic case the autopsy on one Westmoreland-based tourist found that he had ingested 275 packets of compressed ganja, weighing about two pounds.[53]

In addition, legal and illegal migration between the United States and the Caribbean facilitates drug-use emulation by West Indians, both at home and in North America. Moreover, because of its economic power and, to some extent, its social structure, North American social practice is a model for many people in the Caribbean (and elsewhere). Hence, people emulate not only what is legitimate and positive about the United States but, unfortunately, also things illegal and negative. And it does not help that the United States is the single largest drug-consuming nation in the world.

The geography feature of the United States–Caribbean consumption link is complemented and reinforced by the powerful U.S. media that penetrate the region. Among other things, this results in the transmission of American attitudes and values, such as materialism, which influence what some people in the Caribbean see as desirable or necessary for social acceptance or upward social mobility. Hence, drug use and the conspicuous consumption and "easy money" associated with drugs become desirable social behavior for some people in the Caribbean. Some analysts see this as part of larger social dynamics. One writer, for example, sees a societal

52. Earle, "25% of Tourists Flock to J'ca for Drugs."
53. Earle and Thompson, "Cops Say Visitors Overdosed," and Morris, "Cocaine Knocking Tourists out West."

transformation in which "our culture is becoming cancerously materialistic and hedonistic," with the result that "the individual's own gratification is the standard of right and wrong."[54]

Conclusion

This chapter points to variability in both production and consumption-abuse—in the levels of production among countries and in the kinds and volumes consumed, among other things. Production and consumption-abuse are not driven by the same set of factors, although there are domestic and international influences on both. Geography and politics have a central place in the production area. Geography also has a role in consumption-abuse. This analysis also indicates that history, economics, and social practice have all featured in both the production and consumption-abuse problems. Hence, the dynamics in these aspects of the region's geonarcotics milieu are complex, making for complexity in the efforts to deal with the consequent threats and apprehensions. But as problematic as production and consumption-abuse are, they are only part of the dilemma. Another critical area is trafficking, the subject of the next chapter.

54. Boyne, "Crime, Corruption, and Civility."

2
Drug-Trafficking Operations

The drug trade learned long ago that where political will is
weak it can establish a modus vivendi with a government.
Trafficking organizations as a matter of course will absorb
losses in a given area if their overall operations in other
areas are profitable. This is the cost of doing business.
—*International Narcotics Control Strategy Report*, 1996

The Caribbean lies at what José Martí once called "the Vortex of the
Americas," making it a bridge or front between North and South
America. This strategic importance was dramatized in geopolitical
terms during the recent Cold War. But the strategic value of the
region lies not only in its geopolitical value as viewed by state actors
engaged in systemic conflict and cooperation. Over the last three to
four decades it has also been viewed as strategic by nonstate drug
actors, also with conflict and cooperation in mind, but in terms of
geonarcotics, not geopolitics. While there is production, consumption-abuse, trafficking, and money laundering in the region, it is
trafficking that best highlights this strategic importance, dramatiz-
ing the importance of geography as a geonarcotics factor. Thus, although Chapter 1, in its examination of production, presented a

geographic profile of the region, an additional comment on geography is warranted with regard to trafficking.

The Caribbean as Vortex

Any discussion of the Caribbean as a vortex needs to begin with what is perhaps the most dominant geographical feature of the region: the Caribbean Sea. The Caribbean Sea is 1,049,500 square miles in area. Its north-south width ranges from 380 miles to about 700 miles. The deepest passage connecting the Eastern Caribbean with the Atlantic Ocean is the Anegada Passage, a sea lane of 48 nautical miles between Anegada and Sombrero Islands. The name Caribbean was introduced in 1773 by Thomas Jeffreys, author of *The West Indies Atlas*. He named the sea after the Carib people, who were native to many of the islands in the area. The islands in the Caribbean Sea form a chain almost 2,500 miles long, but never more than 160 miles wide, creating a bridge between North and South America.[1]

Aspects of both the physical and social geography of the Caribbean make it conducive to drug trafficking. Generally, physical-geography considerations are more important than social-geography features, and the key physical-geography elements are island character and location.

Except for mainland Belize, French Guiana, Guyana, and Suriname, Caribbean countries are all island territories. Some are plural island territories, examples being St. Vincent and the Grenadines, with several islands, and the Virgin Islands, comprising about 100 islands and cays. Indeed, one—the Bahamas—is an archipelago of 700 islands and 2,000 cays. This island character permits entry into and use of Caribbean territories from the surrounding sea at literally hundreds of different places. For the mainland states, access is possible at various places along the Atlantic Ocean in the case of Guyana, Suriname, and French Guiana, and along the Caribbean coast in Belize's case.

The region's physical location highlights another feature: proxim-

---

1. Griffith, *The Quest for Security in the Caribbean*, 51.

ity. This proximity is dual: to South America, a major drug supplier, and to North America, a major drug consumer. On the supply side, the world's cocaine is produced in South America, coming notably from Colombia, Peru, Bolivia, Brazil, Ecuador, and Venezuela. Colombia alone produces about 80 percent of all the cocaine in the world, although only about 20 percent of worldwide coca-leaf cultivation is done there. (Colombia's coca cultivation is reported to have grown 13 percent in 1995, making that country the world's second largest coca producer, after Peru. Bolivia's place is now reduced from second to third.) A significant proportion of global heroin and marijuana also comes from South and Central America, especially from Colombia, Mexico, Peru, Paraguay, Brazil, and Guatemala.[2]

On the demand side, the United States has the dubious distinction of being the world's single largest drug-consuming nation. An analyst at the Congressional Research Service reported as follows in 1988: "America is consuming drugs at an annual rate of more than six metric tons (mt) of heroin, 70–90 mt of cocaine, and 6,000–9,000 mt of marijuana—80 percent of which are imported. American demand therefore is the linchpin of one of the fastest-growing and most profitable industries in the world."[3] By 1993, however, State Department estimates placed consumption of cocaine alone at 150 to 175 metric tons, valued at U.S.$15 billion to $17.5 billion.[4] In April 1995, General Barry McCaffrey, then the head of the U.S. Southern Command, now the U.S. drug "czar," estimated that about 300 metric tons of the approximately 575 metric tons of cocaine available worldwide in 1994 was consumed in the United States.[5]

As Figure 4 and Tables 3 and 4 show, there is not much distance either between the Caribbean and South America or between the Caribbean and the United States, especially the southern and eastern parts of the United States. Some countries, like the Bahamas, Cuba, Haiti, Jamaica, and the Cayman Islands, are just "a stone's

2. For a recent discussion of Latin American drug production in a global context, see Bagley and Walker, *Drug Trafficking in the Americas,* chaps. 5–10, 14, 15, 17, 18, 22, and 23; United Nations, *Report of the International Narcotics Control Board for 1995,* 29–36; and *INCSR* (1996), 61–158.

3. Surrett, *The International Narcotics Trade,* 1.

4. *INCSR* (1993), 16.

5. General McCaffrey, "Lessons of 1994: Prognosis for 1995 and Beyond."

Fig. 4 Maritime Trafficking Routes in the Caribbean

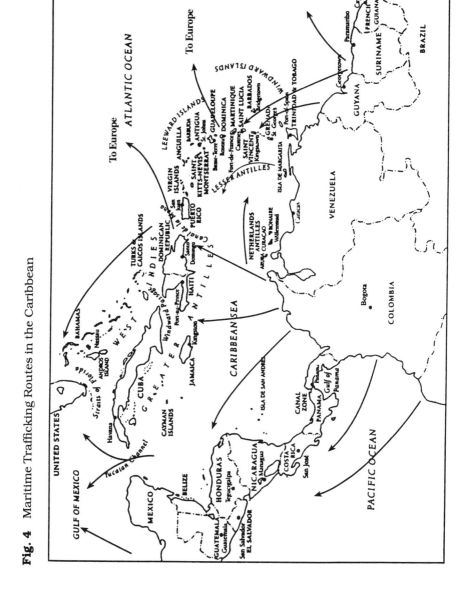

throw" away from Miami. Table 3 reveals that, except for French Guiana and Suriname, all Caribbean countries are less than 2,000 miles from Miami, and only seven of them are more than 2,000 miles from Atlanta and Washington, D.C. Table 3 only gives distances for six states and the District of Columbia in the United States. However, these are not the only places that feature in Caribbean drug trafficking; they are places with ports of entry that are among the heaviest used for trafficking from and through the Caribbean. As for distances between the Caribbean and some main South American drug centers, twenty-four of the twenty-nine Caribbean countries in Table 4 are less than 1,000 miles from Caracas, and all except Belize (in relation to Caracas), French Guiana (in relation to Cali and Medellín), and Suriname (in relation to Medellín) are less than 1,500 miles away from Bogotá, Cali, Caracas, and Medellín.

The distances shown in Tables 3 and 4 are calculated using air distances from Caribbean capitals and from international-airport locations where noncapital cities are involved. Because of this the tables mask the reality that for some trafficking purposes the distances involved are even shorter, given that there are places in some Caribbean territories, outside the capitals, that are closer to U.S. or Latin American territory, and traffickers exploit this greater proximity. Nassau, for example, is only 183 miles away from Miami, as Table 3 shows, but Bimini, also in the Bahamas, is even closer to American territory: 40 miles from the Florida Keys. A mere 90 miles separate Cuba from the United States. As Table 4 indicates, the distance between Trinidad (Port of Spain) and Venezuela (Caracas) is 371 miles. However, it is only 7 miles between La Brea in southwestern Trinidad and Pedernales in northeastern Venezuela, a strait called Serpent's Mouth. Moreover, the town of Lethem in southwest Guyana is a mere 75 miles away from the city of Boa Vista in northeastern Brazil; and Eteringbang, Guyana, is only 28 miles from El Dorado, Venezuela.[6]

Europe is also a huge drug-consuming area, with cocaine, heroin,

6. I am grateful to Brigadier David Granger (ret.) for the Guyana-Brazil and the Guyana-Venezuela data, and to Dr. Ricardo Mario Rodríguez of the Venezuelan Mission to the OAS for the Trinidad-Venezuela information, all provided during May 1995.

Table 3 Caribbean-U.S. Distances (miles)

Caribbean/U.S.	Atlanta	Baltimore	Boston	Miami	New York	Philadelphia	Washington, D.C.
Antigua-Barbuda	1,811	1,767	1,827	1,332	1,787	1,767	1,763
Aruba	1,716	1,881	2,057	1,133	1,960	1,912	1,867
Bahamas	726	980	1,244	183	1,100	1,030	953
Barbados	2,114	2,082	2,133	1,611	2,099	2,081	2,077
Belize	1,135	1,646	1,992	809	1,812	1,727	1,620
Bonaire	1,798	1,931	2,088	1,223	2,001	1,957	1,917
British Virgin Islands	1,613	1,606	1,690	1,117	1,632	1,609	1,593
Cayman Islands	1,007	1,398	1,702	454	1,542	1,465	1,375
Cuba	741	1,163	1,476	227	1,306	1,233	1,130
Curaçao	1,770	1,916	2,081	1,191	1,989	1,944	1,903
Dominica	1,916	1,892	1,950	1,412	1,907	1,890	1,882
Dominican Republic	1,378	1,489	1,648	829	1,456	1,509	1,470
French Guiana	2,856	2,810	2,822	2,342	2,808	2,799	2,804
Grenada	2,065	2,080	2,161	1,535	2,112	2,086	2,073
Guadeloupe	1,867	1,839	1,898	1,375	1,844	1,837	1,829
Guyana	2,497	2,509	2,572	1,957	2,534	2,512	2,503
Haiti	1,286	1,452	1,640	712	1,530	1,485	1,427
Jamaica	1,181	1,462	1,717	586	1,580	1,515	1,443
Martinique	1,966	1,945	2,003	1,468	1,959	1,729	1,934
Montserrat	1,810	1,782	1,843	1,322	1,800	1,780	1,772

	Atlanta	Baltimore	Boston	Miami	New York	Philadelphia	Washington, D.C.
Puerto Rico	1,547	1,564	1,674	1,045	1,608	1,576	1,556
St. Kitts–Nevis	1,758	1,731	1,795	1,265	1,747	1,729	1,720
St. Lucia	1,997	1,978	2,042	1,490	2,001	1,980	1,972
St. Maarten	—	1,667	1,738	1,223	1,692	1,669	1,661
St. Vincent & the Grenadines	2,033	2,031	2,097	1,508	2,049	2,031	2,019
Suriname	2,681	2,664	2,697	2,154	2,671	2,658	2,655
Trinidad & Tobago	2,148	2,174	2,259	1,611	2,208	2,182	2,167
Turks & Caicos	1,171	1,245	1,440	647	1,337	1,296	1,306
U.S. Virgin Islands	1,600	1,597	1,693	1,107	1,635	1,606	1,590
Atlanta	—	576	946	595	755	667	548
Baltimore	576	—	370	945	179	91	28
Boston	946	370	—	1,258	191	280	398
Miami	595	945	1,258	—	1,092	1,013	921
New York	755	179	191	1,092	—	89	207
Philadelphia	667	91	280	1,013	89	—	119
Washington, D.C.	548	28	398	921	207	119	—

SOURCES: Gary Fitzpatrick and Marilyn Modelin, *Direct-Line Distances*, Int'l ed. (Metuchen, N.J.: Scarecrow Press, 1986); and *Official Airline Guide*, June 1994.

NOTES: Distances are air-mile distances.
Distances between countries are calculated on the basis of distances between country capitals.
Distances between noncapital cities are on the basis of the (major) international airports of cities.

Table 4 Caribbean–Latin American–European Distances (miles)

Caribbean	Bogotá	Cali	Caracas	Medellín	Amsterdam	London	Paris
Antigua-Barbuda	1,201	1,244	563	1,198	4,310	4,092	4,172
Aruba	606	768	244	574	4,899	4,683	4,775
Bahamas	1,425	1,488	1,215	1,301	4,528	4,354	4,484
Barbados	1,155	1,340	526	1,193	4,427	4,208	4,270
Belize	1,322	1,261	1,539	1,169	5,443	5,204	5,386
Bonaire	655	823	137	644	4,846	4,629	4,714
British Virgin Islands	1,147	1,309	568	1,118	4,417	4,141	4,229
Cayman Islands	1,124	1,138	1,131	979	5,024	4,816	4,949
Cuba	1,374	1,409	1,328	1,246	4,864	4,667	4,814
Curaçao	625	796	174	610	4,871	4,654	4,742
Dominica	1,134	1,313	511	1,146	4,393	4,152	4,242
Dominican Republic	989	1,130	575	924	4,578	4,364	4,471
French Guiana	1,499	1,671	1,076	1,603	4,598	4,379	4,394
Grenada	987	1,171	369	1,025	4,576	4,357	4,423
Guadeloupe	1,148	1,325	534	1,153	4,370	4,122	4,199
Guyana	1,106	1,285	650	1,197	4,567	4,504	4,545

Haiti	962	1,084	661	877	4,683	4,462	4,574
Jamaica	927	1,001	839	812	4897	4,689	4,811
Martinique	1,124	1,307	487	1,145	4,417	4,190	4,260
Montserrat	1,158	1,332	531	1,155	4,352	4,128	4,207
Puerto Rico	1,094	1,256	543	1,060	4,413	4,197	4,293
St. Kitts–Nevis	1,164	1,336	546	1,155	4,342	4,120	4,200
St. Lucia	1,102	1,286	467	1,127	4,439	4,220	4,289
St. Maarten	1,183	1,356	573	1,169	4,313	4,095	4,182
St. Vincent & the Grenadines	1,056	1,240	421	1,087	4,502	4,279	4,344
Suriname	1,306	1,481	866	1,629	4,659	4,437	4,465
Trinidad & Tobago	957	1,142	371	1,009	4,643	4,424	4,486
Turks & Caicos	1,176	1,291	805	1,088	4,479	4,265	4,378
U.S. Virgin Islands	1,124	1,291	556	1,098	4,379	4,159	4,248

SOURCES: Gary Fitzpatrick and Marilyn Modelin, *Direct-Line Distances*, Int'l ed. (Metuchen, N.J.: Scarecrow Press, 1986); and *Official Airline Guide*, June 1994.

NOTES: Distances are air-mile distances.
Distances between countries are calculated on the basis of distances between country capitals.
Distances between noncapital cities are on the basis of the (major) international airports of cities.

and marijuana imports coming through and from the Caribbean.[7] However, despite the relatively great distance between that continent and the Caribbean region, as Table 4 points out, the Caribbean is a major transit area for drugs bound for Europe. Several factors explain this. One is the proximity of the Caribbean to South America, and a second is the commercial, communications, and other linkages between Europe and the Caribbean, which provide the infrastructure, institutional and otherwise, for trafficking.

The third factor is the political linkages involving countries in Europe and territories in the Caribbean. Because French Guiana, Guadeloupe, and Martinique are Départments d'Outre Mer (DOMs) of France, and Anguilla, Bermuda, British Virgin Islands, Cayman Islands, Montserrat, and the Turks and Caicos Islands are British dependencies, and Bonaire, Curaçao, Saba, and St. Maarten are integral parts of the Kingdom of the Netherlands, there are certain customs, immigration, and transportation arrangements and facilities between these territories and their respective European "owners," and these are exploited by traffickers.[8] Some of the arrangements are similar to those involving the United States and Puerto Rico and the U.S. Virgin Islands, which also facilitate trafficking aimed at destinations in the continental United States.

Each of the elements of the physical geography factor discussed above—island character and location—by itself conduces to trafficking. However, the region's vulnerability to trafficking and the prospects for continued trafficking can be better appreciated when it is recognized that these factors are often mutually supporting and reinforcing and that they interact with aspects of social geography. One way to understand these dynamics is to examine patterns and routes of trafficking in and through the region.

Trafficking Patterns and Routes

Apart from trading their own marijuana in the United States, some Caribbean countries are important transshipment centers for

7. For recent assessments of European drug operations and their Latin American and Caribbean (and other) connections, see *INCSR* (1996), 315–432; MacDonald and Zagaris, *International Handbook on Drug Control*, chaps. 14–18; and Lee and MacDonald, "Drugs in the East."

8. For an examination of the political configurations between European countries and Caribbean territories, see Sutton, *Europe and the Caribbean*.

South American cocaine, heroin, and marijuana bound for Europe and North America.

For more than two decades the Bahamas, Belize, and Jamaica dominated this business. In the case of the Bahamas, its geography makes it an excellent candidate for drug transshipment, given its hundreds of islands and cays and its strategic location in the airline flight path between Colombia and South Florida. Anthony Maingot once observed: "In a way, geography had always been the Bahamas' main commodity, and they had always marketed it with great skill."[9] This, of course, is true of other countries.

Although most of the Bahamian islands could be used for drug smuggling, the trade has been concentrated over the years in a few strategic places: Bimini, the Exumas, Andros, Grand Bahama, Abaco, Berry Islands, Cat Islands, Ragged Island, Mayaguana, Eleuthera, Long Island, San Salvador, and Inagua.[10] For a typical cocaine-trafficking mission, aircraft depart from the north coast of Colombia and four to five hours later arrive in the Bahamas, where their cargo is dropped. The cargo is then either transferred immediately to waiting vessels for the final run to a U.S. point of entry or is collected and held for later shipment. However, this is not the only modus operandi. Traffickers use other tactics, including use of Cuban waters to evade OPBAT (Operation Bahamas and the Turks and Caicos) efforts, drop-offs by aircraft making only momentary landings, and development of a cocaine route through Jamaica.[11]

The Bahamas has also become (in)famous for the marijuana and hashish traffic, from South America as well as Jamaica. In fact, when the Bahamas first became a transshipment center, the drug involved was mainly marijuana, with a few consignments of hashish.[12] There is evidence of drug trafficking dating as far back as 1968, when 250–300 pounds of marijuana were flown from Jamaica to Bimini. One of the earliest cocaine seizures was made in 1974: 247 pounds of pure cocaine, with a 1974 street value of U.S.$2 billion, at an airport in George Town, Exuma. That same

9. Maingot, "Laundering the Gains of the Drug Trade," 168.

10. For a detailed examination of the use of Bimini and other areas for trafficking, see Bahamas, *Report of the Commission of Inquiry*, 9–51; idem, *Bahamas Narcotics Control Report, 1991* (1992); and U.S. General Accounting Office, *Drug Control: Anti-Drug Efforts in the Bahamas*, esp. 14–28.

11. *INCSR* (1995), 160.

12. Bahamas, *Report of the Commission of Inquiry*, 31.

year, the Bahamas police discovered off Grand Bahama a store of marijuana over six feet high and more than two miles long.[13]

There have been undulating patterns of drug seizures since the mid to late 1980s, reflecting differences in the use of countries, successful countermeasures, and consequent trafficker adaptations. For example, as Table 5 shows, cocaine seizures dropped from 490 kilos in 1994 to 390 kilos in 1995, while marijuana seizures increased dramatically from 1,420 kilos in 1994 to 3,530 kilos in 1995.[14] There are also, understandably, fluctuations in the number of trafficking arrests. In all cases both locals and foreigners are arrested. U.S. citizens always constitute the largest group of foreign-

Table 5   Caribbean Drug Seizures, 1991–1995 (kilos)

Country		1991	1992	1993	1994	1995
Antigua-Barbuda	C	NA	500	NA	130	110
	M	NA	NA	10,095	3,380	217
Bahamas	C	5,260	4,800	1,800	490	390
	M	1,180	1,000	650	1,420	3,530
Belize	C	13	850	100	140	840
	M	800	5,200	93,000	4,800	2,800
British Virgin	C	15	24	709	450	1,194
Islands	M	NA	NA	NA	1,000	235
Dominican Republic	C	1,810	2,360	1,070	2,800	3,600
	M	400	6,450	310	6,800	NA
Guyana	C	7	41	463	76	51
	M	NA	93,000	15,600	54,800	10,900
Haiti	C	188	56	157	716	550
	M	330	NA	2,520	500	NA
Jamaica	C	60	490	160	180	570
	M	4,300	3,500	7,500	4,600	3,720
Trinidad & Tobago	C	NA	NA	NA	311	110
	M	NA	NA	NA	3,977	1,634

Source: U.S. Department of State, *International Narcotics Control Strategy Report* (various years).

C = Cocaine.
M = Marijuana.

13. Ibid., 7–8.
14. *INCSR* (1996), 166.

ers, followed by Jamaicans, Colombians, and Haitians in varying order. However, nationals of places far away from the Bahamas also engage in trafficking. For example, in August 1990, a Nigerian woman was given a seven-year sentence by the Bahamian Supreme Court following her arrest in 1989 for attempting to smuggle 4.1 pounds of heroin and 1.25 pounds of cocaine out of the country.[15] In 1994, 1,025 people were arrested for trafficking; the figure for 1995 was 1,565.

The geography and topography of Belize also make that country ideal for drug smuggling. Apart from a long coastline and contiguous borders with Guatemala and Mexico, two major heroin and marijuana producers, there are dense unpopulated jungle areas and numerous inland waterways. Moreover, there are about 140 isolated airstrips and virtually no radar coverage beyond a thirty-mile radius of the international airport at Belize City. And recently there has been increasing use of maritime routes.

Crack has also been featuring more prominently. According to the 1994 *INCSR*, in 1993, "for the first time, there was evidence of Belizean export of crack cocaine to the United States."[16] Belize officials agreed with the 1992 U.S. government assessment that the country's "growing importance as a transshipment point for South American cocaine is now the[ir] most important narcotics-related challenge."[17] That assessment has remained credible over the ensuing years. Indeed, while 141 kilos of cocaine were seized in all of 1994, two seizures in January 1995 alone netted 636 kilos. Overall, 1995 cocaine seizures amounted to 840 kilos.[18]

Jamaica has long been key to the drug trade, given its long coastline, proximity to the United States, its many ports, harbors, and beaches, and its closeness to the Yucatan and Windward Passages, as Figure 4 shows. Trafficking takes place by both air and sea. For the maritime traffic, use is often made of pleasure boats with storage compartments to ferry small quantities of drugs. Large loads are put aboard commercial cargo and fishing vessels. Both large

15. See Bahamas, Ministry of National Security, *Summary Report on the Traffic in Narcotic Drugs Affecting the Bahamas in 1990*, 13.
16. *INCSR* (1994), 136.
17. *INCSR* (1992), 141.
18. The January 1995 seizure is reported in *INCSR* (1995), 122; the 1995 total figure comes from *INCSR* (1996), 122.

and small amounts are also smuggled by air, and arrests of couriers at the country's two international airports are almost daily occurrences. Jamaicans also have an asset as far as South American operators are concerned: a long track record of ganja smuggling.

Jamaica Defense Force (JDF) sources indicate that both legal and illegal airstrips are used for trafficking. In December 1994 the JDF was aware of forty-nine illegal airstrips, about 50 percent of which were capable of being brought into operation. Many of them are only 1,200–1,500 feet long, just enough length for use by Pipers, Cessnas, BE-100s, and KingAir aircraft. The largest known illegal strip, 3,000 feet, was on the south coast. Jamaica's west and south coasts are the most popular areas for air trafficking because of their physical geography. Apart from landings on strips designed or adapted for drug operations, landings have been made on roads, in cane fields, and on legal strips owned by bauxite and sugar companies. The JDF has destroyed close to a hundred illegal airstrips and airfields but, as the JDF chief of staff explained, given the heavy limestone in many of the popular landing areas, operators are often able to make fields serviceable within ten days of destruction.

Most of the aircraft recovered from forced landings or after crashes are leased craft with U.S. registry. However, most of the pilots are Bahamian or Bahamas-based. It frustrates JDF officials that most of the time the aircraft are recovered by their owners using legal and administrative technicalities and loopholes. Planes now rarely come to a complete stop for trafficking operations. Loading and unloading is done by "loaders," who run alongside the aircraft, putting on or taking off the cocaine and or marijuana. Partly because of this, unless there is a crash, pilots are rarely caught; the loaders are the ones arrested. Most of the cocaine air operations using Jamaica involve San Andres and Bogotá in Colombia, the Bahamas, Panama, and Curaçao. Furthermore, traffickers do not rely only on illegal flights; they also use legal commercial flights. Particularly popular, and problematic for Jamaican officials, was the commercial link between San Andres and Montego Bay. That connection was suspended in September 1994, but there are still commercial flights linking Jamaica and Bogotá. Now, according to military intelligence sources, the drugs go from San Andres to Bogotá, and then to Montego Bay or Kingston.[19]

19. Interviews with Rear Admiral Brady, Lieutenant Colonel Douglas, and Captain Edwards, December 1994.

Jamaican drug seizures are sometimes dramatic because of the quantity of drugs seized. In April 1989, for instance, U.S. Customs found 4,173 pounds of marijuana on an Air Jamaica A-300 Airbus in Miami. The drugs were packed in eighty-eight boxes labeled "wearing apparel" and consigned to Joseph and Schiller, Inc., of Miami, coming from Threadways Garments of Jamaica. That same April 5,000 pounds of marijuana was seized in Gramercy, Louisiana, on board MV *Kotor,* which was there to deliver a shipment of Jamaican bauxite. The drugs were discovered after violent clashes between two rival drug gangs over its ownership.[20]

As Table 5 indicates, marijuana seizures in 1993 were 7,500 kilos, up from 3,500 kilos the previous year. The actual amount of cocaine seized in 1993 was 160 kilos, down from a 1992 high of 490 kilos. The 1992 figure was exceptional because of one dramatic operation where 412 kilos were confiscated. Heroin and hashish oil continue to be transshipped, with confiscations of the latter amounting to 235 kilos in 1993. There were 1,416 arrests in 1993, up by 267 from the 1992 figure of 1,149. During 1994, 886 people were arrested for drug trafficking (and production). The 1995 figure was considerably higher: 3,905.

March 6, 1995, saw a large seizure in Jamaica: 4,000 pounds of marijuana, along with weapons and ammunition, in the St. Paul's district of Manchester. There was also a large seizure on March 3, 1995: 10,000 pounds of marijuana, valued at J$20 million, in twenty-seven barrels concealed by unfinished furniture in a twenty-foot container at the Kingston Wharf, awaiting shipment to Miami. In October 1995, 814 pounds of cocaine was seized at Montego Bay's international airport. The drugs were found in the cargo section of a Chilean passenger aircraft on stopover in Jamaica, en route from Chile and Colombia to Miami.[21] And in December 1995, 43,000 pounds of marijuana in 856 boxes labeled "ceramic tiles" was found at the docks in Jamaica aboard a freighter that had brought the consignment from Cartegena, Colombia.[22]

Although the Bahamas, Belize, and Jamaica are still important drug-trafficking centers, countermeasures there and in South and

20. *New York Carib News,* "Jamaica Under Drug Siege"; idem, "Questions Surround Air Jamaica Drug Find"; and idem, "Politicians United Against Drugs."

21. *Gleaner* (Jamaica), "Major Ganja Find in Manchester," and *New York Carib News,* "Jamaica: 800-Pound Cocaine Haul."

22. *New York Carib News,* " Police Seize Colombian Ganja."

Central America have prompted traffickers to seek and develop alternative routes, bringing eastern and southern Caribbean countries into greater prominence since the early 1990s. The shifts are of such a magnitude that in November 1994 Puerto Rico and the U.S. Virgin Islands were designated by U.S. authorities as high-intensity drug trafficking areas (HIDTAs),[23] a designation surely appropriate to other areas in the region. As confirmation of this designation, one study declared that "Puerto Rico has become the primary transshipment point into the southeast United States" and that "Puerto Rico and the U.S. Virgin Islands accounted for 26 percent of the documented attempts to smuggle cocaine into the continental United States during 1994."[24] In one case in Puerto Rico, two huge drug shipments—1,650 kilos of cocaine worth U.S.$166 million—were found in one day: July 20, 1996.[25]

Puerto Rico's high-intensity drug operations are not only large and numerous but also daring, often conducted within military perimeters. In one September 1995 case, guards at the naval base at Vieques alerted law-enforcement authorities of 728 kilos of cocaine partly buried in the sands along the base's southern flank. The cocaine, worth U.S.$10 million, was the second cocaine discovery on navy property in as many years.[26] Because of the increased drug activity in the eastern Caribbean, in July 1995 the Drug Enforcement Administration (DEA) upgraded its presence in Puerto Rico from "Office" to "Field Division." It increased the staff and assigned a special-agent-in-charge—Félix Jiménez—to oversee the Caribbean, which was formerly done from Miami. The division became operational on October 1, 1995.[27]

In Barbados, a joint army-police interdiction operation on July 4, 1992, confiscated over 2,000 pounds of marijuana, worth about

23. Puerto Rico and the U.S. Virgin Islands together constitute one of six "gateway" HIDTAs, the others being the southwest border, Houston, Los Angeles, Miami, and New York. There are also other types of HIDTAs. Washington, D.C./Baltimore, for example, is a "distribution" HIDTA. For more on HIDTAs, see U.S. Office of the President, *National Drug Control Strategy: 1996*, 71–73.

24. U.S. General Accounting Office, *Drug Control: U.S. Interdiction Efforts in the Caribbean Decline*, 5.

25. *Caribbean Week*, "Puerto Rico: 1,650 Kilos of Cocaine."

26. Ross, "Drug Shipments Under the Navy's Nose."

27. See Beard, "Drug Money Laundering Puts Pressure on DEA," and Hutt, "The DEA Opens Caribbean Office in Puerto Rico."

B$6 million, and arrested two Barbadians and one Canadian with arms and ammunition. Later that month, 26.5 kilos of cocaine, worth about TT$35 million, was seized at Cali Bay, Tobago, following transshipment from Venezuela. Three couriers were caught in 1993 trying to use Barbados to transport Colombian heroin from Venezuela to Europe. Cocaine seizures in Barbados during 1994 amounted to 240 kilos, and the marijuana confiscated totaled 464 kilos.

In January 1993, 2,761 pounds of cocaine—worth some U.S.$17 million—was seized in St. Vincent following a raid on a family residence in Glamorgan, just outside Kingstown. St. Vincent is now described by the U.S. government as "a pipeline for drugs transiting to the United States and French Islands." The report by the St. Vincent government of a mere 2.5 kilos of cocaine and 881 kilos of marijuana as 1994 seizures is considered by both U.S. and Caribbean observers as a gross undercount. In Antigua, over 150 kilos of cocaine bound for the United Kingdom was seized on a private boat during spring 1994, and 130 kilos of cocaine, 169 pieces of crack, and 3,380 kilos of marijuana were also confiscated during the year.[28]

In February 1993 alone, 3,240 kilos of ganja with an estimated street value of U.S.$16.2 million were recovered from waters around the British Virgin Islands.[29] Trinidad and Tobago had its biggest single cocaine seizure on June 10, 1994, when a forty-one-foot cabin cruiser, *Aquarius,* was intercepted with 226.2 kilos of cocaine—worth an estimated U.S.$18 million—in plastic fuel drums. The cruiser was bound for Antigua. Three Antiguans were arrested and later indicted on conspiracy and trafficking charges.[30] As is true for other places in the Caribbean, trafficking use of Trinidad and Tobago often involves citizens from faraway places. On October 21, 1996, for instance, a thirty-six-year-old Liberian, Janet Paaseve, was arrested at the Piarco International Airport with 720 grams of

---

28. Griffith, "$6M Ganja Haul"; *Stabroek News,* "Trinidad and Tobago Police Make Big Cocaine Seizure"; *Caribbean Daylight,* "St. Vincent Top Cop Wants Legal Loopholes Tightened"; United Nations International Drug Control Program, *Subregional Program Framework for the Caribbean, 1994–1995,* 8; and *INCSR* (1995), 194–98.

29. Sutton and Payne, "The Off-Limits Caribbean," 92.

30. De Leon and Taitt, "T&T Biggest Drug Haul Seized at Sea," and Alonzo, "Third Antiguan Charged with Trafficking in 'Coke.'"

heroin strapped to her legs. She was later given a four-year hard-labor prison sentence.[31]

In the U.S. Virgin Islands 860 pounds of cocaine worth about U.S.$10 million was seized on August 25, 1994. That same month two seizures in St. Martin netted 2,185 pounds of cocaine, and two months later fishermen found 1,766 pounds of cocaine on an uninhabited island between St. Barthelemy and St. Martin. (Of the total 1994 cocaine seizure of 1.2 metric tons in the French Caribbean, 990 kilos were taken in St. Martin alone.) Added to that, in November 1994, 1,320 pounds of cocaine were seized in Guadeloupe.

Elsewhere among the dependencies, 1994 seizures were as follows: Anguilla—832 kilos of cocaine, 75 rocks of crack, and 28 kilos of marijuana; Cayman Islands—5 kilos of cocaine, 25 kilos of hashish oil, and 1.8 metric tons of marijuana; Turks and Caicos Islands—45 kilos of cocaine, 160 rocks of crack, and 15 kilos of marijuana. Further, in January 1995, 742 pounds of marijuana was recovered off the Cayman Islands. The drugs were in burlap sacks bearing the words "brown sugar made in Jamaica." In July 1995, 9 bales with 500 pounds of cocaine worth U.S.$22.3 million were found floating in the British Virgin Islands, between the islands of Fallen Jerusalem and Virgin Gorda. In January 1996, while operating off Grand Cayman, the British frigate HMS *Brave* recovered U.S.$200 million worth of cocaine that had been dumped at sea earlier. All together there were 3,000 pounds of cocaine in 40 bales. Overall for the Cayman Islands in 1995, 548 people were arrested for trafficking. The drugs confiscated were 314 kilos of cocaine and 2.6 metric tons of marijuana.[32]

Aruba and the Netherlands Antilles are said to serve as vital links in the transshipment of cocaine and heroin from Colombia, Venezuela, and Suriname to the United States and Europe. As shown in Table 4, the ABC islands (Aruba, Bonaire, and Curaçao) are very close to Venezuela, from which much of the drugs confiscated in the ABC islands comes. Trafficking in the Dutch Caribbean generally involves commercial and private airlines, air-cargo flights, and

31. Marajh, "Operation Crack Attack Is Here."
32. See Anderson, "$10M Coke Haul off St. Thomas"; Hierso, "Two Bodies Found in St. Martin"; *New York Newsday*, "Marijuana Floating off Caymans"; *INCSR* (1995), 199–201; *Miami Herald*, "$22.3 Million in Cocaine Found"; *New York Carib News*, "British Warship Makes Cocaine Haul"; and *INCSR* (1996), 209.

cruise ships, although ship containers have also been used. In Suriname, for example, one huge seizure in 1994 netted 207 kilos of cocaine concealed in cargo waiting to be shipped to Europe.

Cuba's strategic location has caused it to be used for trafficking, apparently both with and without official sanction. One 1983 DEA report dates official Cuban involvement to 1991, suggesting that there were economic and political motives involved. Cuban officials have often been indicted in the United States for trafficking. One of the earliest cases of importance was in November 1982, when four senior officials were convicted *in absentia:* Rene Rodríguez Cruz of Dirección General de Inteligencia, Cuba's intelligence service, then also a Cuban Communist Party Central Committee member; Vice Admiral Aldo Santamaría Cuadrado, also a Central Committee member; Fernando Ravélo Renédo, former ambassador to Colombia; and Gonzalo Bassols Suarez, a former minister counselor of the Cuban embassy in Colombia. Ravélo Renédo and Basols Suarez reputedly directed arms-for-drugs deals involving the Medellín cartel and Colombia's M19.[33]

Andrés Oppenheimer asserts that Fidel Castro and Colombian drug operators had a long-standing and close association, based mainly on political convenience. Castro is said to have first ordered his intelligence agencies to penetrate the Colombian drug networks in the 1970s to gain access to what then appeared as potentially one of Latin America's most powerful economic and political forces. Indeed, says Oppenheimer, "When the Carter Administration launched exploratory dialogue with the Castro regime in the late 1970s, one of the things the Cubans offered was to help stop drug smuggling through the Caribbean. The proposal died when normalization talks collapsed."[34]

Cuban involvement in trafficking and questions about officially sanctioned involvement commanded the greatest attention in 1989, when several top military officials were convicted and given harsh sentences for trafficking, corruption, and other infractions. The chief defendant was division general Arnaldo Ochoa Sanchez, then a hero of Cuba's Africa campaigns, who had in 1984 been awarded

33. See Ehrenfeld, "Narco-Terrorism and the Cuban Connection," 58, and MacDonald, *Dancing on a Volcano,* 135–36.
34. Oppenheimer, *Castro's Final Hour,* 41.

Cuba's highest military honors: Hero of the Cuban Republic and the Máximo Gomez Order, First Class. All fourteen defendants were found guilty. Ochoa, Captain Jorge Martinez Valdez, Colonel Antonio De La Guardia, and Major Amado Padrón were sentenced to death. Brigadier General Patricio De La Guardia and Captain Miguel Ruiz Poo were each given thirty years in prison, and the eight others were given prison terms ranging from ten to thirty years.[35]

Several analysts indicate that military officials participated in the smuggling of drugs and other commodities not so much to profit individual officers as to satisfy economic needs of the military in particular and economic and political interests of Cuba generally. Evidence suggests that both the military and the political high command in Cuba knew about the trafficking in drugs and other contraband, and that they gave it tacit approval. But they turned on the architects of the operations when it became politically inexpedient to have the operations continue. Oppenheimer claims, for instance, that "[i]n 1988, the Commandante had asked [interior minister and division general Jose] Abrantes to sell 10 thousand kilos of cocaine that was in storage at Havana's Cimeq Hospital, if possible through Eastern European countries. Abrantes was to seek $50 million for the cocaine, which originated largely from Cuban coast guard seizures."[36]

Ever since the Ochoa affair, there have been periodic allegations of collusion by Cuban officials in drug trafficking, the most recent of which was the July 1996 claim that Fidel Castro himself was deeply implicated in the attempt to smuggle 5,828 pounds of cocaine seized the previous January, a claim that, of course, the Cuban authorities denied.[37] U.S. authorities also later questioned the plausibility of the claim.[38] But although there is little hard evidence of present Cuban government involvement in trafficking, there is considerable evidence of trafficking involving Cuba.

In April 1992, for example, twenty-nine Cubans in the city of Camaguey were found guilty of possessing and trafficking cocaine.

35. Ibid., 115.
36. Ibid., 127.
37. See Leen, "Traffickers Tie Castro to Drug Run," and *Gleaner* (Jamaica), "Cuba Not Trafficking in Drugs—Havana Official."
38. See Lyons, "Smuggler Ties Cuba to Drugs," and Leen, "Castro Drugs Probe Collapses in Heap of Dead Ends, Lies."

Some were also convicted of currency- and weapons-possession charges.[39] Cuban officials reported that 3.3 metric tons of cocaine were seized in seventy-nine different cases during 1993. Reported seizures for 1994 were 238 kilos of cocaine and 1.1 metric tons of marijuana.[40] Cuba's national prosecutor is reported to have indicated the following in a November 1995 interview with *Granma:* "Years ago, since this merchandise had no commercial value, everyone who found a packet of this type handed it over to the authorities. Now people have discovered how much that's worth and they don't always hand it over."[41] Moreover, in August 1996, Carlos Abat, who heads Cuba's national counternarcotics operations, reported that Cuban authorities had confiscated the following during the first quarter of 1996: more than 1,000 kilos of cocaine, 1,400 kilos of marijuana, smaller quantities of heroin and hashish oil, weapons, eleven motor boats, and state-of-the-art equipment. Between January and June 1996, forty-five foreign drug runners were arrested. They were of varying nationalities, including Colombians—the largest group—Jamaicans, Bahamians, Spaniards, Dutch, British, Italians, and Irish.[42]

Several features of the Dominican Republic also make that country a prime trafficking candidate: proximity to Colombia, the Bahamas, Puerto Rico, and the southern United States; a long, often desolate border with Haiti; and poorly equipped police and military authorities. The scope of their problem is reflected in the fact that in 1993 the country's National Drug Control Directorate, supported by the navy, seized 1,070 kilos of cocaine, 310 kilos of marijuana, 1,444 grams of crack, and other drugs. Also confiscated were 183 vessels, 222 motorcycles, and 164 firearms. These were the results of 812 antidrug operations where 5,635 people were arrested.

In 1994, the seizures were as shown in Table 5: 2,800 kilos of cocaine (a 160 percent increase over 1993) and 6,800 kilos of marijuana. Arrests numbered 3,000. The 1995 cocaine seizures totaled 3,600 kilos. Although clandestine airstrips are used less now, offshore airdrops between the Dominican Republic and Puerto Rico continue. Moreover, drugs are smuggled over the border from Haiti

39. *Miami Herald,* "Cocaine Found on Coast Brings 29 Before Court."
40. *INCSR* (1995), 166.
41. This interview is reported in Lee, "Drugs: The Cuba Connection," 57.
42. *Gleaner* (Jamaica), "Cuba Not Trafficking in Drugs—Havana Official."

using the same techniques, routes, and resources used to smuggle oil into Haiti during the embargo.[43]

Haiti itself has several factors that have facilitated trafficking: geographic location, poorly monitored coasts, mountainous interior, about twenty unpatrolled airstrips, inadequate law-enforcement resources, and corruption. The complicity of military and other officials in trafficking has been well established.[44] The DEA estimated in 1993, for instance, that two to four tons of cocaine then passed through Haiti, mostly with the blessings of military officials. In April 1994, Gabriel Toboada of the Medellín cartel told a U.S. Senate Foreign Relations Committee hearing that Lieutenant Colonel Joseph Michel François, then commander of Haiti's police, collaborated in the shipment of tons of cocaine during the 1980s. According to the testimony, the deal had been sealed in 1984 following François's visit to Medellín. Haiti was used as a bridge to the United States, with both the flights and the cargo protected by the military.[45] (On March 7, 1997, indictments for trafficking were handed down in Miami against François.)

One Haitian security expert indicates that Haiti emerged significantly onto the international drug-trafficking scene in 1985. This was in the context of the vigorous policy pursued by the Reagan administration against the Colombian cartels, and of the enhanced interdiction programs with the Bahamas and the Turks and Caicos Islands. Haiti thus became an alternative site of operation. Moreover, since "the government of Jean Claude Duvalier was about to collapse and U.S. aid was no longer as generous as in the past, Colombian drug dealers were able, with some success, to make important inroads into the corrupt governmental system. Some officials in the government and the military took this opportunity to enlarge their income and in the process capitalized and accumulated hard currency as well."[46]

According to Laguerre, the period between 1985 and 1987 wit-

43. *INCSR* (1994), 184, 185, and *INCSR* (1995), 168–69.

44. See U.S. Senate, Committee on Foreign Relations, *Drugs, Law Enforcement, and Foreign Policy;* French, "U.S. Says Haiti's Military Runs Cocaine"; Marks, "Haiti's Military May Dig in Heels to Keep Lucrative Drug Trade"; and Laguerre, "National Security, Narcotics Control, and the Haitian Military."

45. Weiner, "Colombian Drug Trafficker Implicates Haitian Police Chief."

46. Laguerre, "National Security, Narcotics Control, and the Haitian Military," 101.

nessed the consolidation of operations involving Haiti. Colombian traffickers were said to have used several different and complementary strategies. These included purchasing legal businesses in Haiti for use as front operations, buying protection from military officers, recruiting military officers as associates, and using Haitian territory as a base for trafficking and storage operations. The period between 1987 and 1994 saw the diversification of market outlets, increased local production and consumption initiatives, and the political destabilization of Haiti.[47]

Officially reported cocaine seizures have been increasing recently, as Table 5 suggests. In 1992, the figure reported was 56 kilos of cocaine; 1993, 157 kilos; and 1994, 716 kilos. However, there was a decline in 1995: 550 kilos.[48] August 22, 1996, witnessed a significant seizure. The significance was both in the quantify of drugs—765.6 pounds of cocaine—and in the fact that it was the first occasion on which the newly formed Haitian Coast Guard had undertaken joint operations with the U.S. Coast Guard. The drugs were taken from an eighty-five-foot fishing boat that had left Coco Solo, Panama, and was headed to Gonave in Haiti.[49]

In the context of trafficking adaptation, Guyana has become an important center of operations. As in many other Caribbean countries, Guyana's trafficking has graduated from marijuana to cocaine and heroin. The earliest known trafficking case was on June 16, 1979, when a trader from the bauxite mining city of Linden arrived from Jamaica with 60 pounds of compressed marijuana.[50] Cocaine and heroin now enter Guyana from all three neighboring countries: Brazil, Suriname, and Venezuela. Data from the Guyana military and police show that cocaine seizures went from 127 grams, with twenty-two arrests, in 1990, to 7 kilos, with forty arrests, in 1991. Cocaine seizures in 1993 amounted to 463 kilos— 1,000 percent higher than in 1992. The exceptional 1993 figure was due to one dramatic seizure; on June 4, 1993, 800 pounds of cocaine was dropped from the air into the Demerara River, along with U.S.$24,000 and a huge quantity of Colombian and Guyanese cur-

---

47. Ibid., 101–2.
48. *INCSR* (1995), 176, and *INCSR* (1996), 177.
49. *Miami Herald*, "U.S., Haiti Cooperate on Drug Seizure."
50. Interview with Assistant Commissioner Felix, June 1994.

rency. Several Guyanese, Colombians, and Venezuelans were implicated in the affair.[51]

As Table 5 indicates, in 1994 the amount of cocaine confiscated declined. However, the smaller amount seized should not create any sense of security, since this does not necessarily indicate a lessening of the quantity being trafficked. As one assessment concluded, "[I]t may be the result of more sophisticated techniques and coordination on the part of drug smugglers or an insufficient drug enforcement unit."[52] There is reason to believe that both of these as well as other factors explain the smaller seizures in 1994. Indeed, both sophistication and inefficiency were revealed in May 1996, when Canadian and Guyanese police smashed a drug network linking Colombia, Venezuela, Brazil, Guyana, and Canada. Seven people, including one Colombian and one Guyanese police detective, were arrested and charged with trafficking and conspiracy in relation to 50 kilos of cocaine.[53]

As with Jamaica, Trinidad and Tobago, Suriname, and elsewhere in the region, there is also marijuana trafficking. Both foreign and local marijuana are involved, the foreign marijuana coming from Colombia, Venezuela, and Brazil. On January 4, 1995, for instance, 5,000 pounds of marijuana valued at U.S.$2 million was discovered behind a false fiberglass wall of a container about to be shipped from Georgetown to Miami.[54]

The air, sea, and land routes developed for smuggling contraband into Guyana from Brazil, Venezuela, and Suriname during the economic crisis of the 1970s and 1980s have now been adapted for narcotics trafficking. Some of these routes are shown in Figure 5. Moreover, traffickers are able to take advantage of the country's relatively large size, the coastal habitation, and the absence of adequate manpower and equipment to police the territory. For example, ninety-two legal aerodromes (private and public) are available for air trafficking. Moreover, as Figure 6 reveals, most them are in remote parts of the country where the physical and social

51. See Khan, "Drugs Dropped by Mysterious Aircraft," and *Stabroek News,* "23 Held in Air-Dropped Cocaine Probe."

52. *INCSR* (1995), 174.

53. *New York Carib News,* "Big Drugs Bust."

54. See *INCSR* (1994), 189; Hassim, "Marijuana Container Valued at US2M"; and *Stabroek News,* "Three Charged for Trafficking."

Fig. 5   Guyana Trafficking Routes

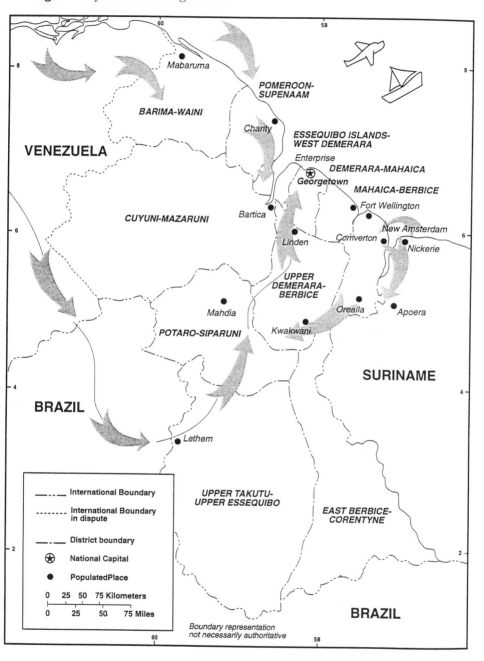

Fig. 6   Legal Aerodromes in Guyana

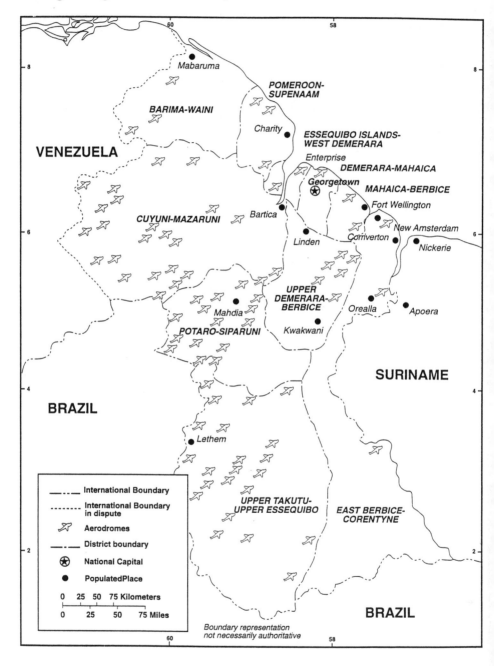

geography provide clear advantages for traffickers. One top military official conceded that "very often we do know what's happening in the some of those places."[55] And this was in relation to the legal airstrips.

Guyana's physical geography—especially its size and location—is a clear facilitator of trafficking. However, the role of social geography is also quite important. Not only is there a low population density—three-quarters of a million people on 214,970 km^2 of territory—but most of the people live along the Atlantic coast. This leaves wide expanses of territory underpopulated and, consequently, underpoliced, providing excellent conditions for trafficking and other operations. (Incidentally, low density and coastal habitation are also found in Belize, French Guiana, and Suriname.)

Given the country's physical and social geography and the corruptibility of some officials, traffickers sometimes aim at establishing their own physical base in a big way. In one case some Colombians and Americans were able to enter the country illegally and to bring a generator, a water pump, two airplane engines, six transmitting sets, tool kits, arms and ammunition, and other supplies over a four-month period. The plan was to build a processing and transshipment center at Waranama, in northeastern Guyana, four hundred miles from the capital, Georgetown, to be part of an international network involving Colombia, Trinidad and Tobago, and the United States.[56] Like elsewhere in the Caribbean, trafficking in Guyana is not done only by air runs dedicated to drug delivery or collection; commercial flights are also used. In one dramatic case, on March 15, 1993, a Guyana Airways Corporation plane—flight GY 714—arrived in New York from Guyana with 117 pounds of cocaine in its paneling.[57] The case is still unsolved.

The country's physical geography also makes it vulnerable to maritime trafficking. Guyana, the "land of many waters," has hundreds of inland rivers and creeks. Thirteen giant rivers flow into the Atlantic Ocean. These rivers and their lengths, from their sources to their Atlantic Ocean estuaries, are Essequibo (667 miles), Ber-

---

55. Interview with Lieutenant Colonel Collins, June 1994.
56. See *Guyana Chronicle*, "Illegal Airstrip Case: Three Colombians, One Guyanese Charged."
57. See Persaud, "117 Pounds of Cocaine Found on GAC Plane," and *Stabroek News*, "GAC Offering G1M Reward for Cocaine Find Leads."

bice (438 miles), Barima (225 miles), Waini (145 miles), Demerara (315 miles), Amakura (88 miles), Pomeroon (109 miles), Moruka (32 miles), Boerasrie (26 miles), Mahaica (91 miles), Mahaicony (89 miles), Canje (169 miles), and Abary (100 miles). Each of these rivers has a network of tributaries. The maritime traffic is also facilitated by the fact that the network of rivers runs into Brazil, Suriname, and Venezuela. For example, the Takatu river in southwest Guyana flows into the Parima, a tributary of the Rio Negro, which flows into the Amazon in Brazil.[58]

The Guyana situation is clear evidence of the vulnerability of Caribbean countries to drug trafficking and other illicit operations. Geography apart, a contributor to this situation is the absence of adequate military and police resources to offer credible countermeasures. In effect, the state lacks the power to exercise proper political and territorial jurisdiction over the nation. Top army, coast guard, and police officials in many parts of the region have expressed frustration not only at the inability adequately to protect their country's borders against trafficking, but also at being the pawns of traffickers who often create successful small interdiction diversions in order to execute large operations.[59]

Conveyance and Organization

Drug trafficking brings out the creativity and ingenuity of drug operators and the people who collude with them. People have used

58. Twelve of the thirteen rivers are listed in Guyana, Ministry of Information, *Guyana in Brief,* 10. The Canje River and the figures on all river lengths were provided by Brigadier Granger (ret.), May 1995.

59. Interviews with, among other officials, Brigadier Joseph Singh of Guyana, June 30, 1994; Commissioner of Police Laurie Lewis, July 1994; Lieutenant Commander Gary Best of the Guyana Coast Guard, July 1994; Commissioner Jules Bernard of Trinidad and Tobago, July 1994; Commissioner Orville Durant of Barbados, July 1994; Rear Admiral Peter Brady of the Jamaica Defense Force; Superintendent Reginald Ferguson of the Royal Bahamas Police Force, December 1994; Commissioner Alvin Goodwin of Antigua-Barbuda, January 1995; Lieutenant Colonel Trevor Thomas of the Antigua-Barbuda Defense Force, August 1996; Commissioner Trueheart Smith of Antigua-Barbuda; Commander Chris Annamunthodo of the Jamaica Defense Force, August 1996; Colonel Trevor Macmillan, commissioner of police, Jamaica, August 1996; Richard King of Jamaica's Port Security Corps, August 1996; Commissioner Errol Farquharson of the Bahamas, August, 1996; Captain Anthony Allens of the Royal Bahamas Defense Force, August 1996.

every possible orifice of the human anatomy, every possible piece of clothing, all kinds of fruits and vegetables, and a variety of craft, furniture, and other things for the conveyance of drugs. Of the human anatomy, use has been made of the vagina, anus, arm pits (to strap packages of drugs), the abdomen and the back (to strap packages), the tongue (by placing drugs under it), natural and false hair, thighs (where drugs are strapped on inner thighs), and the stomach and intestines. Indeed, there are people—called swallowers or mules—who specialize in the use of the stomach and intestines.

In one 1996 case, a twenty-seven-year-old Jamaican-born U.S. permanent resident, Herman McGregor, packed sixty-six cocaine-filled balloons in his stomach in Montego Bay, Jamaica, and brought them to Miami on February 27. McGregor recounted how he had used porridge and milk in the ingestion process, but had been unable to "flush" all of the balloons out of his intestines. He then became ill and sought treatment at the Florida Medical Center. The remaining balloons were discovered during the medical examination. They had to be removed surgically, during which process the police waited outside the operating room to collect the evidence for prosecution.[60]

One eastern Caribbean official related a case in which a leg wound was used. Condoms with cocaine were found in the wound and within its bandages. Drugs have also been found in fish, rice, cake, pepper sauce, coconuts, yams, bananas, "coffee beans" (where the beans are cocaine pellets stamped to the shape of beans and dipped in coffee syrup), cheese, butter, cans of beer, juice, and fruit, ice cream, false tops of drums, cigarette packaging (purported to contain cigarettes), vegetables, detergent, furniture and furniture fixtures, lumber, piñatas, false legs (of amputees), the waistbands of underwear, dolls, cylindrical drums of air compressors, wood carvings, Bibles, mannequins, bales of cloth, mail (letters, packages, and mail bags themselves), ceramic tiles, video tapes, surfboards, fiberglass dog kennels, bottles of shampoo and mouthwash, frozen vegetables, concrete posts, wooden coat hangers, rum (actually liquid cocaine, purported to be coconut rum), and countless other objects.

60. Larrubia, "Man Charged with Smuggling Cocaine in Stomach."

All sorts of clothing are used, including footwear with false soles and heels. So too are picture frames and suitcases with false sides and bottoms. Both dead and live animals and birds are also used to convey drugs. In one horrible case, on December 1, 1994, U.S. Customs agents in New York found ten cocaine-filled condoms weighing close to five pounds sewn into the abdomen of an English sheep dog that had arrived from Bogotá, Colombia, aboard Avianca Flight 020. The four-year-old dog, which had been shipped as cargo, looked emaciated and lethargic on arrival, prompting officials to order an X-ray, which revealed the drugs. The person who attempted to retrieve the dog, twenty-two-year-old John Erik Roa of New Jersey, was arrested and charged with cocaine smuggling. He later pled guilty and was sentenced, on April 26, 1995, to three years and one month in prison.[61]

One official in the eastern Caribbean recounted a case in which a guitar was made entirely of compressed marijuana. I call it "the case of the guitarganja." Not only are cars, vans, trucks, planes, and boats used to convey large and small quantities of drugs and people and objects with them, but drugs are often stashed in unbelievable places in these vessels: in car batteries and tires; paneling and upholstery; false hulls and bottoms of boats; false gas tanks, even in the gas itself; false floors and walls of trucks and vans; life jackets; and ship containers, some with false sides and bottoms, some without.

The following are some of the more incredible cases, all but the last of which were included in one *New York Times* report:

- dead cocaine-filled eviscerated parrots among a shipment of live parrots sent from Grenada to China in 1991
- a bust of Jesus Christ molded of cocaine and spray-painted gray
- over 6,000 pounds of cocaine in bricks inside ice-packed cases of broccoli, found in Fort Lauderdale, April 1992
- 1,000 pounds of cocaine packed into hollow plaster shells shaped and painted to resemble yams
- heroin- and cocaine-filled condoms discovered in the stomachs of race horses at the San Ysidro crossing of the U.S.-Mexican border

61. *Miami Herald*, "NY Drug Agents Find 10 Cocaine-Filled Condoms Inside Dog," and idem, "Man Sentenced for Bid to Smuggle Coke in Dog."

- 37 pounds of cocaine, in condoms, sewn into the rectums of live boa constrictors that arrived in Miami in June 1993
- 192 kilos of cocaine hidden in cans of tomato sauce sent from the Dominican Republic to Puerto Rico in April 1995.[62]

Moreover, on August 1, 1996, 6,043 pounds of cocaine was retrieved from a hill of coffee beans at the Port of Miami.[63]

Apart from risking discovery and prosecution, some traffickers risk physical injury and even death. Swallowers, for example, risk both, although they often drink coconut, olive, or some other oil to line the stomach and intestines before swallowing the condoms with cocaine, heroin, or compressed marijuana. As a matter of fact, scores of them have died when packages have broken in their stomachs or intestines.[64] Breakages occur for various reasons, including physiological reactions, improper packaging, and flight delays that extend the time of drug retention beyond the safe period, which itself varies from drug to drug. According to one Caribbean police official, "[T]he worst thing that could happen to a mule is for his/her flight to be delayed or canceled." In one dramatic March 1994 case in Jamaica, a trafficker died from a combination of factors, most notably the extremely large quantity of drugs ingested. The autopsy found that he had ingested 275 packets of compressed ganja, weighing about two pounds. This caused his stomach literally to explode.[65]

Swallowers are known to have been murdered by people who wanted to get the drugs they were carrying. One gruesome case in 1995 involved Henry Vega, a twenty-one-year-old Colombian living in Miami, who was murdered following a smuggling trip from Cali, Colombia, to Miami on January 30. His stomach was slit open with a box cutter and the contents removed, but the postmortem revealed that he still had drugs in him: two condoms of heroin in his esophagus.[66] Despite the risks involved, swallowing has become a

---

62. Spart, "The New Drug Mules," 44–45. The tomato-sauce case was reported in Pilarte, "A Latin Mecca for Laundering Drug Money."

63. May, "Drug Trade Is 'Booming.'"

64. See Swarns, "At Huge Risk, Smugglers Swallow Drugs for Money."

65. Earle and Thompson, "Cops Say Visitors Overdosed," and Morris, "Cocaine Knocking Tourists out West."

66. See Hancock and Sheridan, "Requiem for a Drug Courier."

popular method of trafficking, because of its high profitability. Indeed, according to the DEA, for heroin alone, the swallowing arrests in the Miami District have increased dramatically: from one person with 0.7 pounds of heroin inside the body in 1990 to three people with 5.6 pounds arrested in 1991; 68 people arrested in 1992 with 109 pounds in them; 106 people with 97 pounds in them in 1993. The 1994 arrests numbered 181, and they carried 184 pounds of heroin in their bodies.[67]

Traffickers are not only creative, they are also adaptive, changing methods and operatives depending on the success of counternarcotics measures. Hence, some of the methods mentioned above are used for a while, then changed. Some are used on a rotation basis, or on different routes. Often, some methods have just a one- or two-time use. Adaptations also take place in relation to trafficking routes. Indeed, the fact that Trinidad, Guyana, and eastern Caribbean countries began to be used heavily after 1990 reflects changed route patterns. As was observed by the U.S. State Department, successful U.S. interdiction in the Bahamas and Turks and Caicos Islands and U.S. military activity around Hispaniola have contributed to increased use of the eastern Caribbean, Puerto Rico, and the U.S. Virgin Islands, such that "[i]n 1994, 26 percent of documented cocaine smuggling attempts into the U.S. came through these Caribbean portals."[68]

Most of the trafficking reflects careful planning and organization by people who are either fully aware of their roles or suspect that they are involved but, because of the unwritten secrecy code or the need-to-know modus operandi, are unsure of the extent of their involvement. Sometimes, however, people are unsuspecting "mules," often under the impression that they are doing a favor for a friend, an associate, or even a lover. For example, as the director of the Narcotics Trial Bureau in the Queens District Attorney's Office, New York, explained, countless gullible Caribbean (and other) women are duped by men who profess love and offer them the prospect of all-expenses-paid trips to the United States or an opportunity to emigrate there. When they make the trip(s), they are given packages to deliver to "friends" or "family" in the United States, only

---

67. *Miami Herald*, "Body Packers on the Increase."
68. *INCSR* (1995), 192.

to discover later when arrested that they are merely being used to traffic drugs.[69]

Family connections are also exploited by drug operators. One such case involved a retired U.S. army captain who was used by a cousin and duped into making a U.S.$300,000 cash delivery that turned out to be part of a drug deal. In March 1995 the retired officer, Mario Vega, who lives in Miami, was asked by his cousin in the Dominican Republic, who operates a money-changing service, to make the delivery to someone who allegedly was negotiating car purchases. By the time law-enforcement authorities cleared Vega and his wife of trafficking complicity and other charges in December 1995, he had lost his house, car, and credit.[70]

Young women are particularly popular couriers in parts of the region. In Jamaica, for instance, police officials reported in 1995 that some 60 percent of all persons arrested at the country's two international airports attempting to smuggle drugs were women from other countries. Between 1993 and 1995 nearly two hundred young American women were caught trying to smuggle drugs out of the country. Investigations have revealed that some women are paid up to U.S.$3,000 per trip. This is small compensation for the value of the product transported and the risks involved, but a huge income for some of the women involved.

As might be expected, given the profitability and lure of drug trafficking, not only "ordinary people" are involved or implicated; members of the region's political, social, and corporate elite have also been involved. A few examples will suffice. One early case, which is discussed more in Chapter 5, involved Chief Minister Norman Saunders and Minister of Commerce and Development Stafford Missick of the Turks and Caicos Islands. They were arrested in March 1985 by U.S. authorities and charged with conspiracy to import narcotics into the United States, among other things. They were later sentenced to eight and ten years, respectively, and each was fined U.S.$5,000.

The following year, Captain Etienne Boerenveen, the Suriname army's second in command was arrested in Miami, convicted of trafficking cocaine, and imprisoned until 1989. As noted earlier, in

69. See Best, "Cupid's Arrow May Do More Than Pierce the Heart."
70. Lyons, "Couple Who Did 'Favor' Freed from Legal Tangle."

1989 General Arnaldo Ochoa Sanchez of Cuba was one of several top officers executed following conviction for trafficking. In November 1990 Rashleigh Jackson, then the long-standing—twelve years—and respected foreign minister of Guyana was obliged to resign following indictment of his son, Martin, on drug-possession charges. Martin had had a previous brush with the law over drugs. In November 1994, following his confession, Frantz Biamby, cousin of deposed Haitian dictator Brigadier General Philippe Biamby, was charged in Miami for shipping 107 kilos of cocaine from Haiti to Miami, through the Dominican Republic, in 1992.[71]

In April 1994, Brian and Daren Bernal, sons of Richard Bernal, Jamaica's ambassador to the United States and the OAS, were arrested at the Norman Manley International Airport in Jamaica and charged with drug trafficking. They had 46 kilos of compressed marijuana in 96 cans of what was purported to be Grace pineapple juice, and were about to board a flight to Washington. Following conviction they were sentenced, in March 1995, to twelve months imprisonment and fined a total of J$115,000. The sentence was appealed, but the Jamaica Court of Appeal dismissed the matter in January 1996.[72] A further appeal was filed, this time with the British Privy Council, which is Jamaica's highest judicial tribunal.

Also in the political-elite arena, in November 1994, 121 pounds of cocaine were found in the home of two of the sons of the deputy prime minister of St. Kitts–Nevis, Sidney Morris. Not only were they arrested and charged with trafficking, but they were later implicated in the murder of a third Morris brother, Vincent. (More on this case in Chapter 5.) Still in the eastern Caribbean, on May 6, 1995, Ivor Bird, a brother of Prime Minister Lester Bird, was charged in Antigua with attempting to smuggle 22 pounds of cocaine brought from Venezuela the previous day by an accomplice, Marcus Alberto Trotman. He was later convicted and fined U.S.$74,000, which he promptly paid. The alternative was two years in prison.[73]

71. Griffith, *The Quest for Security in the Caribbean*, 229; *Stabroek News*, "Singh Brothers Fined $150,000 in Drug Case"; *St. Croix Avis*, "Drug Scandal Rocks St. Kitts"; *Miami Herald*, "Antigua," May 8, 1995; and idem, "Antigua," May 18, 1995.

72. Williams, "Envoy's Son Testifies He Unknowingly Smuggled Drugs to US"; telephone interview with Glen Andrade, April 1995; and *New York Carib News*, "Jamaica: Appeal Dismissed in Bernal Drug Case."

73. *Miami Herald*, "Antigua," May 8, 1995, and idem, "Antigua," May 18, 1995.

One 1995 example in the corporate elite area involved Cecil Abrams, a leading businessman in Guyana, who was convicted of trafficking, along with his wife and others. The case involved 5,000 pounds of marijuana concealed in a ship container waiting for departure to Miami. Abrams was also convicted on weapons and ammunition charges. And in May 1996 Farouk Razak, a top executive of Swiss House Cambio, one of the oldest and largest cambios (nonbanking finance businesses) in Guyana, was one of several people arrested in a smuggling operations involving Colombia, Canada, and Guyana.[74] Religious leaders have also been involved in the illegal movement of drugs. In one Puerto Rican case, Rev. John McCurran Drake was arrested on January 3, 1997, during a routine visit to a jail in the San Juan suburb of Bayamon, when corrections officers found cocaine taped to his testicles. (A search at his church residence later produced fourteen bags of marijuana.)

People of all ages and of both sexes are involved in trafficking. Old women are sometimes used because they do not fit law-enforcement agencies' trafficker profile. But some have been caught. In one case, a sixty-three-year-old Honduran-born American citizen was arrested in Guyana with 6 pounds of cocaine in her underwear. She was about to board a British West Indian Airways (BWIA) flight to New York when one of the packages fell from under her. The woman, Gwendolyn Martinez, a grandmother, later admitted that she had been recruited in Brooklyn for the job. Upon conviction she was sentenced to ten years in jail.[75] Martinez was one of several "granny mules" arrested during 1993 and 1994 in Guyana and Trinidad. Even children are used. Their tender age and innocence are often good camouflage. Use also has been made of cadavers, of both adults and children. In the latter respect, a military official cited the 1994 case in which a sixteen-month-old dead baby was used to convey cocaine from Kingston, Jamaica, to London, England. The suspicion of an alert air hostess who found it unusual that the "child" had not cried or fidgeted once throughout the eight-and-a-half-hour flight led to the discovery.[76]

Some trafficking is done on an individual basis, but most of it is

---

74. Davidson, "Businessman Abrams Convicted on Illegal Ammunition Charges," and *Caribbean Daylight*, "Guyana: City Businessman on Drug Charge."
75. *Stabroek News*, "10 Years in Jail for Honduran."
76. Interview with Captain Edwards, December 1994.

based on simple or elaborate organizational structures and networks, including posse networks, which are examined closely in Chapter 4. Some operators are trained in armed combat, counternarcotics surveillance, evasive driving, and other areas. And, of course, traffickers are able to buy the services of specialists such as lawyers, pilots, accountants, and engineers. U.S. law-enforcement agents have found cells of Latin American cartels with operation manuals outlining specific protocols and security measures for contact, drug and money delivery, and money collection.[77]

Some operations are very sophisticated, using digital encryption devices, high-frequency transmitters, cellular telephones, beepers, radar-tracking devices, flares and sensors for airdrops, and other equipment. According to one source:

> Drug traffickers are using sophisticated communications technology and global positioning systems to avoid detection when airdropping cocaine to boats in the transit zone. . . . [They] use cellular phones and global positioning systems to determine drop coordinated prior to departure. The traffickers relay the coordinates to the boats which will pick up an airdrop. According to U.S. officials, the global positioning systems are available commercially and are accurate within 10 meters of a target. Because of these systems, traffickers do not have to openly communicate as frequently as they did in the past.[78]

Most of the trafficking structures and networks could not exist and deliver without the collusion of people in government and private agencies in various positions and at all hierarchical levels: people in shipping companies, customs and immigration agencies, warehouses, police forces, the military, airlines, export and import companies, stores, cruise ships, trucking companies, farms, factories, bus and taxi operations, and so forth. Some officials collude

---

77. See McGee, "Drug Smuggling Is Built on Franchises."

78. U.S. General Accounting Office, *Drug Control: U.S. Interdiction Efforts in the Caribbean Decline,* 8. Interestingly enough, the global positioning systems were designed originally for military use. They are now available commercially, and handheld versions are often sold at marine electronics stores for as little as $200–$300, says another report. See Adams, "Drug Runners Paradise," 4A.

through acts of omission: they just fail to perform certain acts, or to go to certain places, or to return to their posts at a certain time. And given their earnings for "doing little" or "doing nothing," one can appreciate how many people are susceptible to the corruption, especially in places with poor salaries specifically or economic deprivation generally.

Trafficking does not always involve direct movement of drugs from place of origin to intended destination; often it is done circuitously. For instance, cocaine may go from Colombia to Jamaica, and then to the United States, sometimes with a further stop in the Bahamas; or from Colombia to Venezuela to Guyana to the United Kingdom, or to the United States, sometimes again with intermediary stops in places like Antigua or Trinidad. And because of the networks mentioned earlier and transportation facilities available in the United States, once there is successful entry into ports at one of the states mentioned in Table 3 or elsewhere, there is often little difficulty in getting the drugs to their final destinations, if those states themselves are not the destinations.

Circuitous routing of drugs is not limited to the Caribbean, of course. The 1995 *INCSR* cited one 1994 case where a trafficking organization managed by Russians and using Ghanian and Nigerian couriers was moving cocaine from Latin American to Europe and the United States through West Africa. In May 1995 officials in the Dominican Republic uncovered trafficking operations in which Colombian cocaine was being shipped to the United States through Spain and the Dominican Republic.[79] The circuitous routing of drugs in the Caribbean often involves "island hopping," which is facilitated by the proximity factor, in this case the closeness of Caribbean countries to each other. The "island hopping" is also possible because of two geographical features mentioned earlier: the island character of most countries, which permits entry at scores, sometimes hundreds, of places; and the physical dispersal of territory in some cases, examples being the Bahamas, the Virgin Islands, and St. Vincent and the Grenadines. Drug-trafficking and migrant-smuggling operations are also often linked. Operators piggy-back one kind of smuggling on the other.

79. See *INCSR* (1995), 1, and *Dutch Caribbean Gazette*, "Authorities Seize Drugs Going to U.S., Coming from Spain."

This circuitous routing itself is a manifestation of the growing international trafficking linkages, which have resulted in increased trafficking by Nigerians and other West Africans in the Caribbean and Latin America, notably since 1994. In parts of Latin America this has led to a situation in which trafficking suspicions are raised whenever foreigners of African descent are seen at airports and seaports and in remote parts of the country. I myself experienced this in Ecuador.

It was November 27, 1996—the day before Thanksgiving. I had just checked in at the American Airlines ticket counter at Mariscal Sucre airport in Quito for my flight—AA 932—having been in the city since November 24 for a European Union–Rio Group conference on security. As I headed away from the ticket counter and toward the immigration control area, I was approached by two undercover cops—one male, the other female. They discreetly flashed their badges, introduced themselves as antidrug police, asked for my passport, and then "invited" me for an "inspection" in the airport police outpost. The officers took possession of my luggage and led me to the police outpost, which was ensconced in the mezzanine of the building. Once we had climbed the two flights of stairs in the L-shaped access to the mezzanine area, I was ushered along a balcony that overlooked most of the interior of the airport, to the outpost. The office was typically Spartan, as police offices in most parts of the developing world go. I was "handed over" to the commanding officer on duty, a boyish but courteous individual who appeared to be in his mid- to late twenties. Another young male officer was also there.

The commanding officer took my passport from the female officer who had taken possession of it earlier. He examined it. I could see a distinct facial expression of relief when he saw that it was a U.S. passport. (There was an additional expression of relief later, when he saw my official conference invitation letter.) He asked five questions: "Where did I live?" "How long had I been in Ecuador?" "Did I go outside Quito?" "Where had I stayed in Quito?" "Was I there as a tourist or for business?" My responses were: "Miami!" "Three days!" "No!" "Hotel Oro Verde!" "Business!" Next came the body search, thankfully not a strip search. Then came the luggage search. I had only two pieces of luggage—a "flight attendant's" bag and a briefcase. Two of the officers started searching them simultaneously. I objected to this attempt and insisted on the right to observe the inspection of each piece—one at a time—since I was not prepared to risk having any drugs "found" in my luggage. The commanding officer readily agreed, and the search proceeded uneventfully.

At the end of the entire process I asked the commanding officer why I had been the only person "invited" for the drug inspection. He tried his utmost to be diplomatic in explaining some of the "new realities" of drug smuggling. It was obvious to me that my presence at the airport, being of African descent, traveling lightly, and taking the first flight of the day to Miami had sent a red flag up the counter-narcotics flagpole at Quito's international airport.

Conclusion

This chapter indicates that of all the elements of the geonarcotics matrix geography is preeminent when it comes to trafficking in the Caribbean. Location is important, but so too are factors of size, island character, and demography. Gone are the days when drug trafficking presented problems only to Belize, the Bahamas, and Jamaica. While there are differences in trafficking history, patterns, and amounts from place to place, trafficking is undeniably a region-wide phenomenon.

Although seizures reveal the nature and scope of trafficking, they expose only a small part of the trafficking iceberg. Some sources estimate that only 15–25 percent of the drugs from and passing through the Caribbean are seized annually. The implications of trafficking go beyond merely the consequences of being transit centers, partly because not everything intended to go through the region actually does so. Some of the cocaine and heroin remain, both by default and by design, as payment for services, for example, in the latter case. Many of these implications are examined later, but I already noted in Chapter 1 a correlation between cocaine trafficking and cocaine consumption-abuse: the countries with high cocaine addiction are the very ones that are major cocaine-trafficking centers. As will be seen later, there are also attendant problems of

crime, arms trafficking, and corruption. Yet, as was observed previously, trafficking is merely one problem area. Two others—
production and consumption-abuse—were examined earlier. The
one that remains to be discussed is money laundering.

3

The Money-Laundering Headache

Money laundering and other financial operations carried out by narco-terrorists in developing countries are a source of grave financial problems to those countries. [Money laundering] brings a new entrepreneur class, the financial power of which is often used in a manner contrary to national and international interests.
—Bruce Zagaris

The two previous chapters examined drug production, consumption-abuse, and trafficking, direct drug problems and hence core geonarcotics issues. This chapter discusses money laundering, which is slightly different; it is not a direct drug problem, yet it is a central geonarcotics problem area. Because of production, trafficking, and other operations, drug operators need to control their money, conceal its origin and ownership, and convert and legitimate it. As this chapter shows, for the Caribbean, money laundering is a headache that involves the dynamics of all the geonarcotics factors—drugs, geography, power, and politics. Understanding the dynamics involved requires an appreciation of some money-laundering methods.

Money-Laundering Methods

Money laundering is the conversion of profits from illegal activities, in this case drug operations, into financial assets that appear to have legitimate origins and uses. Generally, three stages are involved: placement, layering, and integration.

Placement is the physical disposal of bulk cash, either by commingling it with revenues from legitimate businesses or by converting currency into deposits in banks, insurance companies, or other financial intermediaries. Layering involves transferring money between various accounts through several complex transactions designed to disguise the trail of the illicit takings. Integration, the last stage, requires shifting the laundered funds to legitimate organizations with no apparent links to the drug trade.[1] Estimates of the amount of drug money laundered worldwide range between U.S.$300 billion and U.S.$500 billion annually.

Money launderers use a variety of banking and nonbanking financial institutions for placement, layering, and integration. Both onshore and offshore banks are used, private as well as public ones. Nonbanking institutions used include travel agencies, exchange houses, finance companies, securities dealers, casinos, real estate agencies, fruit shops, import and export firms, trucking companies, trust companies, jewelry stores, credit unions, savings and loan associations, investment banks, express-delivery services, and gold and other precious-metals dealers. Money launderers also use antique dealers, auction houses, bars, pizza parlors, pharmacies, car dealers, hotels, restaurants, scrap-metal dealers, shoe-repair shops, supermarkets, vending-machine companies, waste-disposal firms, and shell companies.[2]

Wholesale and retail drug operations are done essentially through cash transactions, although purchases are sometimes done using credit cards. However, cash is both unwieldy and heavy. For example, one money-laundering operation in New York that was smashed in 1989 required a tractor-trailer to remove the $19 mil-

---

1. U.S. Senate, Committee on Foreign Relations, *Drug Money Laundering, Banks, and Foreign Policy*, 5.
2. Thompson, "Strategies to Combat Money Laundering and Predicate Crimes," 4, and *INCSR* (1995), 472.

lion in small bills seized.[3] The placement of cash generally requires smuggling it. In one November 1991 case, U.S. Customs agents in New York arrested a passenger bound for Ghana with U.S.$53,000 in cash, concealed as follows: $6,000 swallowed in balloons, $24,000 among bed sheets in her hand luggage, $22,400 in bottles of shampoo, and the remainder in balloons inserted in her vagina.[4] Of course, in addition to the actual drug transactions, cash is used for direct payment of various production and other workers, which often also requires that it be smuggled.

It was precisely this use—direct payment—as well as the need to place and layer proceeds, that motivated some massive cash-movement attempts during August 1996. On August 12, U.S. authorities raided a warehouse in north Miami and confiscated U.S.$6,269,400, mostly in small bills. The cash was cached in interesting containers: in television sets, battery chargers, hot-water heaters, microwave ovens, audio speakers, video recorders, and electronic toys and games. The merchandise with the cash was to be shipped to Colombia. One freighter with an illegal cash shipment—*Christian 1*—actually made it to Colombia that same month, but was made to return to Miami. Even more cash was involved: U.S.$9,192,659. The money was stashed in the same kinds of merchandise as the previous case, in eighty-one items. Quite ironically, one of the favorite games used for that smuggling attempt was Monopoly, the junior edition, where the play money was replaced by U.S.$20,000 sets of cash. Thus, in one week, and in Miami alone, a total of U.S.$15,462,059 was seized.[5]

Partly because of the difficulty of smuggling cash, noncash instruments are important. These include cashiers checks, bearer bonds, gold and jewels, false and inflated invoicing, and merchandise. The use of postal money orders for layering has increased over

3. U.S. Senate, Committee on Foreign Relations, *Drugs, Money Laundering, Banks, and Foreign Policy,* 4.

4. Möbius, "Money Laundering," 3.

5. Markowitz, "Cash Cache," and idem, "Drug Money Haul Puts Week's Total at $15 million Plus." That same month, on August 12, 1996, four people were removed from a Caracas-bound Avensa flight at Miami International Airport and searched, along with their luggage, which totaled forty-eight pieces. The search revealed the attempt to smuggle almost $1 million, some of it in the luggage and some in layers of underwear. See Robles, "Alleged Smugglers Carried Lots of Cash—and Ex-Cops' IDs."

the years; one 1994 seizure alone involved U.S.$1.2 million in postal money orders clearing through a U.S. bank from a *casa de cambio* in Cali.[6] Express-mail services are used to send cash and other layering instruments. The 1995 *INCSR* reported that following an investigation of express-mail traffic between New York's JFK airport and Colombia, sixty-one of sixty-five express-mail packages examined were found to contain U.S.$6.1 million.

Placement and layering often involve several different mechanisms. In "smurfing" for example, operators go to banks and either buy cashiers checks, money orders, or drafts for under U.S.$10,000, the threshold that triggers a cash-transaction report, or make deposits of sums below that threshold in different accounts. Smurfing can also involve commodities, which are bought and then traded at a loss. In one case lobster tails were bought from fishermen in Puerto Cabezas, Nicaragua, for $15 per pound, $9 above the going rate. In the loan-back method, operators deposit cash in a foreign country, usually in a tax haven, and then transfer it to a bank in another country. The operator then approaches his or her own banker for a loan, using the assets in the other country as collateral. The bank loans the money, which is used for "investment," and repayment comes from the assets in the other country.[7]

Underground banks are also used for money laundering. These banks, which are usually based on trust or family connections, range from highly sophisticated operations by Chinese groups to relatively informal barter and smuggling arrangements in Africa. Many underground banks do not involve the movement of actual cash; they depend instead on different kinds of tokens with set cash values. In a typical operation, the money launderer deposits funds with an underground banker. The latter notifies an associate in the receiving city or country that a certain amount of money has been deposited and will give the depositor a special "chop" or token. The depositor presents the token in the appropriate city or country and receives the value of the deposit, in local currency if it is a foreign country, less a transaction fee. Underground banking systems reportedly involved in narcotics (and other) money laundering are the

6. *INCSR* (1995), 473.
7. Möbius, "Money Laundering," and Johnson, "Hitting Rock Bottom."

Chinese "chit" or "chop" houses and the "Hawala" systems of Europe, South Asia, and the Middle East.[8]

Narcotics money launderers take full advantage of some of the sophisticated technology in the world of commerce and finance and the latest banking practices. One such banking practice is direct-access banking, in which select customers are given a bank's software and allowed to process transactions directly through their accounts. The concern is that this system limits the bank's ability to monitor account activity, such as joint-account use and "pass-through" banking, the latter of which is reputedly a traditional method of layering. Money-laundering specialists indicate that by creating accounts within accounts this practice creates considerable headaches for regulators.

Major drug operators are also able to buy the services of specialists in banking and nonbanking financial institutions and of people with knowledge of the latest technology. Accountants, lawyers, and other professionals are also often in their employ, as the cases involving Marlene Navarro, Michael Abbell, Joel Rosenthal, and others show.[9] There are also real concerns that free trade agreements and regional economic and commercial pacts that create trading and economic zones increase the use of international trade as a money-laundering mechanism. The liberalization of border and other customs controls, liberalized banking procedures, and freedom of access within such trading zones create added risks.[10]

The Caribbean Connection

Caribbean countries have been used for many of the placement, layering, and integration arrangements and instruments mentioned above. All the geonarcotics factors—drugs, geography, power, and politics—feature in the Caribbean money-laundering

8. Rider, "Taking the Profit out of Corruption," 16–17; Möbius, "Money Laundering," 5; and *INCSR* (1995), 468.

9. See McClintick, "Capturing the Butterfly," and Lyons, "Ex-Prosecutors Charged with Aiding Drug Bosses."

10. *INCSR* (1996), 500.

connection. As with trafficking, the geography factor relates to the region's proximity to South America, a critical drug supplier, and North America, a vital demand area. The demand-supply dynamics between the two generate money that needs placement, layering, and integration, and the Caribbean is geographically convenient.

Yet, for money laundering geography does not command a place of prominence equivalent to its position in trafficking. This is because for some money-laundering operations technology dwarfs geography. For instance, electronic highways that link banking and nonbanking financial institutions worldwide to facilitate global trade and finance are often used for money laundering, and these highways make geography irrelevant. Hence, geography alone does not explain the region's vulnerability to money laundering. The region possesses other factors that, while considered assets or requirements for economic growth and development by its political and corporate elites, have become part of the money-laundering infrastructure for narcotics operators. These factors include political stability, bank secrecy, low or little taxation, and relatively well-developed telecommunications.

Regarding the power and politics aspects of geonarcotics, a former U.S. congressional investigator observed that countries that facilitate money laundering, by whatever means, provide economic and political power to criminal elements. "This power may come through influence as a prominent member of the business community or society; prominence gained through illicit wealth. Political power may be earned through political contributions or favors. Or it may be gained through simple bribery." "However gained," Morley continued, "once held, the political power of organized criminal groups is difficult to dislodge."[11]

Some of the conditions for economic growth mentioned above, which are part of the money-laundering infrastructure, are central to a money-laundering mechanism for which the Caribbean has become (in)famous: offshore banking. Offshore banking developed as an important service sector in some countries that lack natural resources and the capacity for meaningful agricultural or industrial development. It was pursued especially by Aruba, the Bahamas, Curaçao, and the British dependencies, notably Anguilla, Ber-

11. Morley, "The Impact of Money Laundering on State Security," 5.

muda, the British Virgin Islands, the Cayman Islands, Montserrat, and the Turks and Caicos.

Lately, Antigua-Barbuda, Barbados, and Belize have also been pursuing it. For instance, regarding Antigua-Barbuda, the 1995 *INCSR* referred to the dramatic growth in the number of offshore banks, amid rumors of investment by Russians whose funds are of unknown origin. Among the prominent Russian banks are: European Union Bank, which was under investigation during 1996 by U.S. authorities, Maxibank, European Federal Credit Bank, and Privat Kredit. Some of the banks run electronically sophisticated operations, including the maintenance of web sites. European Union Bank, for example, maintains a site at www.EUB.com.[12] Offshore banking in Antigua-Barbuda dates to 1982, when the International Business Corporations Act was passed. The first offshore bank—Swiss American Bank—was established the following year. The marketing of Antigua-Barbuda as an offshore center now highlights the fact that "[a]ll offshore transactions are exempted from any exchange control or taxes and can be freely moved inward and outward via wire transfer or foreign drafts, managed through an established network of correspondent banks."[13] Some sixty offshore banks were said to be operating in Antigua-Barbuda at the end of 1996.

In developing its financial-services sector, Barbados is reaching out to Canadian companies. Indeed, Barbados, which in 1993 gained U.S.$65 million in net foreign exchange from the international business sector, was commended in 1995 by the International Monetary Fund (IMF) for its approach to this sector. The IMF feels that "unlike [most] other Caribbean islands involved in the provision of offshore services as no-tax jurisdictions, Barbados is a low-tax jurisdiction and can, therefore, negotiate double taxation treaties with major trading countries."[14] The IMF also thinks that Barbados's ability to exploit the advantage of the global offshore financial sector is enhanced by its hybrid economic policies that tem-

12. I am grateful to Douglas Farah of the *Washington Post* for this information, provided on September 17, 1996.
13. Stuart-Young, "The Antiguan Advantage," 62. Stuart-Young himself is business development manager of the Swiss American Banking Corporation and director of Antigua International Trust, Ltd.
14. Cited in *New York Carib News*, "Barbados Offshore Market Secure."

per its dependence on financial services. Belize is also developing this sector, and had some 1,800 international business corporations (IBCs) in 1994, with no more than U.S.$100 said to be needed to create an IBC. Offshore banking laws were adopted in 1995. These new moves, which include use of the Belizean flag as a "flag of convenience" for international shipping, worry several analysts. They are concerned that "Belize [will] become a mecca for money launderers, tax cheats, and flim-flam men."[15]

In his book *The Poor and the Powerless,* respected economist Clive Thomas explained that the rapid expansion of offshore banking in the Caribbean had less to do with the region's needs and more with the restructuring of global finance, which started in the 1950s, particularly with the development of Euromoney markets. Despite the name, this market depended on the growth of banking transactions in any currency other than that of the country where the bank in question was located. It first developed in Europe, with banks dealing in deposits denominated in U.S. dollars. Estimates for 1988 placed the market at U.S.$3 trillion, 80 percent of which was held in U.S. dollars.[16] Because of this market's operation, Euromoney has been called "money without a country." One writer describes it as "a Cheshire cat which disappears at the end of a telex trail into foreign legal jurisdictions and business practices. . . . Euromoney never leaves its country of origin. It is parked temporarily under anonymous cover and shuffled back and forth from one sovereign jurisdiction's shell bank to another."[17]

In relation to the Anglophone Caribbean, Clive Thomas noted that overseas banking had been around for quite some time. The Currency Board systems, which the British operated until the 1960s, linked the currencies of British Caribbean countries to the pound sterling at fixed and unchangeable exchange rates and also required the authorities issuing currencies to back each unit of currency with its equivalent in sterling. Such an arrangement ensured that banks in Britain carried no greater exchange-rate movement and convertibility risks in their operations in the colonies than they did in Britain itself. The subsequent decline of Britain in the Carib-

---

15. *Miami Herald,* "Belize Fast Turning into Offshore Financial Haven."
16. Thomas, *The Poor and the Powerless,* 169.
17. Lindsay, "Caribbean Offshore Banking," 41.

bean and the increased influence of the United States brought adaptations of overseas banking by individuals and corporations other than those from Britain.[18]

The genesis of offshore banking in the Dutch Caribbean goes even further back, however, to World War II. Scott MacDonald and Bruce Zagaris recount that when the Netherlands was conquered by the Germans in 1940, the headquarters of many Dutch companies were transferred to Curaçao. This was done to prevent both their capture by the Germans and confiscation as enemy assets by the Allies. Although companies such as Royal Dutch Shell and Phillips left the Dutch Antilles when the war ended, a foundation of legal and financial expertise had by then been established. For nominal fees, the Netherlands Antilles offered an attractive registration location for Dutch and non-Dutch companies.[19]

Irrespective of the historical context for offshore banking and financial services in the region, many Caribbean countries have come to possess *Euromoney*'s ten factors for successful offshore banking: little or no direct taxation; free movement of funds in and out of the territory; guarantee of client confidentiality, preferably legislated and judicially enforceable; minimal bureaucratic delays; a cadre of relevant professionals, notably lawyers, bankers, and accountants; fairly well-maintained physical infrastructure; reliable and impartial legal systems and legislation, to reduce uncertainty and arbitrary administrative rulings; modern hotel and meeting facilities in a pleasant environment with easy accessibility by plane from major cities; a favorable international image; and political and social stability.[20]

As Table 6 suggests, offshore banking and financial services do not have uniform importance in the Caribbean, or even among the countries where they are developed. Whereas, for example, business and professional licenses generated 0.7 percent and 13 percent of 1985–89 tax revenue for Barbados and the Cayman Islands,

18. Thomas, *The Poor and the Powerless*, 167–68.
19. MacDonald and Zagaris, "Caribbean Offshore Financial Centers," 151.
20. Cited in Blackman, "Tourism and Other Services in the Anglophone Caribbean," 68–69. For a detailed discussion of Caribbean offshore banking/tax-haven facilities and environment, see U.S. Senate, Committee on Governmental Affairs, *Crime and Secrecy;* U.K. House of Commons, *Report of Mr. Rodney Gallagher;* Spitz, *Tax Haven Encyclopedia;* and MacDonald and Zagaris, "Caribbean Offshore Financial Centers."

Table 6 Caribbean Revenue Sources, 1985–1989 Aggregatcs
(millions of U.S. dollars and percentages)

Tax Category[a]	Barbados	Cayman Islands	Dominican Republic	St. Kitts–Nevis	Trinidad & Tobago
Total revenue & grants	4,526.2	358.6	18,266.5	455.9	27,345.7
Tax revenue	4,178.4	299.1	15,817.5	342.5	21,918.5
Tax on income, profits, capital gains	1,143.7 [27.4]	—	3,316.1 [21.0]	52.0 [15.2]	15,481.5 [70.6]
Taxes on property	223.2 [5.3]	36.6 [12.2]	141.1 [0.9]	6.2 [1.8]	149.4 [0.7]
Domestic tax on goods & services	1,103.9 [26.4]	61.9 [20.7]	4,385.9 [27.7]	55.1 [16.1]	3,852.0 [17.6]
Taxes—use, perm. to use goods	134.2 [3.2]	45.8 [15.3]	387.1 [2.4]	9.2 [2.7]	848.5 [3.9]
Business & prof. license	27.2 [0.7]	38.7 [12.9]	207.1 [1.3]	3.6 [1.1]	91.9 [0.4]
Taxes—int'l trade, transactions	582.4 [13.9]	141.4 [47.3]	6,927.4 [43.8]	168.4 [49.2]	2,267.4 [10.3]
Stamps	453.6 [10.9]	46.7 [15.6]	114.3 [0.7]	15.2 [4.4]	168.2 [0.8]

SOURCE: *Government Finance Statistics Yearbook, 1994.*

NOTES: Numbers in square brackets ([ ]) are percentages of tax revenue.
The percentage figures for countries do not total 100 because not all revenue categories are shown here.

[a]These are selected categories shared by most countries.

respectively, it provided only 1.1 percent and 0.4 percent of the revenue in St. Kitts–Nevis and Trinidad and Tobago, respectively. The latter two countries relied much more on taxes on income and capital gains, in the case of Trinidad and Tobago, and on import and export duties, in the case of St. Kitts–Nevis. But for the Caymans the importance of the offshore sector is obvious: when one totals the revenue categories related to that sector—use and permission to use goods, business and professional licenses, and international trade taxes—these amount to over 75 percent of tax revenue.

The Cayman Islands and the Bahamas have long been two of the leading offshore banking centers, and are among the places deeply implicated in money laundering over the past two decades. In fact,

in 1995 the U.S. Department of State declared: "The Cayman Islands, one of the largest offshore financial services centers in the
world, is the primary British territory in the Caribbean in which
money laundering is a significant threat."[21] U.S. congressional investigators reported in 1985 that although the Caymans had only
one or two banks and virtually no offshore business in 1964, "when
subcommittee staff members visited the Caymans in late 1981 the
island had 30 multilateral full service 'Type A' banks and more than
300 hundred 'Type B' brass plates banks which are allowed to conduct only off-shore business." The growth was such that "by late
1983 the Caymans was said to have 425 banks. Moreover, the number of offshore companies jumped from about 15,550 in 1981 to
36,000 in 1985."[22]

A study commissioned by the British House of Commons—*The
Gallagher Report*—recorded 525 international banks and trust
companies with offices in the Caymans in 1989. The Caymans accommodated 46 of the world's 50 biggest banks, including Dai Ichi
Kangyo and Fuji, Japan's two largest banks; Bank America; Bar-
clays of Britain; Swiss Bank Corporation; and the Royal Bank of
Canada. Banking-sector assets at the end of 1987 were reported as
U.S.$250 million, "a remarkable figure for so small an island," as
The Gallagher Report observed. Official Cayman records for 1987
indicated that 18,264 companies were registered there, with interests in international investment, sales trading, shipping, insurance, real estate, and other areas. The Caymans have no income,
corporate, or withholding taxes. Companies that operate mainly
outside the Caymans can register there as nonresident companies
or incorporate as exempt companies, with the ability to issue bearer
shares to nonresidents, and thus avoid disclosure of beneficial
owners. Moreover, bank secrecy is guaranteed under the 1976
Preservation of Confidential Relations Act. According to the 1995
INCSR, in 1994 the Caymans was home to 450 banks, with deposits
of over U.S.$400 billion.[23] The November 11–24, 1995, edition of
Caribbean Week reported that the Caymans now has 560 class A

21. *INCSR* (1995), 509.
22. U.S. Senate, Committee on Governmental Affairs, *Crime and Secrecy*, 30–31.
23. U.K. House of Commons, *Report of Mr. Rodney Gallagher*, 90; *INCSR*
(1995), 510.

and B banks, 380 insurance companies, and 31,162 registered companies, making it the world's fifth largest financial center.

One writer has made a statement that both highlights the importance of the Cayman Islands in global offshore financing and demonstrates some of the peculiarities of the offshore-banking business. It warrants full replication:

> The financial district in George Town, the capital, boasts the highest density of banks and fax machines in the world. The 548 banking outposts here—a who's who of global banking— holds assets of some $400 billion, a fivefold jump in the past decade, placing it just behind Switzerland as an international banking center. There are, however, no skyscrapers or concrete canyons in George Town, for most of the banks are so-called plaque banks or booking centers—that is, loans or deposits are recorded on the books in the Caymans. Booking centers require no vaults, no tellers, no security guards, not even a bank building. They traffic in electronic debits and credits in a computer, which is where most money is in modern finance. The banking operations in the Caymans can be little more than a brass plate, with the paper work handled by a sponsor bank with offices in George Town and most of the transactions done by fax and phone from elsewhere.[24]

Anguilla, another dependency, was home to 2,400 registered companies in 1988, including 38 banks and 80 insurance companies. The inducements are freedom to move capital without exchange controls, no domestic taxes, minimum disclosure requirements, and the availability of professional services. The British Virgin Islands has a tax regime, although a light one. They had 13,000 IBCs registered in 1988. Although they now have only six major banks, money launders reportedly use their services extensively. However, British Virgin Islands and U.S. authorities have been able to obtain vital bank records and freeze drug-related money. In 1991, for example, over U.S.$3 million was transferred

24. Lohr, "Where the Money Washes Up," 27.

to the United States for forfeiture and sharing between the United States and the British Virgin Islands.[25]

According to the *Tax Haven Encyclopedia*, over 395 banks were incorporated in the Bahamas or had branches there in 1991. An IBC could be incorporated in the Bahamas with minimal formality, and usually within twenty-four hours. The identity of the beneficial owners need not be a matter of public record, since the shares may be held in the names of nominees, whose names appear in the public register. Only limited filing requirements are necessary: company name, registered agent's name and address, and the company's memorandum and articles of association. The names and addresses of the company's directors are not registered in the Bahamas. Hence, IBCs offer considerable confidentiality. Registration fees vary depending on the IBC's authorized capital. Those with capital of B$5,000 or less pay B$100 for registration and the same amount for annual renewal; those with capital between B$5,000 and B$50,000 pay B$300 for registration and renewal; those with capital exceeding B$50,000 pay B$1,000 for registration and the same sum for renewal. According to the 1995 *INCSR*, the Bahamas has over 30,000 IBCs.

The situation is different for banks and trust companies, though. Application for a license requires details on the company, its local officials, directors, partners, managers, and auditors, along with the charter, certificate of incorporation, or memorandum of association. Initial and renewal fees are the same: B$100,000 for a dealer's license; B$60,000 for an agent's license; B$25,000 for a license for general banking or trust operation; and B$15,000 for a license for limited operations. Regarding taxation, there are no taxes on income, profit from capital gains, royalties, dividends, inheritance, or sales, nor are there estate duties or probate taxes.[26]

These fees are pretty small when one considers the volume of business and profit generated by some of the banking and non-banking operations that operate out of the Bahamas and other tax havens. But the fees develop greater meaning when viewed in the context of the small economies involved. Table 6 clearly suggests

---

25. U.K. House of Commons, *Report of Mr. Rodney Gallagher,* 10; *INCSR* (1991), 367–68; and *INCSR* (1992), 421–22.
26. Alexiou, "The Bahamas."

this. The Cayman Islands, just 260 km² of territory with 29,000 people (in 1994), derived U.S.\$146 million in revenue from goods and services, use and permission to use goods and services, and business and professional licenses for the period 1985–89. However, Table 6 does not reveal the full picture. It does not show, for example, that Montserrat, with 102 km² and a population of 12,000, earned U.S.\$762,577 in registration and renewal fees in 1988.[27] Moreover, in the British Virgin Islands company registration fees reportedly provide 35 percent of the government's revenue.[28]

As implied earlier, offshore banking and other financial institutions do not necessarily entail physical structures. One 1992 report noted that "[o]f the Caymans' registered banks, only 68 have offices and staff in George Town. . . . the financial district's office buildings are five stories or less, owing to an old statute declaring that no building should be higher than the tallest tree. The building edict is one of the few regulatory curbs on business."[29] Indeed, many of the banks and other businesses have been described as "little more than a smart title and a letterhead" and "nothing more than a few documents in a lawyer's filing cabinet."[30]

Looking at the Caribbean in a global context, Anindya Bhattacharya, a financial specialist, reported in 1980 that its offshore banking market was nearly one-fifth of the gross size of Eurocurrency operations, and that the Bahamas, the Cayman Islands, and Panama accounted for more than half of all offshore banking transactions undertaken in 1975–77 by banks reporting to the Bank of International Settlements.[31] Using 1976 figures, Bhattacharya indicated that the sector employed 10 percent and 3 percent of the labor force, and that fees from banks and trust companies generated 6 percent and 13 percent of local government revenue, in the Bahamas and the Caymans, respectively. Moreover, there were—and still are—indirect benefits, including generation of local business in printing, law, accounting, and office equipment, and investment and income from telecommunications and construction.

27. Treaster, "On Tiny Isle of 300 Banks."
28. Thorndike, "Making Money in the Sun," 70.
29. Lohr, "Where the Money Washes Up," 28.
30. Treaster, "On Tiny Isle of 300 Banks," and *Economist*, "Stormy Weather."
31. "Offshore Banking in the Caribbean," 37.

However, Bhattacharya's contention was that "the overall contribution of the banking sector to the economic development of the Bahamas and the Cayman Islands is relatively insignificant because it provides less than 10 percent of the national income derived from the islands' principal industry—tourism."[32] Nevertheless, the sector in the region has grown over the years, contributing in the Caymans to an increasingly significant proportion of their GDP, as Table 7 shows. In 1987, for instance, the combined contribution of banking and business services to the GDP was about 32 percent, justifying the observation in *The Gallagher Report* that offshore financial services and related business there constituted about one-third of their total economic activity.[33]

It is impossible to determine exactly how much money is laundered through offshore banks in the Caribbean, but Caribbean and

Table 7 Cayman Islands GDP by Economic Activity (CI$) millions

	1972	1983	1984	1985	1986	1987
Agriculture/fishing	2	1	1	1	1	1
Quarrying	—	1	1	1	1	1
Manufacturing	1	3	4	4	4	4
Electricity/gas/water	2	5	6	7	7	9
Construction	11	32	30	26	27	25
Wholesale/retail	14	37	40	41	43	47
Hotels/restaurants	12	17	19	20	22	28
Transport/communications	3	22	25	28	31	37
Financial services[a]	10	32	35	35	41	46
Business services	17	40	43	45	48	53
Governmental services	3	24	25	27	28	30
Community/social/personal	5	15	16	17	18	20
Subtotal	80	230	245	252	271	300
Adjustments Less imputed bank service charges	—	−9	−10	−11	−12	−12
Plus import duties	—	20	20	20	23	27
GDP (output measure)	80	241	256	262	281	315

SOURCE: *Report of Mr. Rodney Gallagher,* 93.

[a]Excluding offshore banks and insurance companies without a physical presence (office) in the Cayman Islands.

32. Ibid., 41.
33. U.K. House of Commons, *Report of Mr. Rodney Gallagher,* 94.

U.S. officials estimate that hundreds of millions of dollars (U.S.) have been placed, layered, and integrated over the years. Indeed, it is partly the money-laundering "reputation" of the Caribbean that made Anguilla the choice for Operation Dinero, a major money-laundering sting operation that ran from January 1992 through December 1994. The American and British authorities involved seized nine tons of cocaine and U.S.$90 million worth of cash and assets, including expensive paintings, one of which was Pablo Picasso's *Head of a Beggar*. They also made 116 arrests and gathered a wealth of data on worldwide drug operations.[34]

Hence, the observation by two investigators into the BCCI (Bank of Credit and Commerce International) debacle about how the Cayman Islands was caught in the money-laundering web is an indictment that, unfortunately, applies elsewhere in the Caribbean: "The criminal element simply slid in comfortably behind the reputable corporations and used the same mechanisms for their own ends."[35] The veneer of respectability created by the respected banking and other financial operators covers the web of narcotics money laundering. Perhaps the thinking of drug operators has been "If it's good for the goose, it must be good for the gander," to use a popular adage.[36]

Offshore banking and other financial services are used in different money-laundering operations. Several noncash instruments are placed and layered in banking and nonbanking financial institutions. IBCs are used as shell companies as well as for layering, and banks and other institutions are used for the kind of loan-back operations described earlier. Nevertheless, the Bahamas and the British dependencies are not the only countries implicated in money laundering. Neither, as suggested above, is offshore banking the only mechanism used. Recently Puerto Rico was used to launder over U.S.$7 million through casinos. Evidence also suggests that postal money orders have been used for layering there. And in fall 1995 authorities in Guyana and the United States began uncovering a multi-million-dollar laundering scheme linking drug money

34. McGee, "US Set Up Fake Bank to Trick Drug Lords"; Sniffen, "International Drug Sting in Anguilla"; and *INCSR* (1995), 483.

35. Beaty and Gwynne, *The Outlaw Bank*, 113.

36. For useful business-oriented summary assessments of offshore centers in the Caribbean and throughout the world, see Cornez, *The Offshore Money Book*, 44–58.

to gold smuggling. The operations have been based in Guyana, but the connections extend to Bolivia, Chile, Colombia, and the United States.[37]

Aruban Exempt Corporations (AECs) are said to facilitate massive money laundering, and offshore banking, the free economic zones, and casinos there and in the Netherlands Antilles are allegedly heavily involved. Reports also claim that a network of ethnic Chinese money launderers based in New York is operating in Aruba through Chinese-owned factories. The Dominican Republic is considered the world's fourth largest shipper of U.S. currency to the United States—notably through Puerto Rico—after Panama, Colombia, and Bolivia. In September 1993 alone, transfers to Puerto Rico reached $650 million, nearly 8 percent of the gross national product (GNP) of the Dominican Republic for that year. The transfers for 1994 totaled $400 million.[38]

Tangible and circumstantial evidence of overall money laundering in the Caribbean has led the U.S. Department of State to place several countries in the top money-laundering category. As Table 8 reveals, six of the seventeen countries ranked in 1995 as "high priority" are in the Caribbean Basin: Aruba, Cayman Islands, Colombia, Mexico, Panama, and Venezuela. In 1996 the Netherlands Antilles was added to the list. Antigua-Barbuda, which had been ranked as "medium priority" in 1995 was moved up the critical list to "medium-high." The rankings, which are based on evidence gleaned from uncovered operations and intelligence reports and on circumstantial evidence, reflect U.S. interests and interpretation. These may change over time, as Table 8 shows, depending on actions by drug operators and countermeasures by the countries concerned, usually in conjunction with the United States and regional and international organizations.

Whether money-laundering operations justify a "high-priority," "low-priority," or other ranking for the country or countries involved, they are a headache for the region. A dangerous, suspicious cloud is cast over all offshore banking operations. This can affect confidence in and the success of a sector that was designed for legal

37. *Miami Herald*, "Guyana Probes Scheme Tied to Gold Smuggling."
38. *INCSR* (1994), 513; Sterling, *Thieves' World*, 230–31; *INCSR* (1995), 364–65, 508–9; and Pilarte, "A Latin Mecca for Laundering Drug Money."

Table 8 Money-Laundering Rankings of Caribbean-Basin Countries

Year	High	Medium-High	Medium	Low-Medium	Low	No Priority
1993	Cayman Islands Colombia Mexico Panama Venezuela		Aruba Bahamas British Virgin Islands Belize Costa Rica Guatemala Montserrat	Antigua-Barbuda Netherlands Antilles St. Lucia	Barbados Dominican Republic Grenada Haiti Honduras Jamaica St. Vincent & the Grenadines Suriname Trinidad & Tobago	Anguilla Cuba Dominica Guyana Martinique St. Kitts–Nevis Turks & Caicos
1994	Cayman Islands Colombia Mexico Panama Venezuela	Aruba Bahamas	Belize Costa Rica Guatemala Montserrat Netherlands Antilles	Antigua-Barbuda St. Vincent and the Grenadines Trinidad & Tobago	Barbados Bermuda British Virgin Islands Cuba Dominican Republic French West Indies Haiti Honduras Jamaica Puerto Rico St. Lucia Suriname	Anguilla Dominica Guyana Nicaragua St. Kitts–Nevis Turks & Caicos U.S. Virgin Islands

The Money-Laundering Headache   111

1995	Aruba Cayman Islands Colombia Mexico Panama Venezuela	Costa Rica Netherlands Antilles	Antigua-Barbuda Bahamas Belize Montserrat St. Vincent & the Grenadines	Cuba Dominican Republic Trinidad & Tobago	Anguilla Barbados Bermuda British Virgin Islands French West Indies Haiti Honduras Jamaica Puerto Rico St. Kitts–Nevis St. Lucia Suriname	Dominica Grenada Guyana Nicaragua Turks & Caicos U.S. Virgin Islands
1996	Aruba Cayman Islands Colombia Mexico Netherlands Antilles Panama Venezuela	Antigua Costa Rica	Bahamas Belize Dominican Republic Guatemala Montserrat St. Vincent & the Grenadines	Cuba Trinidad & Tobago	Anguilla Barbados Bermuda British Virgin Islands French West Indies Haiti Honduras Jamaica St. Kitts–Nevis St. Lucia Suriname	Dominica El Salvador Grenada Guyana Nicaragua Turks & Caicos U.S. Virgin Islands

Source: *International Narcotics Control Strategy Report*, 1993, 1994, 1995, 1996.

ends and that has become essential to the economic viability of several countries.

The pursuit of the neoliberal economic agenda in the region also has money-laundering implications. That agenda includes divestment, trade liberalization, and equity participation in state companies by local and international investors. There is every risk that these agenda items will create greater opportunities for money laundering and more instruments for layering. Added to this, economic circumstances are such that in a few places, as with production and trafficking, mechanisms that are vulnerable to money laundering are viewed in terms of economics and survival; morality, and sometimes legality, are relatively unimportant.

For Caribbean countries implicated the situation is complicated by the linkages between the legal economy and the underground economy, of which money laundering is a part. One British expert asserts that "[m]ost underground systems will [also] at some stage have to interface with conventional financial or banking institutions."[39] This is partly because the distinction between formal and informal economies lies not so much in the "economic" nature of activities as in their legal character.[40] Hence, money laundering becomes even more complicated, for as Anthony Maingot correctly argued, "Once a given economy—whether it be an individual island or a specific U.S. city—decides to build on the proceeds of the informal flows . . . it is virtually impossible to untangle the strictly legal from the verifiably illegal."[41] Moreover, in some countries with severe economic hardships, laundered money is said to influence both the availability of foreign currency and the foreign-exchange rate. In Guyana, for instance, countermeasures against traffickers and money launderers during 1993 are credited with reducing the supply of U.S. dollars such that there was a rise in the cost of the U.S. dollar against the Guyana dollar in the informal economy. That in turn influenced the exchange rate in the cambios and banks in the formal economy. The exchange rate shifted from U.S.$1–G$124 at the beginning of the year to U.S.$1–G$137 by year-end.[42]

---

39. Rider, "Taking the Profit out of Corruption," 16.
40. Thomas, "Foreign Currency Black Markets," 146.
41. "Laundering the Gains of the Drug Trade," 183.
42. See *Stabroek News*, "Drug Seizures Said to Be a Factor in US$ Rate Rise."

Conclusion

This chapter indicates that the Caribbean's geography, political stability, social tranquillity, and development needs have made it vulnerable to narcotics money laundering. Offshore banking, a sector
that several countries chose to propel economic growth, if not development, has become part of the infrastructure for placement, layering, and integration schemes. Surely not all offshore operators are
involved in money laundering. But, as one such operator himself
acknowledged, there are many shady operators.[43] Because of its
complexity and transnational nature and the resource limitations
of Caribbean countries, battling money laundering, which has been
called the fifth column of the drug trade, is no simple task. However,
as will be seen in Chapter 7, several countermeasures have been
adopted.

Along with narcotics money laundering, the problems of drug
production, consumption-abuse, and trafficking, which were discussed earlier, have several security implications for Caribbean
countries. The implications are both direct and tangential, both
manifest and latent, and they exist in political, economic, military,
and other areas. In the next three chapters, I examine the nature,
scope, and impact of some of these implications.

43. Interview with Roy Bouchier, chief executive officer of International Trade and
Investments, Ltd., Nassau, August 1996. The e-mail of one "investor" who contacted
Bouchier to explore business relations read, in part: "I would like for you to send
any information on how I could open an account with you. I will be using large sums
of cash, not checks or money orders. We are heavy hitters from South of the border.
Will this be a problem? I'm looking to start at around a million U.S. dollars or so and
change. Please contact my accountant and personal representative. His e-mail is as
follows . . ." The e-mail address was provided.

PART II

SECURITY
IMPLICATIONS
AND
COUNTERMEASURES

4

Crime, Justice, and Public Order

> What kind of criminal laws a society makes, and how it
> chooses to interpret and enforce those laws, will largely
> shape that society's definition of crime and, more impor-
> tant, determine how it will deal with criminal occurrences.
> —Bernard Headley

The drug operations described in the preceding three chapters have
multiple ripple effects on criminal justice and other public-policy
areas, including health, education, and economic policy. The focus
here is on criminal justice. This chapter deals essentially with the
power and politics elements of the geonarcotics milieu. It indicates
some of the nonmilitary threats presented by drugs to the Caribbean.

Caribbean countries pay a high price for trying to meet the criminal-justice challenges presented by drugs. Among the criminal-
justice costs are those related to crime education, enforcing drug
laws, prosecuting and punishing violators of those laws, and protecting private and government property through improved security
measures. With regard to property protection, for example, many

parts of the region have witnessed a dramatic increase in the number of private security agencies used by industrial and commercial companies and diplomatic missions. In Jamaica, for example, 231 private security companies with some 15,000 guards registered in 1994 under the Private Security Regulation Authority Act, introduced in 1992 to regulate the growing private security subindustry. By mid-1996 the number of guards had exceeded 20,000.[1] One report about Barbados noted that "the security business is growing, boosted by a downturn in the economy and attendant crime. . . . High security fencing, high-tech burglar alarms systems, and trained guard dogs are becoming more prevalent here."[2] Thus, the costs involved are borne not only by governments but also by corporate agencies and, eventually, by entire societies.

Criminal Behavior

There is an obvious relationship between drugs and crime: drug operations are illegal, and they lead to or require other criminal conduct. One study sees two basic categories of drug crime: enforcement crimes and business crimes. The former involves crimes among traffickers and between traffickers and civilians and police, triggered by traffickers' efforts to avoid arrest and prosecution. The latter category encompasses crimes committed as part of business disputes, and acquisitive crimes, such as robbery and extortion. Another typology posits three types of crime: consensual crimes, such as drug possession, use, or trafficking; expressive ones, such as violence or assault; and instrumental or property crimes, examples being theft, forgery, burglary, and robbery.[3]

Either typology can be used in the Caribbean context, but I am partial to the second one mainly because it offers more crime categories and permits better analysis of causes, consequences, and linkages. However, irrespective of which typology is used, the range

1. Jamaica, Parliament, *Presentation of the Hon. K. D. Knight* (1994), 36, and *Jamaica Herald*, "Security Industry Regulation Takes Hold."
2. *Miami Times*, "Security Now Big Business in Barbados."
3. See Kleiman, *Marijuana*, 109–17, and Anglin and Speckart, "Narcotics Use and Crime," 198.

of drug-related criminal activity in the Caribbean is wide. Table 9 shows a progressive increase in drug offenses reported for most countries between 1985 and 1995, and early 1996 evidence shows that this has continued in most places. The table also points to increased theft and fraud for some countries, and homicides and serious assaults for others.

There is no empirical evidence of regionwide causal linkages between drug activities, on the one hand, and fraud, homicide, theft, and assault, on the other. However, considerable circumstantial evidence points to connections. Three observations are in order. First, these are precisely the crime categories likely to be associated with drug production, trafficking, and money laundering. Second, in a few countries there *is* evidence of the association. For instance, in Jamaica, where there were 561 reported murders in 1991, according to the Planning Institute of Jamaica, "[t]here was a 75 per cent increase [over 1990] in the incidents of murder linked directly or indirectly to drug trafficking."[4] Jamaica had 780 murders in 1995, a 13 percent increase over the 1994 figure of 690.[5] The 1996 murder figure was 921—17 percent more than that of 1995, and the highest number of homicides since the political violence of 1980. Third, although Table 9 does not show this, the places with the high and progressive reports in the theft, homicide, and serious-assault categories are the same ones that have featured prominently over the past decade as centers of drug activity, namely, the Bahamas, Belize, the Dominican Republic, Guyana, Jamaica, St. Kitts–Nevis, Puerto Rico, Trinidad and Tobago, and the U.S. Virgin Islands.

In the U.S. Virgin Islands, for instance, 75 percent of the 1993 burglaries and a significant proportion of the robberies were attributed to drugs. Puerto Rico, which was designated in November 1994 as a HIDTA, had 980 murders during 1994, 60 percent of which were drug-related.[6] Although there were fewer murders in 1995, in some respects the 1995 situation was worse. According to one report, "Puerto Rico has the highest per capita murder rate in the United States, [DEA special agent Félix] Jiménez said, and 64 percent of the 850 murders there in 1995 were drug-related. The

4. *Economic and Social Survey, 1991* (1992), 21.3–21.4.

5. Jamaica Constabulary Force, *Annual Report, 1995*, 13.

6. Claxton, "Virgin Islands Drugs Linked to Antigua," and Navarro, "Puerto Rico Reeling Under Scourge of Drugs and Rising Gang Violence."

Table 9 Volume of Crime in the Caribbean[1]

Country	Year	Homicides	Sex Offenses	Serious Assaults	Thefts (All Kinds)	Fraud	Drug Offenses	Total[2]
Bahamas	1985	68	150	210	10,149[a]	416	1,161	12,154
	1986	69	158	157	11,539	549	1,259	13,731
	1987	75	177	197	12,425	397	1,214	14,485
	1988	111	228	233	12,555	446	948	14,521
	1989	93	201	243	11,618	448	955	13,558
	1990	134	301	295	12,288	441	1,172	14,631
	1991	NA	NA	NA	NA	NA	NA	NA
	1992	151	303	196	12,336	282	1,135	14,403
	1993	156	427	177	14,322	266	1,023	16,371
	1994	216	458	335	14,131	374	997	16,511
Barbados	1985	16	101	200	4,088	317	259	4,981
	1986	10	134	215	4,401	308	274	5,342
	1987	24	118	234	4,644	321	401	5,742
	1988	NR	NR	NR	NR	NR	NR	—
	1989	18	137	292	6,389	334	510	7,680
	1990	30	150	280	7,057	448	555	8,520
Dominican Republic	1985	588	815	5,791	47,048	286	1,121	55,649
	1986	608	1,323	4,010	38,609	339	1,358	46,247
	1987	780	1,066	15,308	38,890	815	1,329	58,188
	1988	837	321	2,162	30,085	335	1,036	35,376
	1989	NR	NR	NR	NR	NR	NR	—
	1990	NR	NR	NR	NR	NR	NR	—

Jamaica							
1983	483	825	681	22,030	1,544	4,250	29,813
1986	449	NR	729	23,949	1,584	4,123	30,834
1987	442	1,007	894	22,055	1,563	4,395	30,356
1988	414	1,118	812	19,769	1,533	3,533	27,179
1989	439	1,090	651	19,684	1,393	4,086	27,343
1990	542	1,006	12,375	16,278	1,297	5,433	37,031
1991	561	1,091	10,698	16,476	1,661	6,711	37,198
1992	629	1,108	12,368	14,521	1,721	6,298	36,645
1993	653	1,121	12,710	15,454	2,039	6,915	38,892
1994	690	1,070	13,855	14,453	1,853	5,859	37,780
1995	780	1,605	14,883	13,766	2,429	6,074	39,537
Trinidad & Tobago							
1985	121	272	334	25,794	242	3,162	29,925
1986	101	276	348	28,131	230	2,175	31,201
1987	118	215	2,032	29,748	377	2,401	34,981
1988	119	377	2,901	33,689	1,839	2,473	41,398
1989	128	311	534	31,971	506	2,361	35,811
1990	104	289	2,031	16,551[a]	423	2,921	22,319
1991	106	305	2,275	30,437	645	2,706	36,474
1992	109	372	2,221	31,764	626	2,317	37,409
1993	111	424	2,686	31,928	682	2,509	39,340

SOURCES: INTERPOL, *International Crime Statistics* (various years); *Economic and Social Survey, 1993*, Jamaica (1994); *Economic and Social Survey, 1995*, Jamaica (1996); Central Statistical Office, *Annual Statistical Digest, 1993*, Trinidad (1996); Royal Bahamas Police Force, *Annual Report, 1994* (1996).

NOTES: [1]Selected crime categories. Figures are the number of cases reported to the police.
[2]This is a total of the categories presented here, not a total of all crimes reported in the country.

NA = Not available.
NR = Not reported.
[a]All categories of crime not reported.

situation has deteriorated to the point where the National Guard has taken over more than 70 housing projects."[7] Murders increased dramatically in 1996—to 868—and 80 percent of them were drug-related, according to Puerto Rican law-enforcement authorities.

One of the few places with reduced crime generally in 1994 was Guyana: reported incidents dropped by 5 percent—from 11,560 in 1993 to 10,979 in 1994. However, there were increases in most serious crimes. Murders, for example, increased from 88 in 1993 to 102 in 1994; armed robberies, from 1,114 in 1993 to 1,161 in 1994; and cocaine possession, from 93 in 1993 to 283 in 1994.[8] However, during 1996, a serious drugs-driven crime wave erupted, during which several Canadians were murdered and assaulted. This prompted the Canadian government to issue a travel advisory for Guyana, and as a result of the travel advisory and understandable local outcry, in September 1996 the Guyanese authorities introduced joint army-police patrols to curb the crime explosion. By the end of the year the situation was largely under control, with some 200 people arrested in the joint operations. The situation was equally atrocious a few hundred miles north of Guyana, in Trinidad and Tobago. In October 1996, for example, Prime Minister Basdeo Panday told journalists in New York that "75 to 80 percent of all crimes in Trinidad and Tobago today are drug related."[9]

Drug criminality has no economic, social, or political boundaries. Indeed, social, economic, or political association or status is often the ideal cover or context for the commission of certain crimes. This is clear from some of the trafficking cases discussed in Chapter 2. On some occasions the web of criminality is deep and wide enough to reach the political foundation of a nation. St. Kitts–Nevis provides the most recent instance of this, as will be seen in Chapter 5.

Drug operations often generate criminal behavior that defies clear "consensual," "expressive," or "instrumental" ranking because of linkages and overlapping. Sometimes the crimes involved have a sharp, traumatic social edge, such as the case in which a thirty-year-old deranged crack addict murdered six people, including his own mother, in a single machete attack on December 9, 1994, at

7. Farah, "Caribbean Key to US Drug Trade," A9.
8. Khan, "Serious Offenses on the Increase."
9. Roberts, "Panday: Crime Is Number One."

Buxton-Friendship, a village along Guyana's Atlantic coast.[10] Drug-related crime can also have a distinctly economic orientation, or a political one, especially when power and politics are elements in the matrix. The 1988–89 Antigua-Barbuda arms-trafficking case, which is elaborated in the next chapter, is an example.

A former Jamaican commissioner of corrections once stated: "Mounting crime and violence have been declared leading national problems, and the issue of law and order has assumed high priority in national planning and policy making. Fear of crime is destroying . . . freedom of movement, freedom from harm, and freedom from fear itself."[11] This statement, first made in 1976, remains relevant two decades later, now even more dramatically so. It was also made mainly in the Jamaican context, but it now has regionwide validity because, for a variety of reasons not explored here, crime has sky-rocketed.[12] The drugs-driven crime situation has deteriorated to the point where even a territorial governor—Governor Roy L. Schneider of the U.S. Virgin Islands—feels compelled to carry a Glock semiautomatic pistol when he does not have his official security detail, a fact he disclosed to the *Washington Post* and the *Virgin Islands Daily News* in January 1997.

As with drug criminality in other parts of the world, drug crimes in the Caribbean are not all random and individually perpetrated. Organized criminal activity has established itself within countries in the region and also links drug operators in the region with some outside the area. Research on the Bahamas, for example, has found that "the Bahamas is [now] seeing the formation of youth gangs which provide an environment where detached youths find money, protection, access to drugs, and a sense of community."[13] However, the most notorious organized crime is perpetrated by groups called posses in Canada, the Caribbean, and the United States, and yardies in Britain.

The posses are organized criminal gangs of Jamaican origin and composed primarily of Jamaicans or people of Jamaican descent.

---

10. Waddell, "Deranged Man Murders Mother, Five Others," and idem, "'Baby Arthur' Was a Crack Addict." "Baby Arthur" was the pseudonym of the addict.

11. Allen, "Urban Crime and Violence in Jamaica," 29.

12. For an excellent analysis of crime in Jamaica, an analysis relevant to other Caribbean countries, see Phillips and Wedderburn, *Crime and Violence.*

13. Jekel et al., "Nine Years of Freebase Cocaine," 20.

One writer has called them "the most disciplined and violent of all inner-city traffickers," the "by-product of Jamaica's pattern of polarized and dependent economic development, the workings of 'retrogressive' politics in Jamaican democracy, and U.S. foreign policy."[14] They also have been described as "an outgrowth of [this] organized crime in Jamaica which uses violence as the organizing principle in the accumulation of 'alternative power' "[15] Although the posses are known most for the trafficking in drugs and weapons, they have also been implicated in money laundering, fraud, kidnapping, robbery, burglary, prostitution, documents forgery, and murder.

In terms of organization, the basic structure of a posse is said to comprise an upper echelon, a middle echelon, and the workers at the bottom of the hierarchy. The upper echelon coordinates the drugs, arms, and other operations. Daily operational management is the responsibility of the middle echelon, and workers perform a variety of tasks, including sales, protection, weapons purchases, rental of apartments and vehicles, and the requisite acts of violence. Nevertheless, not all posses are that structured; some are loose networks. As might be expected, there is variation in posse size, scope and length of operation, and implication in crime. For instance, the Gullymen posse, the majority of whose members come from McGreggor Gully in Jamaica, is said to have been in operation since 1979. And the Shower posse, which started in Tivoli Gardens, first came to the attention of U.S. authorities in 1984 after INTERPOL asked the Bureau of Alcohol, Tobacco, and Firearms (ATF) for assistance in tracing some firearms that had been recovered in Jamaica.[16]

Swift and brutal violence is a posse trademark. For instance, Jim Brown, also known as Lester Coke, coleader of the Shower posse, was reputedly responsible for sixty-eight murders and the shooting of thirteen policemen in Jamaica during the first six months of 1990 alone. Brown was tried for murder on fourteen occasions, but he was always acquitted because witnesses either disappeared or were killed. Incidentally, Brown was murdered in 1993 in a mysterious

14. Harrison, "Drug Trafficking in World Capitalism," 119.
15. Stone, "Crime and Violence," 29.
16. Brana-Shute, "Jamaican Posse Gangs," 2–3, and Gunst, "Jamaica Drug Gangs," 549, 567.

fire in the Jamaica prison where he was being held pending hearings for extradition to the United States for trial on several murder and other charges.

Law-enforcement officials have noted certain commonalities of posse-related homicides, 4,915 of which were said to have been committed in the United States between 1985 and 1992: gunshot wounds at the back of the neck; multiple gunshots from several different weapons; setting victims on fire; shooting in the face; firebombing; throat slashing; and dismemberment. Sometimes several methods of killing are used, and there are reports of people being shot first and then dismembered, their bodies disposed of in different parts of a city. Victims' heads are sometimes left as a warning, and parts of entire families are known to have been liquidated by posses.[17]

The posses first trafficked and sold marijuana that came mainly from Jamaica. Gary Brana-Shute explained: "The Jamaican posses were unique because they controlled the importation, distribution, and sale of marijuana down to the retail (street) level. The organization was self-contained and self-reliant."[18] But as the posses gained a foothold in the narcotics enterprise, their leaders recognized the potential for expanding the range of drugs and related "services." As their networks became overextended and their need for manpower increased, the posses began to recruit from outside the Jamaican national group, using "outsiders" primarily as mules and street-level dealers to minimize their vulnerability to law-enforcement countermeasures. African-Americans, Guyanese, Panamanians, Trinidadians, and Nigerians are now increasingly brought into posse operations. Cooperation with Colombians and Dominicans is also said to be on the rise. More than this, however, white females are reportedly now used as couriers and arms purchasers. Chinese, whites, and Indians of Jamaican descent are also said to be recruited.[19]

Like their Latin American organized criminal counterparts, posses often control their own money laundering. Most of them are said

---

17. Brana-Shute, "Jamaican Posse Gangs," 20–21, and U. S. Department of Justice, National Drug Intelligence Center, *Jamaican Organized Crime* [hereafter *Jamaican Organized Crime*].

18. "Jamaican Posse Gangs," 6.

19. Ibid., 6–9, and *Jamaican Organized Crime*, 5.

to avoid using large financial institutions, relying instead on Western Union and other wire-transfer services. They allegedly purchase legitimate businesses as fronts and invest in real estate, restaurants, hair salons, bakeries, car-rental agencies, trucking companies, auto-repair shops, and the entertainment business. And like other criminal groups, they are able to succeed in their pursuits partly because of adeptness at getting or creating documents and flexibility of operations. As one narcotics intelligence report indicates: "Identification of posse members is extremely difficult due to their proficiency in obtaining and/or producing false documentation, their ability to blend into lower income neighborhoods, and their mobility. It is not unusual for posse members to have a dozen aliases and a sophisticated array of fraudulent identification cards."[20]

Female posse members once performed mainly menial roles as "baby mothers" (to provide sexual pleasure and bear children), couriers, and renters of cars and apartments. However, women now perform middle-echelon duties. Indeed, one posse, the Classic posse, is allegedly an all-woman group. But whatever the gender composition, almost all posses engage in some social investment by "taking care" of their communities of origin in material terms. As Laurie Gunst put it: "Like the singer-gunfighter played by Jimmy Cliff in [the movie] *The Harder They Come,* many a 'Johnny-too-Bad' becomes a ghetto hero in Kingston [and other places], a Robin Hood who steals from the rich and gives to the sufferers."[21] Partly for this reason, Carl Stone once said: "Whereas conventional crime must be seen as having had a negative impact on the [Jamaican] economy, the drug trade represents an area of crime where the impact has been mainly positive."[22]

Three migration factors, some with economic underpinnings, are credited with the extension of the Jamaican criminal networks into the United States and elsewhere. One factor is the migration of known senior "top-ranking" drug dealers from Jamaica, men usually between ages thirty and forty, with established criminal records—Bucky Marshall and Claudie Massop, who emigrated to

20. *Jamaican Organized Crime,* 5.
21. Gunst, "Jamaica Drug Gangs," 568.
22. Stone, "Crime and Violence," 47.

the United States in the 1970s, being two examples. A second factor is the migration of a younger generation of "rude bways," primarily men in their teens to early twenties. They may have only minor criminal records in Jamaica, but their upbringing in West Kingston and other tough urban areas makes them as feared and as fearsome as some of the "top-ranking."[23]

The final factor is first- and second-generation youths born in North America and Europe to Jamaican parents:

> Although Americans by birth, their roles and entire systems of identification—as well as sense of belonging—lie with their home country ("a yard") and with select sectors of the overseas Jamaican community. More concretely, the identities and definitions of reality of the "Jamericans"—many of them born in the slums of America's large urban centers—are shaped in a constant process of mutual sharing and primary interactions with immigrants arriving regularly from Jamaica. These interactions include—but are not necessarily limited to—association with the "rude bways" coming from the streets of West Kingston. Eventually, for the "Jamericans," these varied levels of contact lead to gang recruitment.[24]

Over the past decade scores of posses are said to have operated within the Caribbean–North American–European drug circuit. These include Allentown, Cats, Cricket Organ, Classic, Dog, Delta Force, Dunkirk, Jungle, Montego Bay, New Kingston, Nineties, Rats, Reema, Rude Boys, Samokan, Shower, Solid Gold, Sprangler, Tel-Aviv, Tivoli Gardens, Untouchable, Shadow, Wilkinsburg, Wonderland, Barbara Daley Organization, Kirkers, Devon Sutherland Organization, Black, Chris Melaglan Organization, Dwight Pratt Organization, Henderson Family, Junglelites, Vernon Stedman Organization, Alverang, Anthony Levy Organization, Apache, Gold Star, Lancelot and Lancelot, Williams Organization, Miami Boys, Paul Black, Wet Skin, Waterhouse, Lickshot, Southies, Backbush, Reema, and Southee. As might be expected, estimates of the num-

23. Headley, "War Ina 'Babylon,' " 77.
24. Ibid. Headley also discusses these factors in his book *The Jamaica Crime Scene: A Perspective,* 35–38.

ber of posse groups and their total membership vary. Figures range between 40 and 110 for posse groups, and between 2,500 and 20,000 for membership.[25]

The Shower, Sprangler, Dunkirk, and Jungle posses are said to be among the largest and best-known groups operating within the United States. One narcotics intelligence source indicates that the Shower posse's distribution network, which is based in New York and Miami, extends to Atlanta, Boston, Buffalo, Chicago, Cleveland, Dallas, Denver, Detroit, Hartford, Kansas, Los Angeles, Philadelphia, Pittsburgh, Seattle, Toronto, Quebec, and Washington, D.C. In Europe, it is known to have operated in Britain, the Netherlands, and Germany. According to the National Drug Intelligence Center, the Shower posse has its own airplanes and pilots for smuggling, as well as a variety of legitimate businesses, such as car-rental and travel agencies, to assist with its money-laundering operations.

Over the years, economic incentives and law-enforcement countermeasures have created shifts in posse operations, from traditional centers in New York and Miami to areas in upstate New York and to Connecticut, Massachusetts, and several midwest and southwest cities. They are also said to have been focusing over recent years on small and medium-size cities along interstate highways and Amtrak lines. The expansion in Canada is beyond Montreal and Toronto to Oshawa, Kitchner, London, Windsor, and Hamilton. In Britain, they have extended from London, especially the Brixton area, to Manchester, Birmingham, and Bristol, among other places. And as might be expected, the organizational networks in Canada and Britain differ somewhat from those in the Caribbean and the United States.[26]

Thus, with their interactions at the level of the group, the nation, and the international system, the workings of the posses demonstrate the transnational nature of drug operations and of the criminal conduct related to them. Moreover, their operations illustrate that drug entrepreneurs employ a wide range of mechanisms for both cooperation and conflict, sometimes using instruments of co-

---

25. Brana-Shute, "Jamaican Posse Gangs," 25–31; Headley, "War Ina 'Babylon' "; and *Jamaican Organized Crime,* 5–6.

26. *Jamaican Organized Crime,* 5–8, and U.S. Department of Justice, National Drug Intelligence Center, *The Jamaica Intelligence Connection.*

ercion that state agents are unable to command or are prohibited from using.

Drug-related criminal activity within some Caribbean countries is complicated and aggravated by the activities of Caribbean nationals who are convicted and sentenced elsewhere and later deported. Many of these deportees are posse members or former posse members. Jamaica's national security minister reported to the country's Parliament in July 1993 that "[n]early a thousand Jamaicans were deported from other countries last year, with over 700 coming from the United States. Most of them, nearly 600, were deported for drug-related offenses. . . . Intelligence indicates that many of them become more involved in criminal activity here."[27] During 1993, 923 deportees were returned from the United States, Canada, and the Cayman Islands; 64 percent of them were implicated with drugs.[28]

The figure for 1994 was even higher: 1,434—511 more than in 1993. Of the 1994 deportees, 874 (70 percent) were sent from the United States, and 872 (71 percent) of them were returned because of drugs and weapons possession and smuggling. The figure was higher still in 1995: 1,563. And between January and July 1996, 465 people were returned to Jamaica, mostly because of drug-related crimes.[29] According to Jamaica Constabulary Force (JCF) sources, for the entire 1996 the number was 1,158, 53 percent of which was drug-related. In Guyana's case, 67 nationals were deported from the United States and scores from Suriname and Trinidad in 1992, 50 from the United States in 1993, and 64 in 1994. The 1995 figure shot up to 721, from twenty countries, and between January and June 1996, 351 people were returned to Guyana.[30] By the end of 1996, the total number of people deported to Guyana was 1,053, a 40 percent increase over 1995. They came from twenty-

27. Jamaica, Parliament, *Presentation of the Hon. K. D. Knight* (1993), 11.

28. Planning Institute of Jamaica, *Economic and Social Survey, 1993*, 23.3.

29. Planning Institute of Jamaica, *Economic and Social Survey, 1994*, 23.3; Jamaica Constabulary Force, *Annual Report, 1995*, 16; and *Jamaica Herald*, "Deportees on the Rise."

30. The 1992 figures come from Philadelphia, "Drug Wars: The Threat to Guyana," 16. "John Philadelphia" was the pseudonym used by Lieutenant Colonel Fabian Liverpool, permanent secretary in the Ministry of Home Affairs. The 1993 figure is from Assistant Commissioner Felix. The 1994 figure is from Khan, "Serious Offenses on the Increase," and the 1995 and 1996 figures are from Jordon, "One Thousand Guyanese Deported in Past 18 Months."

three countries. Moreover, there was a 200 percent increase in the number of individuals returned for drug-related offenses, sent mainly from the United States.[31]

Government officials throughout the Caribbean have noted that the deportees tend to become involved locally in trafficking and other criminal networks. Jamaica's 1995 *Economic and Social Survey* reported that deportees are heavily involved in crime, "particularly the importation and use of firearms, the drug trade, and money laundering." The situation is so grave that new legislation was adopted in Jamaica in 1994 to allow the police to monitor the movement of deportees and take preemptive action.

The new legislation—the Criminal Justice (Administration) (Amendment) Act, 1994—provides for deportees to be deemed restricted persons. And under section 54(C) restricted persons are subject to the imposition of orders, for up to twelve months at a time, to restrict their residence, force their registration, and compel them to report to police authorities on a weekly basis. They are also required to inform the police about intended absences from the registered address when the absence is for more than a week, and about any planned change of address. The new law provides for a central register of restricted persons as well as for twelve-month prison terms for violation of monitoring provisions or for false reporting. The act also creates a five-member Restricted Persons Review Tribunal to hear appeals from persons placed under restriction and to advise the government on the maintenance of the system.[32] Guyana plans to emulate Jamaica's legislative lead in this respect.[33]

Guyana and Jamaica are, however, not the only places with deportee problems. The Dominican Republic and some of the eastern Caribbean countries also face them.[34] The Dominican Republic, for example, had 1,124 deportees from the United States alone in 1995. One important difference between the problems in Guyana

31. *Stabroek News Online*, "Number of Deportees Up by 40%."

32. I am grateful to Glen Andrade, Jamaica's director of public prosecutions, for providing a copy of the legislation.

33. See *Stabroek News*, "Deportees to Come Under Close Scrutiny," and *Weekly Gleaner* (U.S.), "Guyana Goes Ahead on Deportee Legislation."

34. Interviews with Commissioner Courtney of Grenada, July 1994, and with Deputy Commissioner Smith of Antigua-Barbuda, August 1996; and conversations with Superintendent Frazer, Superintendent Clarkson, Chief Secretary Farrier, and Deputy Commissioner Harry in January 1995.

and Jamaica and those in the eastern Caribbean is the size factor. Because of the very small size of the populations of eastern Caribbean countries, and hence of their migrant populations, and the smaller scale on which their nationals become involved in drug crimes, they have far fewer deportees. Yet precisely because of their small size the (re)introduction of criminal behavior into those societies by deportees has a dramatic and traumatic effect.

Not only is the problem taxing the resources of eastern Caribbean and other countries, but, as one official who requested anonymity told me, many of the deportees are former servicemen of the U.S. Army or Marines, and they bring their military training and knowledge of weapons and military hardware to their criminal enterprise, creating both a greater sense of apprehension in law-enforcement officials and a bigger practical headache for them. According to that official, "They leave our islands as high school criminals and are returned to us as postgraduate criminals." Moreover, over recent years throughout the Caribbean there has been increasing weapons use in the commission of crime, by individuals and posses, whether deportee or not. In Jamaica, for instance, firearms were used in 58 percent of the 780 murders committed during 1995.[35] Guns are being used more not only in murders but also in theft, rapes, and robberies.

Drug-related criminality in the region has given rise to an increasing problem related to witnesses. Witnesses are not only being intimidated, but murdered. This has necessitated the development of witness-protection programs. There are two kinds of witness protection: short-term law protection, which may or may not involve temporary relocation, before and during a trial; and long-term protection, involving permanent relocation after a trial is completed. These programs are logistically problematic, given the small size of Caribbean countries and communities. They are also very costly. Puerto Rico, for example, spends $4 million a year protecting witnesses in drug cases.[36]

The natural inclination of authorities in many countries facing this problem is to seek external assistance, both in managing programs within the various islands and in providing havens for wit-

35. Planning Institute of Jamaica, *Economic and Social Survey, 1995,* 23.2.
36. Navarro, "Puerto Rico Is Sending Many Drug-Case Witnesses to Florida."

nesses who give testimony in crucial cases. The United States and
Canada have often provided assistance with one or both types of
protection. However, because of a variety of financial, constitutional, and political problems in potentially sympathetic countries—both within and outside the Caribbean—the prospects for
continued witness relocation are not very good, especially in relation to permanent relocation.

The tensions between Puerto Rico and Florida, which were pub-
licly aired in October 1996, are symptomatic of wider problems.
Florida has been the venue where Puerto Rico has relocated a high
proportion of its 127 witnesses and 187 family members between
1994 and 1996, with most settled in Orlando and Miami. This has
caused some resentment from the settlement communities and dis-
gruntledness from Florida law-enforcement agencies, which in turn
has prompted Florida's governor, Lawton Chiles, to ask his Puerto
Rican counterpart, Pedro Rosselló, for details of Puerto Rico's witness-protection program. He also ordered Florida's State Department of Law Enforcement to pursue the establishment of a protocol
to govern witness relocation that would include disclosure procedures and the right to refuse witnesses based on their criminal history.[37] Following two months of discussions, the protocol was
signed by Governors Chiles and Rosselló on January 20, 1997. It
stipulates that Puerto Rican authorities must notify Florida's Department of Law Enforcement of the date and place of the relocation
of any witness who has a criminal record, is suspected of involvement in criminal activity, or is "at significant risk of imminent physical harm or strong likelihood of harmful retaliation" because of his
or her role in a prosecution. The agreement also calls for the sharing
of photographs, fingerprints, and criminal histories of witnesses
and likely witnesses.[38]

These problems apart, the integrity of witness relocation has
often been compromised because of the combined effect of corruption and the networks of the criminal organizations and individuals
implicated, such that on occasion relocated witnesses have been
murdered.[39] Witness protection has been particularly problematic

37. Ibid.
38. Navarro, "Puerto Rico Accepts Plan for Relocating Program Witnesses."
39. See, for example, *Daily Observer* (Jamaica), "Crown Witness Murdered."

for Trinidad and Tobago, Puerto Rico, Jamaica, the Dominican Republic, St. Kitts–Nevis, and Guyana.

Legislative and Judicial Responses

Attention to the criminal-justice impact of drugs must, however, extend beyond crime itself, to law enforcement, adjudication, and punishment. Financial, personnel, and technical limitations place serious constraints on Caribbean countries in all of these areas. Drug offenses are taxing the agencies responsible for these areas beyond their capacities. Illegal drug operations and the problems they generate have created the need for new and expanded drug units for intelligence and prosecution, and new and additional drug courts. One country—Guyana—even plans to create a special corruption court to deal with one of the serious consequences of the drug phenomenon.[40] And Trinidad and Tobago plans to create special drug courts during 1997.

New and revised legislation also has become necessary. And, as Table 10 shows, most of the laws have been introduced since the mid-1980s, reflecting what was noted in the Introduction: it was during the mid-1980s that drugs began to develop regionwide crisis proportions in the Caribbean. Subsidiary and ancillary laws are also often needed. In Trinidad and Tobago, for example, the Transfer of Prisoners Act was passed in 1993 to permit accession to the 1983 International Convention on the Transfer of Sentenced Persons, a move prompted by increased drug-related prisoner-exchange activity.[41] Yet, more vital than new or revised laws is their implementation. For reasons ranging from administrative lethargy to technical, financial, and other limitations, the implementation record is very poor in the region.

40. See Naraine, "Plans for Corruption Court Moving Ahead." Minister of Home Affairs Mohammed indicated in our interview that the corruption court had become necessary because of the alarming number of drug and other corruption cases that were creating judicial bottlenecks. The establishment of the court was, however, delayed by financial and staffing problems.

41. Subsidiary administrative law also became necessary in Trinidad and Tobago. The Exchange of Prisoners Regulations and the Exchange of Prisoners Order were adopted in May and June 1994, respectively.

Table 10 Antidrug Legislation in the Caribbean

Country	Principal Legislation		Subsidiary Legislation	
Anguilla[a]	(i)	Drugs (Prevention of Misuse) Ordinance, No. 17 of 1988	The Dangerous Drug Rules, 1942 (continued in force)	
	(ii)	Drug Trafficking Offences Ordinance, No. 14 of 1988		
	(iii)	Drug Trafficking Offences (Amendment) Ordinance, 1990		
	(iv)	Mutual Legal Assistance (USA) Ordinance, 1990		
	(v)	Drugs (Prevention of Misuse) (Amendment) Ordinance, 1993		
	(vi)	Mutual Legal Assistance (USA) Ordinance, 1996		
Antigua-Barbuda[a]	(i)	Misuse of Drugs Act, 1973	(i)	Dangerous Drugs Rules, 1942
	(ii)	Misuse of Drugs (Amendment) Act, 1987	(ii)	Dangerous Drugs (Relaxation) Order, 1953
	(iii)	Misuse of Drugs (Amendment) Act, No. 1 of 1993	(iii)	Dangerous Drugs (Application) Order, 1954
	(iv)	Proceeds of Crime Act, No. 13 of 1993		
	(v)	Mutual Assistance in Criminal Matters Act, No. 2 of 1993		
Aruba[b]	(i)	Narcotic Drugs Act		
	(ii)	Precursor Law, 1991		
	(iii)	Land Ordinance on the Penalization of Legal Entities, 1995		
	(iv)	Land Ordinance on the Import and Export of Essential Chemicals		

The Bahamas[a]	(i) Dangerous Drugs Act, Chapter 213 (rev. 1987) (ii) Dangerous Drugs (Amendment) Act, 1998 (iii) Dangerous Drugs (Amendment) Act, 1989 (iv) Tracing and Forfeiture of the Drug Trafficking Act, Chapter 86 (Rev. 1987) (v) Mutual Legal Assistance (Criminal Matters) Act, 1988	(i) Dangerous Drugs (Dispensing of Narcotics) Rules, 1952 (ii) Dangerous Drugs (Methaqualone) Order, 1981 (iii) Dangerous Drugs (Prescription of Minimum Amounts) Rules, 1989 (iv) Tracing and Forfeiture of the Proceeds of Drug Trafficking (Designated Countries and Territories) Order, 1990
Barbados[a]	(i) Drug Abuse (Prevention and Control) Act, No. 14 of 1990 (ii) Proceeds of Crime Act, No. 13 of 1990 (iii) Mutual Assistance (Criminal Matters) Act, No. 8 of 1992	Drug Abuse (Prevention and Control) Regulations, 1993
Belize[a]	(i) Misuse of Drugs Act, No. 22 of 1990 (ii) Criminal Justice (Amendment) Act, No. 26 of 1992 (iii) Criminal Justice (Amendment) Act, No. 6 of 1994	
Bermuda[a]	(i) Misuse of Drugs Act, 1972 (ii) Misuse of Drugs (Amendment) Act, 1987 (iii) Misuse of Drugs (Amendment) Act, 1988 (iv) Drug Trafficking Suppression Act, 1988	(i) Misuse of Drugs (Designation) Order, 1973 (ii) Misuse of Drugs (Supply to Addicts) Regulations, 1974

Table 10 (continued)

Country	Principal Legislation		Subsidiary Legislation	
British Virgin Islands[a]	(i)	Drugs (Prevention of Misuse) Act, 1988	(i)	Dangerous Drugs Rules, 1942
	(ii)	Drug Trafficking Offences Act, 1992	(ii)	Dangerous Drugs Application Order, 1954
	(iii)	Assets Seizure Act, 1993		
	(iv)	Criminal Justice (International Cooperation) Act, 1993		
Cayman Islands[a]	(i)	Misuse of Drugs Law, 1973		Misuse of Drugs Order, 1988
	(ii)	Misuse of Drugs (Amendment) Laws, 1986, 1987, 1988		
	(iii)	Mutual Legal Assistance (USA) Law, 1990		
	(iv)	Misuse of Drugs (Amendment) Law, 1995		
Cuba[c]	(i)	Drug Trafficking Law, No. 1 of 1979	(i)	Decree No. 72 of 1990
	(ii)	Public Health Law, No. 41 of 1983	(ii)	Decree No. 150 of 1994
	(iii)	Law No. 62 of 1988		
Dominica[a]	(i)	Narcotics Control Act, No. 23 of 1969	(i)	Prevention of Misuse Regulations
	(ii)	Drugs (Prevention of Misuse) Act, No. 20 of 1988	(ii)	Drugs (Notification of and Supply to Addicts) Regulations
	(iii)	Mutual Assistance in Criminal Matters Act, 1990		
	(iv)	Proceeds of Crime Act, 1993		

Dominican Republic[c]	(i) Narcotics Drugs Act, No. 168 of 1975 (ii) Law No. 105 of 1987 (iii) Drugs and Substance Control Act, No. 50 of 1988 (iv) Law No. 39 of 1990 (v) Drugs and Substance Control (Amendment) Act, 1995	(i) Decree No. 2787 of 1985 (ii) Law No. 62-82-21 of 1986 (iii) Decree No. 339 of 1988 (iv) Decree No. 356 of 1988 (v) Decree No. 6 of 1989
Grenada[a]	(i) Dangerous Drugs (Expert Witness) Act, 1979 (ii) Proceeds of Crime Act, 1992 (iii) Drug Abuse (Prevention and Control) Act, 1992 (iv) Mutual Assistance (Criminal Matters) Act, 1993	Misuse of Drugs Regulations
Guyana[a, d]	(i) Narcotic Drugs and Psychotropic Substances (Control) Act, 1988 (ii) Narcotic Drugs and Psychotropic Substances (Amendment) Act, No. 10, 1989 (iii) Narcotic Drugs and Psychotropic Substances (Amendment) Act, No. 14, 1989 (iv) Administration of Justice (Fines) Act, 1989	Narcotic Drugs and Psychotropic Substances (Control) Regulations, 1988
Haiti[c]	(i) Decree of December 18, 1975	

Table 10 (continued)

Country	Principal Legislation		Subsidiary Legislation	
Jamaica[a]	(i)	Dangerous Drugs Act, Chap. 90 (1973 rev.)	(i)	Dangerous Drugs Regulations, 1948
	(ii)	Dangerous Drugs (Amendment) Act, 1974	(ii)	Dangerous Drugs (Authorization Condition) Regulations, 1948
	(iii)	Dangerous Drugs (Amendment) Act, No. 17		
	(iv)	Dangerous Drugs (Amendment) Act, No. 2, 1987		
	(v)	Drug Offences (Forfeiture of Proceeds) Act, No. 16, 1994		
	(vi)	Dangerous Drugs (Amendment) Act, No. 30, 1994		
	(vii)	Mutual Assistance in Criminal Matters Act, 1995		
Montserrat[a]	(i)	Drugs (Prevention of Misuse) Ordinance, 1989		
	(ii)	Drug Trafficking Offences Ordinance, 1990		
	(iii)	Mutual Legal Assistance in Criminal Matters (USA) Ordinance, 1991		
St. Kitts–Nevis[a]	(i)	Drugs (Prevention of Misuse) Act, No. 11 of 1986		Dangerous Drugs Regulations (continued in force by virtue of S.37(2) of the 1986 act)
	(ii)	Proceeds of Crime Act, 1993		
St. Lucia[a, e]	(i)	Drugs (Prevention of Misuse) Act, 1986	(i)	Dangerous Drugs (cocaine, morphine, etc.) Regulation
	(ii)	Proceeds of Crime Act, 1992	(ii)	Dangerous Drugs (raw opium and coca leaves) Regulation, 1957
	(iii)	Prevention of Misuse (Amendment) Act, 1993	(iii)	Dangerous Drugs Order, 1958

St. Vincent & the Grenadines[a]	(i) Drugs (Prevention of Misuse) Act, Chap. 219 (1991 rev.) (ii) Drugs (Prevention of Misuse) (Amendment) Act, 1993 (iii) Mutual Assistance in Criminal Matters Act, 1993 (iv) Drug Trafficking Offences Act, 1993	(i) Raw Opium and Coca Leaves Regulation, 1940 (ii) Dangerous Drugs Regulations, 1940
Suriname[b]	(i) Opium Law, 1955 (ii) Narcotics Act, 1996	
Trinidad & Tobago[a]	(i) Dangerous Drugs Act, No. 38, 1991 (ii) Dangerous Drugs (Amendment) Act, 1994	Dangerous Drugs Regulations, 1950 (continued in force)
Turks & Caicos[a]	(i) Misuse of Drugs Ordinance, 1971 (ii) Control of Drugs Ordinance, 1976 (iii) Control of Drugs (Trafficking) Ordinance, 1988 (iv) Mutual Legal Assistance (USA) Ordinance, 1990 (v) Control of Drugs (Amendment) Ordinance, 1992 (vi) Criminal Justice (International Cooperation) Ordinance, 1992	Customs Ordinance, 1971

SOURCES: UWI–UNDCP Drug Control Legal Training Program; Attorneys-general chambers of various countries; UNDCP.

NOTE: This table does not cover money-laundering legislation, except where money laundering is an aspect of legislation on trafficking or abuse. It also does not list all the pieces of legislation pertaining to drugs issues, just the major ones.

[a]Common-law tradition.
[b]Roman-Dutch law tradition.
[c]Civil-law tradition.
[d]This legal system also uses Roman-Dutch law significantly.
[e]This legal system also uses French civil law significantly.

Calls have been made for capital punishment for certain drug offenses,[42] but generally the new laws impose stiff fines and terms of imprisonment and provide for the confiscation of property acquired through drug trading. The scope and gravity of drugs activities prompt many judges to apply provisions of some laws fully, as when, in March 1992, the chief magistrate of Guyana (now a judge), Claudette La Bennett, refused bail to a nine-month pregnant woman accused of possessing weapons and ammunition and six pounds of cocaine. The woman, Sharon Morgan, appealed La Bennett's decision and was released on G$100,000 bail. While on bail she delivered her baby, but then failed to attend trial on three occasions. She was later convicted and sentenced to four years in prison, *in absentia*. In another case, Justice Lennox Deyalsingh of Trinidad and Tobago in June 1994 sentenced thirty-three-year-old Nizam Mohamed to life imprisonment for possessing fifteen rocks of crack cocaine.[43]

Some of the provisions of the new laws border on violation of the civil rights of citizens, or have that potential. Four examples will suffice. Section 24(1) of the 1987 Jamaica legislation permits *any constable* to search, seize, and detain, *without a warrant,* any conveyance he or she reasonably suspects is "being or has been used for the commission of any offense under this Act." The Guyana law has a similar provision—section 93(1). These provisions permit considerable police power, which, regrettably, has often been misused. Second, under section 26 of the Jamaica legislation, section 78 of the Guyana legislation, and section 20 of the Trinidad and Tobago law, the burden of proof rests on the accused. This is an exception to the normal provision for the burden of proof to rest with the party bringing the charge or making the complaint, which, in these cases, is the state.

Third, provisions of Belize's Crime Control Bill, introduced in Parliament in December 1994 to combat spiraling drug-related and other crime, cover the protection of citizens who act in self-defense,

---

42. See, for example, *Stabroek News,* "Trinidad Senator Advocates Hanging for Drug Traffickers," and *New York Carib News,* "[Dominica Prime Minister] Charles Says No to Drugs: Hang Them."

43. See *Stabroek News,* "Court Refuses Bail to Nine-Month Pregnant Accused"; idem, "Drugs Accused Sentenced to Jail in Her Absence"; and *Guyana Chronicle,* "Cocaine Trafficker Jailed for Life."

weapons restrictions in public places, and harsher penalties for juveniles. There is also a provision for accelerated adjudication using auxiliary judges for summary trials rather than trials by indictment, which tend to be lengthy. All of these are laudable. However, two of the critical features of the legislation provide for a virtual suspension of civil rights in crime-ridden neighborhoods declared "special areas." Attorney General Dean Barrow explained that "special-area declarations" would grant security forces the power to cordon off areas and to search, arrest, and detain people without warrants for up to ninety days.[44] Empirical evidence indicates that while Belizeans generally favor drug countermeasures, including criminal sanctions, they are apprehensive about increased police power.[45]

Finally, the Criminal Justice (Administration) (Amendment) Act introduced in Jamaica in 1994 to help deal with the deportee headache has serious implications for constitutionally guaranteed freedoms of association and movement. The government has argued that its actions are constitutional given the "exception clauses" of the fundamental-rights section of the constitution. For example, a provision under section 23 of the constitution, which guarantees freedoms of assembly and association, states: "Nothing contained in or done under the authority of any law shall be held to be inconsistent with or in contravention of this section to the extent that the law in question makes provision (a) which is reasonably required (i) in the interest of defense, public safety, public order, public morality, or public health, or (ii) for the purpose of protecting the rights and freedoms of other persons." Nevertheless, the government's chief prosecutor himself anticipates that the law's constitutionality will be challenged with the very first case brought under it, because of the delicate constitutional issues involved.[46]

Hence, there is justifiable concern about civil rights, justice, and actual and potential abuse of power because of the wide discretion and power that the provisions of some laws give to law-enforcement officials. While he was Jamaica's attorney general, Carl Rattray—

44. Eggleston and Flanagan, "Belize Civil Rights."
45. See Weigand and Bennett, "The Will to Win," esp. 205–14.
46. Telephone interview with Glen Andrade, April 1995. In an interview with Andrade in Jamaica in August 1996, he indicated that, as of then, no one had been charged under that law, since the criminal-justice authorities were awaiting some administrative arrangements to make the legislation effective.

now president of the Jamaica Court of Appeals—had just this in mind when he observed:

> In our effort to rid our societies of the scourge of drugs and with some international pressures we are being invited to reverse burdens of proof and adopt a retroactive confiscatory regime. All this is understandable. The perceived danger is real, the consequences of the mischief which we would excise disastrous. As we contemplate effective measures, the nagging question, though, for all of us remains: Are they just?
>
> I remember too that in Jamaica, the mongoose was imported from India to kill out the snakes. It did a very good job. The snakes were eliminated. The mongoose then turned its attention to the chickens. There is a lesson in this. Effective measures against vermin may be turned to effective use by the ill-intentioned against decent and law abiding citizens.[47]

The resource constraints mentioned above not only limit the capacity of criminal-justice agencies to execute their mandates meaningfully, they also cause considerable frustration among policy makers and the line and staff personnel involved in counternarcotics efforts. In relation to Guyana, one writer found a wide gap between what the legislation mandates and what criminal-justice officials accomplish. He noted that "the difference between persons charged and those found guilty suggests either a certain limitation in the court system or inefficiency in the enforcing organization," and that "over the period 1989 and 1992, *in spite of several seizures of property, not one case of forfeiture has been completed to date.*"[48]

Guyana is not unique, though. Officials in Grenada, Jamaica, and Trinidad and Tobago also reported similar problems, stemming, as in the Guyana case, from loopholes in the legislation and

47. Jamaica, Ministry of Justice, *Crime and Justice in the Caribbean*, 7.
48. Philadelphia, "Drug Wars: Can Guyana Win?" 14, emphasis added. Unlike the author, who senses *either* limitations *or* inefficiency, I see both. The assets-seizure dilemma was also raised by Minister Mohammed, Permanent Secretary Frazier, and Assistant Commissioner Felix in my interviews with them.

from bureaucratic and judicial deficiencies.[49] Given the tough, often mandatory prison sanctions in some of the draconian counternarcotics legislation, successful drug arrests and prosecution create the need for more prison space, something that does not exist. Indeed, most Caribbean prisons are overcrowded. In Guyana, for example, prisons director Cecil Kilkenny indicated that the Georgetown prison, which was built to house 350 prisoners, was forced to accommodate over 800 in 1994 and had accommodated as many as 1,000 prisoners during early 1992.[50] As Table 13 shows, the Georgetown prison now has a higher official capacity, but significant overcrowding still exists in every Guyanese prison except that at Mazaruni and New Amsterdam.

In Jamaica the total inmate population of the adult prisons in December 1991 was 3,705, about 33 percent above the official capacity of 2,781.[51] The justice minister himself acknowledged that "[t]he overcrowding in our two maximum security correctional institutions, the General Penitentiary and the St. Catherine District Prison, is serious, and has triggered serious problems over the years. Each of these prisons contains about twice as many inmates as they were designed to hold."[52] As Table 11 shows, in 1994 the overage was "only" 611; in 1995 it was "merely" 508. One inquiry, the Wolfe investigation, highlighted the appalling conditions of Jamaican prisons. Prisoners were required to eat with their hands for security reasons, a situation deemed "inhuman and degrading." Meals were found to be generally "revolting in appearance and taste." In some places, "the diet fed to the cell occupants should be consumed only by pigs." The Wolfe investigation found that prison indiscipline abounded and that all sorts of malfeasance and abuse occurred in Jamaican prisons.[53]

49. Interviews with Lance Selman, director of the Strategic Services Agency, July 1994; Commissioner of Police Bernard, July 1994; Colonel Macmillan, August 1996; and Glen Andrade, August 1996. Regarding Grenada, the issue was raised by the attorney general, Dr. Francis Alexis, in an interview in July 1994.

50. *Guyana Review*, "Prison Problems."

51. Planning Institute of Jamaica, *Economic and Social Survey, 1991*, 21.7. An interesting fact also reported here is that 72 percent of all female admissions for 1990 were for drug offenses.

52. Jamaica, Parliament, *Presentation of the Hon. K. D. Knight* (1993), 78.

53. See Jamaica, *Report of the National Task Force on Crime*, 55–70. The report is often called "The Wolfe Report" after the task force chairman, Justice Lensley Wolfe. Wolfe is now chief justice of Jamaica.

Table 11   Jamaica's Adult Prison Population, 1987–1995

Year	Official Capacity	Population	Overage
1987	2,861	3,681	820
1988	2,861	3,697	836
1989	2,781	3,516	735
1990	2,781	3,610	829
1991	2,781	3,705	924
1992	2,781	3,379	598
1993	2,781	3,284	503
1994	2,781	3,392	611
1995	2,781	3,289	508

SOURCE: Planning Institute of Jamaica, *Economic and Social Survey*, various years.

In the case of Trinidad and Tobago, one study shows that most of the country's six penal institutions house three and four times the number of people for which they were intended.[54] Table 13 also points to the dangerous overpopulation in Trinidad and Tobago. The Port of Spain prison, for instance, built in 1812 to accommodate 250 inmates, had a 1993 daily average inmate population of

Table 12   Trinidad and Tobago Prison Population and Expenditure

Year	Committed During Year	Daily Average Population	Spending (TT$000)	Change (%)
1985	4,231	1,110	49,053	—
1986	6.264	1,282	59,095	+ 16.99
1987	6,945	1,562	47,812	− 23.59
1988	5,715	1,988	47,647	− 0.23
1989	15,506	2,497	44,257	− 7.65
1990	36,697[a]	3,059	45,656	+ 3.06
1991	16,027	3,308	57,829	+21.04
1992	20,359	3,336	66,333	+12.82
1993	22.852	3,317	66,699	+ .55
1994	21,083	3,753	75,896	+12.12
1995	21,293	4,019	92,756	+18.18

SOURCES: Central Statistical Office, Trinidad and Tobago, *Annual Statistical Digest, 1991* (1992); Office of the Commissioner of Prisons, September 1996.

[a]This large figure reflects law-enforcement activities related to the July–August 1990 coup attempt. A new prison had to be constructed to help relieve the pressure.

54. See Hagley, "Crime and Structural Adjustment in Trinidad and Tobago." This article has some useful data on prison population size and characteristics for the period 1935–90.

Table 13   Prison Accommodation: Guyana and Trinidad and Tobago

Guyana			
Prison	Official Capacity	Highest Pop., 1995	Highest Pop., 1996
Georgetown	510	1,009	941
Mazaruni	300	187	172
Sibley Hall	80	75	84
New Amsterdam	300	278	297
Lusignan	100	138	139
Timehri	80	93	95

		Trinidad and Tobago					
Prison	Official Capacity	Daily Averages					
		1990	1991	1992	1993	1994	1995
Port of Spain	250	898	944	916	978	1100	1052
Carrera	185	504	503	483	493	510	567
Golden Grove	532	1,261	1,436	1,534	1,458	1,910	1,073
Women	120	78	105	115	114	120	123
Youth Training Center	225	189	183	200	225	250	234
Tobago Convict Depot	30	30	33	42	49	50	48

SOURCES: Ministry of Social Development, Trinidad and Tobago, *Report of the Cabinet Approved Committee to Examine the Juvenile Delinquency and Youth Crime Situation in Trinidad and Tobago* (January 1994); Trinidad and Tobago Prison Service, *Administration Report, 1993* (July 1994); Office of the Commissioner of Prisons, June 1995; Office of the Commissioner of Prisons, September 1996; Ministry of Home Affairs, Guyana, September 1996.

NOTE: Trinidad and Tobago also has a Remand Center, built to accommodate 655 people. The daily average there in 1995 was 922.

978, up from the 1992 figure of 916. As Table 13 shows, this prison housed an average of 1,100 people during 1994, and somewhat fewer in 1995. The serious overcrowding presents several critical problems affecting (a) the provision of medical services, especially given the high incidence of prisoner addiction, (b) the maintenance of discipline, particularly since there is increased gang and other violence in prison, (c) the physical safety of prison officers, and (d) the provision of recreational facilities.[55]

55. Interview with Commissioner Baptiste and Deputy Commissioner Watson, July 1994, who also intimated that a new maximum-security prison was being built at Arouca near the present Golden Grove prison. It will house 1,200 inmates and have a 2,000 expansion capacity. It was to be ready for occupancy in June 1995. Batiste noted during a June 1995 telephone interview that construction problems

As might be expected, despite the increased prison funding reflected in Table 12 the budgetary outlays in no way matched actual demands. According to the 1993 prison-services report, the allocation of TT$62,218,271 for 1993 was TT$34,477,449 less than the amount proposed for the year. This budget cut had tremendous effects on all aspects of correctional services: food, training, telephones, electricity, uniforms and supplies, vehicle maintenance, medical services, and other areas. (The cost of maintaining each prisoner increased from TT$44 per day in 1990 to TT$51 in 1993.) Contractors withheld supplies and services because of nonpayment of bills. "Food at institutions was the main item targeted by suppliers for cessation of supplies. Timely intervention by ministerial personnel forestalled inmate revolts or food riots during the year under review."[56]

The report also indicates that "security and communication were also under threat," with frustratingly frequent cuts in service by the Trinidad and Tobago Electricity Corporation and the Telephone Service of Trinidad and Tobago due to nonpayment of outstanding bills. Indeed, given all this, plus the "threat of cholera, hepatitis, and tuberculosis within the prison system," it seems reasonable that Trinidad prison officials would assert that "the result is that little has been achieved and the Prison Service remains in the dark ages."[57] Guyana's chief magistrate, K. Juman-Yassim, is one of several judicial officials in the region to advocate legislative reform to alleviate the bottlenecks in both courts and prisons. He calls for reform of the bail provisions and sentencing mandates of the 1988 Guyana drug legislation, which are similar to many others in the region.[58]

For many countries the growing internationalization of the criminal-justice clientele is an added difficulty. The increasing variety of countries from which suspects and convicts originate creates a host of translation and interpretation demands, and complications with

---

had delayed the prison's opening. Trinidad officials indicated in October 1996 that the prison was mostly completed, but occupancy was delayed by problems with the locking system.

56. Trinidad and Tobago Prison Service, *Administration Report, 1993*, 4.

57. Ibid., 5.

58. See *Stabroek News*, "Magistrate Calls for Parliamentary Revision of Drug Sentences."

diplomatic representation and prisoner exchange. For example, in 1994 Trinidad and Tobago had prisoners from Russia, the United States, Venezuela, Guyana, Barbados, Scotland, Nigeria, Canada, Grenada, St. Vincent and the Grenadines, Aruba, Dominica, Britain, and Jamaica. Among the 250 prisoners in Aruba in October 1996 were people from Colombia, Jamaica, Haiti, the Dominican Republic, Peru, the United States, Canada, Nigeria, and Pakistan. In highlighting the problem in Jamaica, a newspaper report in April 1996 carried the following headline: "Foreigners Languishing in Prison."[59] Thus, while the situation reflected in Tables 11, 12, and 13 is not uniform throughout the region, the situation is critical or near critical in most places. Physical facilities are insufficient, and often in disrepair; trained personnel are in short supply; medical attention is woefully inadequate; and prison rehabilitation is simply nonexistent.

Many courts fare no better in terms of facilities and resources. Indeed, a former Jamaican parliamentary ombudsman has referred to the many "squalid, dilapidated, and decaying court rooms; dark, dank, and ill-ventilated chambers" in the region.[60] In relation to the Dominican Republic one report stated: "The judicial system is outdated, ineffective, and corrupt. Dominican law enforcement attempts to convict traffickers and seize assets are often undermined by long delays, poor preparation by prosecutors, and release of suspects."[61] A serious indictment against Jamaican due process was also issued by the Wolfe Report: "Many serious criminal cases are often concluded without a word of evidence being breathed in a court in support of the allegations."[62] This is true also of several other countries.

The report of a CARICOM study on judicial delays revealed some of the inadequacies and pressures under which courts work. Among many things, it indicated that court resources and facilities have been overloaded, especially at the level of the magistrates courts. Several reasons account for this: increased litigation, an inadequate number of judges and magistrates, poor support-staff resources, a shortage of basic supplies, and outdated equipment,

59. *Gleaner* (Jamaica), April 25, 1996, 2A.
60. Green, "The Role of Governments," 311.
61. *INCSR* (1995), 170.
62. Jamaica, *Report on the National Task Force on Crime*, 76.

technology, and techniques. On the last matter, for example, rules of evidence in many places do not allow for admission into court of evidence obtained from tape recordings. The study also pointed to a dramatic increase in the length of trials over the five years preceding the 1993 survey. Seven main factors were found to have contributed to this development. The most important ones were the absence of witnesses or complainants, the absence or unpreparedness of prosecutors, the absence of defense lawyers from court sessions, and the inefficiency of court registries, where files are often lost or misplaced and relevant individuals are often not served the appropriate notices.[63] Nevertheless, delays are not the result of any single factor or set of factors acting alone; the factors tend to be interrelated, so that a deficiency in one area may send a ripple through the rest of the system. For instance, the judicial and support-staff shortages stem partly from a resource deficiency: there are few judicial officers partly because of unattractively low salaries, poor working conditions, and inadequate facilities, caused mainly by budget constraints. This has led to increased workload for the officers available, which creates numerous postponements and a huge backlog of cases.

In reporting on the factors that contributed to the delays, the CARICOM study proved the maxim "Where you stand depends on where you sit": to officials surveyed, the relative importance of factors reflected their own administrative priorities and assessments. For example, judges, attorneys general, and police commissioners tended to rank the factor "Insufficient number of magistrates and judges" higher than did defense attorneys or solicitors general. On the other hand, the factor "Inadequate support staff, facilities, resources, and equipment" was relatively more important to solicitors general, directors of public prosecution, and court registrars than to many other categories of officials. And though similar divergence of opinion separated officials of the larger states from those of the smaller ones, 80 percent of the interviewees felt that the administration of justice in the region had either stagnated or worsened over the previous five years.[64]

Maureen Crane-Scott, former head of the UWI-UNDCP Drug Con-

---

63. CARICOM, *Report on Delays in the Administration of Justice,* 11.
64. Ibid., 6–9.

trol Legal Training Program, provided additional explanations for the judicial bottlenecks and inefficiency, pointing out direct linkages with drug criminality. She noted that although in most Caribbean countries drug-control legislation provides for drug offenders to be tried either indictably, in the High Court, before a judge and jury, or summarily, before a magistrate, magistrates have to adjudicate a disproportionately larger percentage of the drug cases brought before the courts. "It is estimated that in reality, at least 90 percent of all drug cases in the Commonwealth Caribbean are tried summarily in the Magistrates Courts, irrespective of considerations such as the quantity of drugs involved or their relative street value."[65]

Crane-Scott suggests that preference for summary trials is due generally to two main factors: perceived risk or threat of subornation in jury trials, and the relative speed of summary trials compared with High Court jury trials, which are time-consuming because of the two-tiered committal procedure. However, the trial route for drug cases is also affected by legislation. The Magistrates Jurisdiction and Procedures Act, which exists in most Commonwealth Caribbean countries, stipulates that once an individual is charged with an offense that carries a six-month prison term or more, a magistrate must ascertain from the accused whether he or she wishes to be tried summarily or indictably. This has to be done before the case is tried. Since most drug offenses carry sanctions in excess of six months imprisonment, magistrates find themselves having to offer this choice. And because of the time and cost factors associated with High Court trials, defendants invariably opt for a summary trial.[66]

One area that requires reform is the security and management of exhibits. There are often huge quantities of drugs to be used as evidence in cases. Under current practice in most countries, as required by law, these need to be kept in police custody and taken to the court each day of a trial. Apart from the logistical problems often presented, exhibits are sometimes stolen, misplaced, or switched while in police custody, thereby affecting both the trial specifically and justice generally, because cases often have to be dismissed for

---

65. Crane-Scott, "The Impact of International Narco-Trafficking," 11.
66. Ibid., 12.

lack of evidence or because of evidence tampering. In Guyana, for example, the chief magistrate freed three defendants in November 1994 because of evidence anomalies. And in the Dominican Republic, over a hundred prisoners were released between December 1994 and February 1995 because of insufficient evidence and legal technicalities.[67] In one March 1996 case, forty-four pounds of white flour were substituted for thirty-two pounds of cocaine at the police forensic laboratory.

Many people, including several Caribbean magistrates and judges, have therefore advocated the adoption of alternative procedures, including some that would allow for evidence to be tested, weighed, and photographed, with selection of a sample for the trial and disposal of the rest. Jamaica's director of public prosecutions, Glen Andrade, however, told this writer in an August 1996 interview that in Jamaica the problems associated with bulk evidence require no legislative remedy, since there is no statutory provision requiring the storage of (large) quantities of seized drugs for the prosecution of drug traffickers. The practice stemmed from "common-law" usage.

A European Union report indicated that the criminal-justice battle would also be aided with the establishment of pools of prosecutors to deal with drug cases. It noted that "such a system would also be of great service to smaller countries, which are particularly vulnerable to the operations of organized crime."[68] The European Union experts advocated two other things: the creation of more regional courts, along the lines of the eastern Caribbean Supreme Court, and the creation of regional courts of appeal for drug-related matters.

Conclusion

This chapter illustrates that the criminal-justice picture in the Caribbean is multifaceted. It also shows not only that there are con-

67. See, *Stabroek News*, "Magistrate Calls for Parliamentary Revision," for the Guyana case. In commenting on evidence generally, the magistrate observed: "The court needs [to have] more forensic help coming from the police." About the Dominican Republic, see *Miami Herald*, "Many Drug Defendants Freed on Technicalities." Incidentally, these have not been the only such cases in Guyana or the Dominican Republic, or in the Caribbean.

68. European Union, *The Caribbean and the Drugs Problem*, 28.

sensual, expressive, and property crimes, but that crime is perpetrated on an organized basis—not just randomly—and that the organized criminal links are both intraregional and extraregional. The discussion also suggests that drug operations in the Caribbean precipitate crime and present a major threat to civil society by overt and covert, and manifest and latent challenges to institutions of public order and to normal social intercourse. Research on the Bahamas has found developments that are common to the rest of the region: a decreased sense of the value of life, a lack of respect for property, and a lesser appreciation for honest work.[69] Drug-related crime is also of great concern for many Caribbean countries because it affects tourism, a vital enterprise in most countries, as will be seen in Chapter 6.

The drugs–criminal-justice situation is such that it is realistic to ask the question, Are we at the dawn of the Colombianization of the Caribbean? In Colombia, the drugs–power-politics combination has driven a catharsis that has caused thousands to be murdered and maimed, wreaked social and economic havoc on communities great and small, and upset the political stability of the entire nation.[70] Exact parallels do not exist between Colombia and the Caribbean, but there is an underlying anomie in many parts of the Caribbean that could very well develop elements of the Colombian reality now that drugs feature so prominently in the region. Yet, the criminal-justice area is not the only one where the battle has been joined. I turn attention next to arms trafficking and corruption, allied subjects that further reveal the dangerous dynamics of drugs.

---

69. Jekel et al., "Nine Years of Freebase Cocaine," 20.

70. For a discussion of drug-related and other violence in Colombia, see Lee, *The White Labyrinth;* Bergquist, Peñaranda, and Sánchez, *Violence in Colombia;* and Bagley and Walker, *Drug Trafficking in the Americas,* chap. 7.

5

Arms Trafficking, Corruption, and Governance

> Corruption undermines the legitimacy of public institutions and strikes at society, moral order, and justice, as well as at the comprehensive development of peoples. . . . The steadily increasing links between corruption and the proceeds generated by illicit narcotics trafficking undermine and threaten legitimate commercial and financial activities, and society, at all levels.
> —1996 Inter-American Convention Against Corruption

Like the previous chapter, this one examines some of the security implications of drugs. The issues examined here have direct linkages: the illegality of arms trafficking necessitates corruption, and they both undermine good governance. But corruption also exists quite independently of arms trafficking. Because of the proscription against drug production, consumption-abuse, trafficking, and money laundering, corruption is a crucial facilitator of these. Moreover, because two or more of these operations exist simultaneously in some places, corruption often involves interlocking networks to facilitate production, consumption, and trafficking; money laundering and trafficking; production, trafficking, and arms smuggling; or other such combinations. The task here is to probe some of the dynamics and linkages involved and consider some of their implications.

Arms Trafficking

The ownership and use of weapons and ammunition are considered vital to the successful conduct of some drug operations, especially production and trafficking. Weapons and ammunition are used for both symbolic and substantive purposes, notably for protection of drugs and drug operatives, commission of robberies and acts of narcoterrorism, and intimidation of clients as well as fellow operators.

Arms trafficking in the Caribbean has been both intraregional and interregional. In the former case it has facilitated some or all of the above-mentioned activities of producers, traffickers, and users within the region. The disastrous consequences of the drugs-weapons connection has been felt in Puerto Rico, St. Kitts–Nevis, Guyana, the Dominican Republic, Trinidad and Tobago, and elsewhere in the region. But perhaps of all places, Jamaica and Puerto Rico provide the most startling evidence of those consequences, with high rates of drug-related homicides and drug-gang activities, a glimpse of which was provided in the last chapter. Indeed, with regard to Jamaica, a 1989 statement still captures the reality today: "Jamaica over the past few years has experienced, through an upsurge in violent crime, the effects of a combination of drugs and money in the form of the naked display of power, through the use of arms."[1] This is certainly also true of Puerto Rico.

In the case of interregional trafficking, the Caribbean is used to facilitate the acquisition of weapons by drug operators based in South America. It is here that the geography factor assumes importance, although, as will be seen later, it is not the only consideration; politics and economics also feature. Both intraregional and interregional trafficking have serious security consequences. But interregional trafficking is relatively more dangerous, partly because of the larger quantities of weapons and funds involved and

---

1. Tulloch, "Terrorism/Drugs Combination Threatens Security."

the notoriety and viciousness of some of the individuals and organizations behind it. One gets a sense of this, and of the geography, power, and politics factors involved, by looking at a couple of the dramatic cases.

In one case, a ten-ton shipment of arms, with an estimated value of J$8 million, arrived in Jamaica on December 22, 1988, on the way to Colombia. The shipment, from Heckler and Koch of West Germany, included 1,000 G3A3 automatic assault rifles, 250 HK21 machine guns, 10 sixty-millimeter commando mortars, and 600 rounds of high-explosive sixty-millimeter mortar shells. The planned trafficking operation involved Germans, Englishmen, Panamanians, Colombians, and Jamaicans. Interrogation of some of the conspirators on January 4 and 5, 1989, revealed that the arms were destined for a leftist insurgent group called the Revolutionary Armed Forces of Colombia (FARC). The operation was underwritten by Colombian cocaine dealers who financed FARC. The arms had been paid for out of a special drug shipment made earlier to Europe. The affair ended on January 6, 1989, when the arms were placed on a Colombian military aircraft and sent to Bogotá. The foreigners were extradited, and the Jamaicans were held on several charges.[2]

More dramatic, however, was the case involving Antigua-Barbuda. On December 15, 1989, the Colombian police killed Gonzalo Rodríguez Gacha and his son Freddy, both of the Medellín cartel. One of the raids made on Rodríguez Gacha's properties uncovered hundreds of Israeli-made Galil rifles and supporting ammunition. Colombia sought an explanation from Israel. The disclosure by Israel that the weapons were part of a larger sale to the Antigua-Barbuda government for the Antigua-Barbuda Defense Force (ABDF) led Colombia to file a diplomatic protest against Antigua-Barbuda on April 3, 1990. The protest prompted Antigua-Barbuda on April 10, 1990, to retain U.S. attorney Lawrence Barcella to investigate the matter. This was essentially an investigation into the international aspects of the matter. As the matter developed, however, it was clear that both domestic and foreign aspects had to be probed. Consequently, an extensive public inquiry by a one-man commission of inquiry was held in Antigua and broadcast on local radio and television.

2. *Sunday Gleaner* (Jamaica), "Arms Shipment: Traffickers, Terrorists Involved," and idem, "Text of Statement Made at a Press Conference at Up Park Camp."

The inquiry, by British jurist Louis Blom-Cooper, uncovered an incredible scheme involving Israelis, Antiguans, Panamanians, and Colombians. Yair Klein, a retired Israeli army colonel, and Pinchas Schachar, a retired brigadier general, then a representative of Israel Military Industries (IMI), were told by Maurice Sarfati, another Israeli, that the Antigua-Barbuda government was interested in acquiring weapons and ammunition. Sarfati presented forged documents showing (a) that he was an authorized Antiguan government representative and (b) that an arms purchase had been authorized by Vere Bird Jr., Antigua's "national security minister," the son of Prime Minister Vere Bird Sr., and Lieutenant Colonel Clyde Walker, the head of the ABDF. Subsequently, the relevant end-user certificate, the official weapons requisition by an arms purchaser, was forwarded to Israel.[3] It should be noted that Sarfati had indeed been a government representative at one time, but in this case the documents were forged. Moreover, there was no person in the Antiguan government designated as "national security minister."

U.S. Senate investigations into the affair revealed that the initial order was for 500 weapons and 200,000 rounds of ammunition, valued at U.S.$353,700. The final order total was U.S.$324,205. A down payment of U.S.$95,000 was made, and between November 14, 1988, and February 13, 1989, thirteen financial transactions, ranging between U.S.$44,000 and U.S.$100,000, were made on the deal. The banks used were Banco Aleman-Panameño, Philadelphia International Bank, Manufacturers Hanover Trust, Bank Hapoalim of Israel, and American Security Bank of Washington, D.C.[4] The weapons were placed aboard a Danish ship, MV *Else TH*, which sailed from Haifa, Israel, on March 29, 1989, bound for Central and South America via Antigua. The consignment was transshipped at Port Antigua to the MV *Seapoint*, a Panamanian ship. The *Seapoint* then took the arms to the real consignee in Colombia, the Medellín cartel. The Antiguans implicated were Vere Bird Jr., minister of public works and communications; Lieutenant Colonel Clyde Walker, ABDF commander; Vernon Edwards, managing director of a shipping and brokerage agency; and Glenton Armstrong and Sean Leitch, customs officers.

3. Blom-Cooper, *Guns for Antigua*, 2.
4. U.S. Senate, Committee on Governmental Affairs, *Arms Trafficking, Mercenaries, and Drug Cartels*, 127–30.

Sarfati, the leading Israeli figure, had first gone to Antigua in April 1983. He cultivated a friendship with Vere Bird Jr., then an attorney in private practice, who was instrumental in gaining approval for a melon-cultivation project, one of Sarfati's pet schemes. The Bird-Sarfati friendship produced many advantages for Sarfati between 1983 and 1990: appointment in October 1984 by Vere Bird Jr. as special adviser on civil aviation; appointment in May 1985 as special envoy in the Ministry of External Affairs, Economic Development, and Tourism; a 1985 OPIC ([U.S.] Overseas Private Investment Corporation) loan of U.S.$700,000; a supplemental loan from OPIC for U.S.$600,000 in 1986; appointment in February 1986 as managing director of Antigua-Barbuda Airways, with a token salary of U.S.$100 but a U.S.$70,000 expense account; and a series of 1987 promissory notes from the Antiguan government, totaling U.S.$4 million.[5]

Thus, Sarfati had developed a relationship with the Antiguan government, and with Vere Bird Jr. in particular, enabling him to exploit the relationship and not account meaningfully for any of his actions. Vere Bird Jr. also benefited from the links. For example, his law firm, Bird and Bird, handled the legal interests of Sarfati's corporate holdings—Roydan Ltd. and Antigua Promoters Ltd. In addition, Sarfati guaranteed Bird's loans, amounting to U.S.$92,000 in November 1988. Blom-Cooper observed: "It seems to me a matter of some significance that at the time the conspiracy was negotiated, Mr. Vere Bird, Jr. was in financial difficulties and was beholden to the bankrupt Mr. Sarfati. He needed money, but he also needed to help Mr. Sarfati earn money." The commissioner made an even more damaging observation: "I entertain no doubt Mr. Vere Bird, Jr. was paid by or at least with, money emanating from Señor Rodríguez Gacha, for the services rendered to the arms transshipment."[6]

The arms transshipment was, however, only part of a larger scheme that was initiated in September 1988 to create a mercenary training outfit using the ABDF as organizational cover. According to the brochure produced by Spearhead Ltd., the project's corporate entity, the aim was to establish a security school to train "corporate

5. Blom-Cooper, *Guns for Antigua*, 47–52, 120–21.
6. Ibid., 116, 117.

security experts, ranging from the executive level to the operational level, and bring them to the highest professional capacity in order to confront and defuse any possible threat." A central part of the enterprise was to be a "specialty shop" to sell small arms, among other things. Blom-Cooper asserted: "To any one with the slightest knowledge of armed forces it was obvious that the training school proffered by Spearhead Ltd., was intended, among other things, to train mercenaries in assault techniques and assassination."[7]

The full extent of arms trafficking in the Caribbean may never be known, for fairly obvious reasons. What is clear from direct and circumstantial evidence, however, is that the cases mentioned above only hint at the extent of Caribbean arms smuggling. Scott MacDonald, for example, recounted an incident originally recorded by Leslie Cockburn in *Out of Control,* a book about the drugs-money-weapons connections of the Iran-Contra affair. The incident involved "Mickey" Tolliver, an American pilot, and a July 1986 air run. The run began in Haiti, where Tolliver picked up a DC-3 with weapons and ammunition. After making a stop in Costa Rica, he flew to Colombia for a consignment of 4,000 pounds of marijuana and 400–500 kilos of cocaine, and then headed for the Bahamas, where all the weapons and ammunition were unloaded.[8]

Guyana, which, as was seen in Chapter 2, has risen to prominence in drug trafficking, is also said to be deeply implicated in arms trafficking.[9] As noted in the drug-trafficking discussion, the contraband smuggling routes linking Guyana with Brazil, Suriname, and Venezuela have been adapted to drug trafficking. These are, no doubt, also being used to smuggle arms. As with drug trafficking, Guyana is vulnerable because of its physical and social geography and its political and economic weaknesses: a large, sparsely populated territory, most of whose small population lives mainly along the Atlantic coast; and long borders with neighboring countries—1,120 km with Brazil, 745 km with Venezuela, and 600 km with Suriname—none of which are adequately policed, largely due to financial and manpower shortages, which also hamper supervision of the scores of landing strips.

7. Ibid., 58.
8. MacDonald, *Dancing on a Volcano,* 111.
9. See *Guyana Review,* "Gun Runnings."

Corruption

Drug-related corruption in the Caribbean, like elsewhere, violates both laws and norms. It involves acts of commission and omission that breach laws and deviate from accepted social, economic, and political norms. Especially problematic are acts by public officials. Drug corruption varies in nature, scope, and impact, but despite the variation, the deleterious effects on governance are unmistakable.

In conceptual terms, although there are different ways to approach the subject of corruption, that of Ethan Nadelmann is most useful for my analysis. It distinguishes networks by size, sophistication, and hierarchical structure, differentiating among sporadic, systemic, and institutionalized corruption. The first is characterized by the absence of broad patterns of corruption; individuals or small groups take bribes without sharing their takings or knowledge of their activities with others.

Systemic corruption has two variants. In the first, corruption is pervasive but poorly organized; although corruption may be rampant, not everyone in the hierarchy is corrupt. The second is distinguished by a hierarchical payoff arrangement in which lower-level officials hand over most of their takings to their superiors. The flow of the takings may also flow in the reverse direction—higher to lower. In institutionalized corruption all lesser "payoff cones" fall within a centralized national "payoff cone," or only one "payoff cone" exists for the entire nation. One example of this would be control of virtually all corrupt schemes of any value by a country's leader, especially with the support of the military and the police.[10]

There has been considerable evidence of sporadic and systemic corruption in the Caribbean. Yet, except perhaps for pre-Aristide Haiti, no contemporary Caribbean country fits Nadelmann's category of institutionalized corruption. However, if one defines institutionalized corruption differently, as does Peter Andreas, several countries may be said to have had institutionalized corruption, as will be seen later. According to Andreas: "Corruption becomes institutionalized when individuals within an institution are complicit in

10. Nadelmann, *Cops Across Borders*, 269–70.

the [drug] trade and the institution acts as a shield against account-ability."[11]

Although they were not named as such, references were made to these three types of corruption in the discussions on trafficking and money laundering, but a discussion of several cases here will serve to demonstrate the nature and scope of corruption in the region. Apart from those earlier references, the discussion of arms traffick-ing above also points to some of the region's corruption. In the Anti-gua-Barbuda case, for example, Blom-Cooper summed up the motives quite well: "Greed, the thirst for power, and finally, unbri-dled corruption."[12]

The 1989 arms-drugs-corruption episode in Antigua-Barbuda was dramatic and dangerous. Yet, given what one scholar called "Antigua's highly distasteful record of corruption, maladministra-tion, and general sleaze,"[13] some observers were not surprised that it occurred. But other, reputedly pristine places do offer surprises sometimes. One such country is St. Lucia. During an extensive Au-gust 1988 interview with Cuthbert Phillips, then that island's police commissioner, about eastern Caribbean security issues, the drug problem consumed much of our attention, and Phillips waxed elo-quent in declaiming against the drug barons and their accomplices. Less than a month later Phillips was implicated in drug-related cor-ruption and inefficiency in the Royal St. Lucia Police Force and was dismissed. (He was later imprisoned also, following a manslaughter conviction.)[14]

Partly because of the central role of the Bahamas in both traffick-ing and money laundering over the years, it has had some of the region's most notorious corruption cases. Repeated allegations of high-level corruption involving the prime minister and other gov-ernment officials prompted an official inquiry in 1983. In its 1984 report, the commission of inquiry noted that widespread trafficking through the Bahamas had adversely affected almost all strata of society. Several top officials were indicted, and five government ministers either resigned or were dismissed. The commission noted

11. Andreas, "Profits, Poverty, and Illegality," 24.
12. Blom-Cooper, *Guns for Antigua*, 131.
13. Thorndike, "Avarice in the Aviary," 181.
14. For more on this case, see Griffith, *The Quest for Security in the Caribbean*, chap. 9.

several questionable practices by Prime Minister Lynden Pindling and observed that between 1977 and 1984 his expenditures and assets far exceeded his official income. For example, his bank deposits reflected U.S.$3.5 million in excess of his salary for that period, but there was no hard evidence of his being on the drug payroll as alleged.

The commission reported being "alarmed by the extent to which persons in the public service have been corrupted by the illegal trade," asserting that there was corruption at both the upper and lower levels of the police force and within the immigration and customs services. It declared: "We were particularly concerned to discover that those corrupting influences made their presence felt at the levels of Permanent Secretary and Minister."[15] Media attention, the commission's report, and the implementation of some of its recommendations have led to treatment of the institutionalized corruption in the Bahamas, but sporadic corruption exists. In March 1992, for example, Sergeant Roger Newman of the Bahamas Police Force was charged with possession and intent to supply six kilos of cocaine. Interestingly enough, Newman worked with the Bahamas special drug court, where he often acted as a prosecutor. More recently, Chief Petty Officer Keith Baker of the Bahamas Defense Force was one of several people convicted in Miami on January 17, 1995, of importing and distributing three tons of marijuana. In a sting operation conducted during the preceding investigations, Baker took a cash bribe of U.S.$25,000 to use a Bahamas Defense Force boat to provide safe haven through the Bahamas to a Colombian ship used for trafficking.[16] However, while these two cases relate to the police and the military, sporadic corruption also exists elsewhere.

Three months after the publication of the Bahamas inquiry report, Chief Minister Norman Saunders and Minister of Commerce and Development Stafford Missick of the Turks and Caicos were among several people arrested in Miami on drug-related charges. The March 1985 arrests followed three months of investigations by the U.S. Drug Enforcement Administration (DEA), in cooperation

15. Bahamas, *Report of the Commission of Inquiry*, 35.
16. *Stabroek News*, "Bahamian Police Charged for Cocaine," and *Miami Herald*, "Three Guilty of Importing Marijuana."

with the British government and Turks and Caicos law-enforcement agencies. The charges included conspiracy to import narcotics into the United States, conspiracy to violate the U.S. Travel Act, and the conduct of interstate and foreign travel to aid racketeering.

During the trial the DEA alleged that Saunders had accepted U.S.$30,000 from undercover DEA agents to guarantee safe stopover refueling on flights from Colombia to the United Sates. Moreover, the prosecution showed a videotape, filmed before the arrests, on which Saunders was shown receiving U.S.$20,000 from a DEA undercover agent. The money was allegedly to protect drug shipments passing through South Caicos Island en route to the United States. All the defendants were convicted in July 1985 on the conspiracy charges, although Saunders was acquitted of the more serious charges of conspiring to import cocaine into the United States. Missick was convicted of the additional charge of cocaine importation. Saunders and Missick were sentenced to eight and ten years, respectively, and each was fined U.S.$50,000.[17]

Curiously enough, after his release from prison, Saunders resumed his involvement in local politics. Although he was repudiated by his former political party, the Progressive National Party, and denied its platform for elections, he was elected to Parliament as an independent candidate in January 1995, winning the South Caicos seat by a mere six votes.

In April 1992, Assistant Commissioner of Police Rodwell Murray of the Trinidad and Tobago Police Service went public with an allegation he had made in 1991 to top National Security Ministry officials: that there was a drug-trafficking cartel operating within the police force. Drug corruption had been uncovered before in Trinidad. In 1987, for example, an inquiry led to the suspension of fifty-one police officers and the eventual resignation of Commissioner of Police Randolph Burroughs, who had earlier been indicted on bribery and other charges but later was acquitted.

That inquiry produced considerable evidence of the violation of both laws and norms and at all hierarchical levels. It noted: "There is abundant evidence of a close relationship between the Commissioner and more than one known drug dealer," and "it is clear that

17. MacDonald, *Dancing on a Volcano*, 120–22, and Cichon, "British Dependencies: The Cayman Islands and the Turks and Caicos," 579–81.

several members of the Police Service have become involved in many ways in illegal drug use, and in its trade, and this unfortunate situation has existed for some years." The report also highlighted the frequency of police officers' "use of drugs, their pushing of drugs, their engagement in the growing and reaping of marijuana, recycling of confiscated drugs for the supply of drug dealers, the operation of protection rackets whereby major drug dealers are assisted in or allowed to pursue their illegal trade without let or hindrance."[18]

Because of the increasing scale of drug trafficking and attendant problems, the seniority of the police officer making the allegations in 1992, and the seriousness of those allegations, Prime Minister Patrick Manning invited Scotland Yard to investigate the situation. The investigation was led by Detective Superintendent Graham Seabry. The Seabry inquiry did not confirm the allegations about the existence of a drug cartel in the police department, but it revealed the scope and extent of institutionalized corruption (in the Andreas sense) there, and several structural and functional factors that facilitated it.

According to the investigators, "corruption in the police service can be described as endemic," existing in many forms, including cash or goods for favors, canteen fraud, theft from colleagues, false claims for extra duty and mileage for travel, and bribery to protect illegitimate enterprises from police interference and to take action against rival enterprises. Blackmail was also cited, with "clear evidence showing cash demanded not to execute warrants, not to charge criminal offenses, not to give evidence at court, or not to be able to locate the prosecution papers."[19] The *Seabry Report* also stated: "The protection of whe whe banking turfs [whe whe being an informal banking scheme] is part of this level of corruption, but it also includes the protection of drug dealers, their supplies, and their supply routes. *This is where the core of the police service gets its money.*"[20]

18. Trinidad and Tobago, Parliament, *Report of the Commission of Inquiry into the Extent of the Problem of Drug Abuse in Trinidad and Tobago,* 19, 20, 21.
19. Trinidad and Tobago, Ministry of National Security, *Final Report for the Government of Trinidad and Tobago on Investigations . . . in Respect of Allegations . . . About Corruption in the Trinidad and Tobago Police Service* [hereafter *Seabry Report*], 24.
20. Ibid., emphasis added.

In what is perhaps the main outline of the structural and functional linkages of the institutionalized corruption in the Trinidad and Tobago police force, the *Seabry Report* declared:

> Two corrupt groups were identified which stretched from the top to the bottom of the organization. Recruits were drawn in from the junior ranks. Such groups protected and promoted their own members, and provided a succession plan or "career structure" for their members. Thus, the groups are self-perpetuating. The two groups appear to be separate entities though the division does not appear to be absolute. The extent of any cooperation between the two groups is not clear, but the requirement to exist unhindered unites them. Their range of corrupt activity is wide. Anything that makes money is in, although protection of drug dealers and whe whe bankers forms a prominent and regular slice of the income. Using rank to frustrate honest police action and grant concessions is an irregular but repeating occurrence that can generate large bonuses. The complete make-up of such groups has not been fully established, but the heads and principal lieutenants have been identified.
>
> It is not realistic to put a figure on the number of corrupt officers. The range of corrupt activities is large and the type of corruption varies greatly. However, the removal of about one hundred specific officers from the service would have a marked effect.[21]

The absence of prosecutable evidence against the hundred officers named, resistance by the police union, and inaction by the police high command combined to thwart efforts to charge any of the officers, although some of them were transferred and brought up on administrative charges. The Seabry probe also identified "ten things that allow corruption to flourish": the police service's operation as a law unto itself; the idea that image must be sustained; a rank-and-status mentality, which is used to avoid responsibility, hinder communication, and promote intense ambition; lack of accountability; insufficient supervision; absence of a clear policy on posting

21. Ibid., 24–25.

and transfers; court delays and procedures; destruction of records; a breakdown of disciplinary procedures; and territorial control that allows local commanders to pursue or condone corruption within their jurisdictions.

Based on the findings, the Trinidad and Tobago government sought to introduce institutional changes, including creation of an independent Police Complaints Authority, a Complaints Division within the force, for internal review, and five new senior positions. The new positions—one deputy commissioner and four assistant commissioners—were to be filled with Scotland Yard officers. This decision infuriated police officers, some of whom demonstrated outside Parliament and police headquarters on February 5, 1993, against what they called "the recolonization of the police force."[22] The staffing plan was later abandoned.

The Trinidad police commissioner acknowledged that corruption existed, but he challenged claims about institutionalization, averring that the police high command had no interest in cover-ups; for him the problem was one of sporadic corruption. He explained the difficulty of getting hard, credible evidence to convict corrupt officers, something that is perhaps reflective of the institutional dimensions of the problem. Another senior government official observed that, regrettably, drug corruption is not limited to the police department. Moreover, because of the corruption networks across agencies, law-enforcement measures are often seriously compromised and sometimes frustrated. One critical area is witness protection. Dealing with corruption is problematic partly because it is a politically charged issue. This explains some of the difficulty in getting legislation passed. But there is a problem beyond legislation— implementation, due to financial and other resource limitations.[23]

Cuban involvement in drug trafficking, which was noted in Chapter 2, points to a hybrid between systemic and (Andreas) institutionalized corruption. According to Andrés Oppenheimer, in *Castro's Final Hour,* military officials participated in drug trafficking and in the smuggling of precious stones, ivory, and other commodities not so much to profit individual officers as to satisfy the eco-

---

22. John, "A Bid to Police the Police," and Viarruel, "Police March in Historic Protest."

23. Interviews with Commissioner Bernard and Lancelot Selman, July 1994.

nomic needs of the military in the first instance and the economic and political interests of Cuba overall. Oppenheimer shows that the military and other institutions protected officials for some time, but turned on them when it became politically inexpedient and administratively awkward to have their projects continue.

While the cases above highlight sporadic and (Andreas) institutionalized corruption, the case of Aruba comes closest to approximating one of the two systemic kinds identified by Nadelmann. Corruption there is reportedly so deep and wide that the late Claire Sterling, widely acclaimed for her works on drugs and crime, said of it: "[T]he world's first independent mafia state emerged in 1993."[24] She argued that Aruba was "bought and paid for" by one of the most powerful Mafia families: the Cuntrera brothers—Paolo and Pasquale—of Italy and Venezuela. From nearby Venezuela the Cuntreras are reported to have bought and corrupted everything of value in Aruba: casinos, hotels, real estate, banks, police and customs officials, the prime minister, the justice minister, and the ruling and opposition parties. This "purchase" is said to have been the culmination of a process that began in October 1987, when a Sicilian-Medellin drug summit agreed to form a strategic alliance of the Italians and the Colombians. However, as noted in Chapter 3, the U.S. Department of State feels that the corruption in Aruba goes beyond the Colombian-Italian connection; ethnic Chinese are also allegedly involved.

From the available evidence, several observations may be made about corruption generally. First, corrupted officials not only violate laws and norms within their own nations; sometimes they cross international boundaries to violate the laws and norms of other nations. In one case, for instance, Rufus Trotman of the Barbados diplomatic mission in Caracas was dismissed in 1988 for his role in an attempt to use the Barbadian diplomatic bag to smuggle four pounds of cocaine out of Venezuela. In a second case, a Barbadian immigration officer was arrested at London's Heathrow International Airport with a large quantity of cocaine he had brought from Barbados. In another case, Sergeant Earl Scott of the Jamaica Constabulary Force was sentenced to seven years in the Cayman Islands on January 6, 1994, following conviction for possessing one

---

24. Sterling, *Thieves' World*, 21.

pound of cocaine with intent to supply. Scott and two female companions—Judith Kerr and Coleen Williams—had gone to the Caymans in February 1992 with the cocaine. Following negotiations with someone who turned out to be an undercover policeman, they had agreed on a sale of the drugs.[25]

Second, the cases discussed here do not reflect the totality of corruption in the Caribbean. In talking about corruption in relation to his country, for example, the justice minister of Suriname, Soeshiel Girjasing, declared in 1995 that "[t]he drug mafia has penetrated the military and the police . . . very deeply." Although reluctant to specify the level of corruption, he admitted that several army and police officials were among the 117 people arrested in 1994 for trafficking. In the Dominican Republic, persistent accusations of drug-related corruption forced President Joaquín Balaguer on November 1, 1995, to dismiss Attorney General Juan Demostenes Cotes Morales and a prosecutor attached to the Santo Domingo Appeals Court, José Leonardo Duran Fajardo.[26] Later that same month court-martial proceedings began against two officers accused of cocaine smuggling: Lieutenant Colonel Luis Rivera Jiménez and First Lieutenant Basilio Alcantara Gonzalez. In August 1996, a top Guyana Airways Corporation executive was held on cocaine-smuggling charges, and the same month—on August 18—constables Kervin Millard and Mervin Matthew of the St. Kitts–Nevis police were arrested and charged with cocaine trafficking.[27]

Third, while most of the sporadic and institutionalized corruption mentioned here pertains to military and law- enforcement agencies, corruption is not limited to these. Other official reports, indictments, and interviews by this writer have implicated a wide variety of government agencies, notably those dealing with customs, taxes, prisons, and banking. Moreover, although the discussion thus far has focused on violations of law and norms by government officials, drug-related corruption is not only a public-sector phenomenon. As

25. Morris, "Bajan Connection Arrested in London"; *Stabroek News*, "Jamaica Police Sergeant Gets Seven Years for Cocaine"; and *Sunday Advocate* (Barbados), "Drug Convict Points to Top DLP Members in Scandal."

26. Cawthorne, "Cocaine Barons Threaten Suriname," and *Miami Herald*, "Dominican Republic: 2 Officials Dismissed in Drug-Related Scandal."

27. *New York Carib News*, "GAC Official, Sons on Cocaine Charge," and *Daily Observer* (Antigua-Barbuda), "Constables in St. Kitts Arrested in Drug Bust."

was noted in Chapter 2 and implied in Chapter 3, the private sector is just as involved: owners and operators of banks, nonbanking financial enterprises, taxi companies, airlines, shipping companies, supermarkets, farms, warehouses, private security agencies, and other businesses are also corrupted. Moreover, especially in an age in which privatization is in vogue and the private sector is being touted as *the* engine of economic growth, private-sector corruption is actually and potentially just as injurious to moral rectitude and good governance.

Finally, although most of the corruption cases cited here and in Chapter 2 identify officials in the executive branch of government, the judicial and legislative branches are not exempt from corruption. Corruption networks extend not just across agencies in a single branch of government, but also across branches. In one place—Puerto Rico—there were serious charges of corruption during 1994 and 1995 in both legislative chambers. In one instance the senate reacted to accusations against four senators by ordering senators to undergo drug tests, and one senator even invited reporters into a public bathroom to vouch for the integrity of the urine sample.[28] (The reporters accepted the invitation.)

Governance and Sovereignty at Risk

Undoubtedly, arms trafficking and corruption have consequences for the observance of laws and norms. Apart from leading to the erosion of respect for law and norms, they also affect the shaping of attitudes and values in societies that are already vulnerable to cultural penetration and the political machinations of state and nonstate actors elsewhere. Anthony Maingot was thus both cute and correct in observing: "The corrupting power of the drug trade does strange things to an otherwise decent people."[29] Some of the "strange things" happen at the individual level, but—and this is worse—many of them happen at the group, national, and interna-

---

28. See Navarro, "Puerto Rico Reeling Under Scourge of Drugs and Rising Gang Violence."

29. Maingot, "Laundering the Gains of the Drug Trade," 173.

tional levels also, affecting governance of Caribbean people and placing at risk the sovereignty of Caribbean states. Thus, both power and politics are involved, and the implications are military, political, and economic.

In military terms, the corruption of military and police officials compromises these agents of national security, and as a consequence, (a) their capacity for effective action is undermined, and (b) individuals and groups become inclined to resort to vigilante tactics because of that diminished capacity or a perception of it. Vigilante operations have long existed in Haiti and Jamaica. However, they are spreading to other places, to the point that National Security Minister Russell Huggins of Trinidad and Tobago was forced to make a national radio and television broadcast on the subject in June 1993, during which he stated "that under no condition will the government condone the formation of vigilante groups [in which people] may choose themselves to be unlawfully armed with dangerous weapons on the pretext of protecting the community."[30] Moreover, in May 1996 Trinidad and Tobago passed legislation to curtail the formation of private militia groups.[31]

The situation is worse when soldiers and police facilitate arms trafficking. Arms trafficking presents real prospects for augmenting the store of illegal weapons within Caribbean countries, since, as with drugs, some of what is trafficked stays within the region, both by default and by design. This can only aggravate the crime problem insofar as increasing weapons stocks enable drug gangs either to engage in violent conflict or to escalate the extant level of violence. Jamaica, Puerto Rico, Trinidad and Tobago, Guyana, the Dominican Republic, Haiti, St. Kitts–Nevis, and St. Lucia bear sad testimony to this.

The undermining of effectiveness mentioned above is partly a function of a loss of public confidence, either in the government as a whole or in certain specific institutions, and both of these have political implications. The October–November 1994 St. Kitts–Nevis drugs-weapons-murder-riot saga, which led to the ouster of the ruling party in the July 1995 elections, reflects the former. Perhaps more than any other recent Caribbean case, that of St. Kitts–Nevis

30. *New York Carib News*, "Crackdown on Vigilantes."
31. *Caribbean Daylight*, "T'dad Govt Moves Against Small Armies."

dramatizes the emerging and dangerous linkages involving politics, power, and drugs, and the crime and other challenges to governability that these precipitate. Particularly since 1993, people in the leadership of the People's Action Movement (PAM), which ruled the country between February 1980 and July 1995, and of the St. Kitts Labor Party (SKLP), which won power in July 1995, have been credibly connected to people involved in the drug trade.

In relation to the PAM government, during the 1980s the ambassador to the United Nations, Dr. William Herbert, had been implicated in money laundering and drug trafficking. In July 1994 Herbert and his family disappeared mysteriously at sea. There was strong suspicion of foul play related to drugs. On October 1, 1994, Vincent Morris, one of the sons of Deputy Prime Minister Sidney Morris disappeared along with his fiancee, Joan Walsh. Later, they were both found murdered in the trunk of a burned vehicle abandoned in a cane field. The following month, two other sons of the deputy prime minister were arrested for trafficking 121 pounds of cocaine and for possessing illegal weapons. They were also implicated in the murders. Meanwhile, on October 13, Superintendent Jude Matthews, head of Special Branch—the agency that protects top government officials—and the lead investigator into the murders, was himself killed on the way to work.

The Morris brothers were granted bail after arraignment. A public protest and a prison riot ensued as a result of the perception by the public and prisoners that the family and political connections of the Morris brothers had influenced the decision granting them bail, manifestly violating equal-treatment norms. Sidney Morris was forced to resign as deputy prime minister. The riot resulted in the complete destruction of the central prison and the escape of over 150 prisoners, necessitating a call for help from the Regional Security System (RSS). (Most of the prisoners were recaptured later.)

Given the erosion of public confidence, the PAM government was forced to concede to a call by the opposition SKLP and a coalition of civic groups for new elections within a year. The elections were held on July 3, 1995—three years before the government's term of office was due to end. The opposition SKLP was victorious, winning almost 50 percent of the popular vote and seven of the eleven elected legislative seats. Predictably, major issues in the election campaign were the escalation of narcocrime, drug-related violence in the country, and the perceived complicity of government officials in drug trafficking. At the same time, the leadership of the SKLP, which formed the new government, was not without its own "skeletons in the closet." In May 1993, for instance, just six months before the controversial November 1993 general elections, Noel "Zamba" Heath, a long-standing business partner of both Dr. Denzil Douglas and Sam Condor, SKLP leader and deputy leader, respectively, was arrested and charged with illegal possession of drugs and ammunition. Heath subsequently pleaded guilty to the illegal-weapons charges and was fined.

As might be expected, the St. Kitts–Nevis affair developed new dimensions after 1994. In May 1996, for example, the U.S. Justice Department charged Charles Miller, Glenroy Matthew, Clifford Henry, and Noel Heath with conspiracy to smuggle cocaine from St. Kitts to the United States. Henry was arrested in Miami. The three others remained free on EC$25,000 (U.S.$9,400) bail each in St. Kitts–Nevis while extradition requests were being processed.[32] Extradition hearings ran from August 19 through 23, 1996, and after a two-month delay, which raised considerable fears and apprehensions in political and judicial circles in the region, magistrate Haynes Blackman on October 28 denied the extradition request and ordered that the seized property and documents of the three suspects be returned to them. The magistrate ruled that the evidence purporting to show conspiracy was not sufficiently extensive, and that overall it was inadmissible under the country's 1870 Extradition Act. He excoriated the prosecution for the poor quality of its affidavits and the duplication and improper inclusion of some affidavits. He also lamented the overreliance on affidavits and the paucity of oral testimony, which would have been subject to cross-examination.[33]

A good example of the second type of confidence erosion, where a specific institution is affected, was highlighted in a recent study of crime in Jamaica. "The solving of crime depends to a large extent upon information supplied to police by citizens. However, the breakdown in [that] relationship has made citizens reluctant to give

32. This discussion is adapted from Griffith and Munroe, "Drugs and Democratic Governance in the Caribbean," and Rohter, "Storm Is Unleashed in St. Kitts, As a Cocaine Case Churns Politics."
33. Mager, "Three Walk Free in St. Kitts."

the police information as they no longer regard the police as a friend of the community. The abuse of citizens' rights and the obvious partiality with which the police execute their duty, have given them a corrupt reputation. The link between police and the criminal element has resulted in a loss of confidence in the police."[34]

Thus, drug corruption has several serious consequences: it undermines the credibility of governments, and, as the St. Kitts–Nevis case clearly shows, it impairs the ability of government agencies to protect the interests of the state, both domestic and foreign. Further, it can diminish the ability of politicians and bureaucrats to define those interests adequately. Clearly all of this hurts good governance and sovereignty. When one bears in mind the political and social penetrability of Caribbean societies, it is relatively easy to understand how the governability and sovereignty of states there can be subverted by drug barons and their accomplices. Indeed, some analysts contend that the April 1, 1989, Air Jamaica seizure—of 4,173 pounds of marijuana—coming just one week after Prime Minister Michael Manley had declared a "war on drugs," resulted from a deliberate act and was meant as a direct challenge to the Jamaica government.[35]

Shridath Ramphal, former Guyanese foreign minister and Commonwealth of Nations secretary-general, highlighted both political and military vulnerability in saying: "It only takes twelve men in a boat to put some of these governments out of business." Military-political dangers were similarly implicit in a remark by one Caribbean diplomat: "A handful of well-armed narcotic soldiers or mercenaries could make a lightning trip to a country, wreak destruction, and fly out before a defense could be mounted by states friendly to the small island."[36]

Insofar as economic implications are concerned, it is not difficult to appreciate how drug operators can corrupt top officials in government, industry, and business: they have the money to do it. As one Chilean scholar has remarked, when drug operators get involved in politics, when they corrupt the state or bribe government officials, it is because they have decided not to attack the state—not directly,

34. Jamaica, *Report of the National Task Force on Crime,* 42.
35. See Griffith, "Some Security Implications of Commonwealth Caribbean Narcotics Operations," 31–37.
36. Sanders, "Narcotics, Corruption, and Development," 84.

it should be added. This is not because doing so is ineffective, but "because it is easier and more useful to buy a government and put it to work in the extending and eventual securing of a transnational network."[37] Andreas is right in suggesting that perhaps the best way to understand the issue is to see the corrupting of officials as the equivalent of paying an informal tax. Levels of corruption—the "tax rate"—depend on the extent of enforcement measures. Thus, as measures increase, so too does the need to pursue corruption.[38] Hence, for drug operators the monetary and in-kind outlays for corruption amount to a business expense.

Conclusion

This chapter suggests that drugs portend the dangers entailed in arms trafficking and corruption, in both individual and collective terms. And some of this danger is clear and present. The dangers of drugs are matched by the uniqueness of the enterprise. Nadelmann captures this uniqueness when he says:

> No other criminal activity comes close in terms of its magnitude, its lucrativeness, its capacity to corrupt the previously uncorruptible, its political consequences, and its impact on international relations. The bribes paid by drug traffickers are much greater, both in an absolute sense and in proportion to government salaries, than those paid by any other type of criminal. Moreover, unlike the sizeable bribes paid by foreign corporations, which are available only to a select group of high-level officials, drug traffickers' bribes are available to all who can place themselves in the right place at the right time.[39]

The direct and indirect links between drug operations and arms trafficking and corruption hold dangers for governance and sover-

---

37. Benavente Urbina, "Drug Traffic and State Stability," 37.
38. Andreas, "Profits, Poverty, and Illegality," 24.
39. Nadelmann, *Cops Across Borders,* 258.

eignty. Arms trafficking and corruption reflect some of the multidimensionality of the drug dilemma, and I have looked at some of the dimensions involved, especially the military and political ones. However, there are economic and policy aspects, not yet examined, that further attest to the gravity of the situation. It is to some of these that I turn next.

6

Economics and Public Policy

The drug menace is intimately bound up with our economic survival. It affects the yam farmer, the worker in the
apparel sector, the hotel employee, the coffee grower, the
entertainer who performs in foreign lands, the Jamaican
traveller abroad.
　　　　　　—Prime Minister P. J. Patterson of Jamaica

Most of the military and political security implications of the Caribbean narcotics phenomenon examined in earlier chapters highlight
its negative aspects. Yet, in looking at the economic security dimension, one is forced to come to terms with both positive and negative
aspects, though the illegality and multidimensionality of drugs
make it impossible fully to evaluate these aspects. Thorough evaluation is confounded also because, as noted earlier, drug operations
and their consequences involve indirect economic costs and social
costs not amenable to easy economic estimation. Nevertheless, a
rough balance sheet of some of the costs and benefits involved
would demonstrate both the gravity of the dilemma and some of
the reasons there is no easy solution. This balance sheet is best

appreciated if placed in the context of the region's economic circumstances.

Economic Portrait of the Caribbean

A survey of the Caribbean economic landscape finds that there are some important natural resources in the region, notably oil, bauxite, gold, diamonds, and nickel. But, as indicated elsewhere, the problem is that very few countries have these resources. Only Trinidad and Tobago and, to a much lesser extent, Barbados have oil industries, although exploration is under way in Cuba and Guyana, and there are refining and transshipment operations in many countries. Bauxite is mined only in the Dominican Republic, Guyana, Jamaica, and Suriname, even though Haiti also has this resource, and diamonds are mined only in Guyana. Only Cuba, the Dominican Republic, and Guyana produce gold, although there is evidence that Belize also has this metal. As for nickel, it is found only in Cuba and the Dominican Republic. This limited mineral-resource availability partly explains why the region's GDP, discounting unlawful activities, rests on such a narrow economic base: (a) agriculture, mainly sugar and bananas; (b) mining and manufacturing, notably of bauxite, oil, nickel, and gold; and (c) services.[1]

Offshore banking and tourism are the two most critical industries in the service sector. As noted in Chapter 3, offshore banking has long been important to Aruba, the Bahamas, Curaçao, and most of the British dependencies in the region, and it is becoming increasingly so to Antigua-Barbuda, Barbados, and Belize. But more important than this industry, both to these countries and the region as a whole, is tourism. Dennis Gayle has explained that tourism is the only industry in the Caribbean Basin that has grown progressively since 1973, generating some U.S.$96 billion in gross expenditure annually. Indeed, "tourism generates more foreign exchange and tax revenues per dollar of investment than any other industry."[2]

1. Griffith, *The Quest for Security in the Caribbean*, 56–58.
2. Gayle, "The Evolving Caribbean Business Environment," 144.

As Table 14 indicates, the Caribbean is characterized by low and negative economic growth, high unemployment, relatively high import food dependency (which is ironic, since agriculture features so prominently in the region), and huge public debts. The 5.5 million people of the English-speaking Caribbean alone had a 1994 foreign debt of some U.S.$9 billion. Cuba's debt is nearly U.S.$7 billion; Haiti's is over U.S.$800 million. However, it is not merely the size of the debts that is problematic, but also their servicing.

Guyana provides dramatic evidence of this. In his February 6, 1995, budget speech, Minister of Finance Asgar Ally (who resigned in May 1995 over policy disputes with President Cheddie Jagan) indicated: "During 1994, total debt service payments stood at U.S.$99.2 million, a 16.6 percent increase on 1993 levels. . . . Even with debt relief of over U.S.$300 million between 1990 and 1994, the ratio of our existing loan portfolio to GDP is still uncomfortably high at over 400 percent with no new borrowing, and the ratio of debt service to merchandise exports is still above what is considered to be the critical level."[3] The new finance minister, Bharrat Jagdeo, told Parliament in January 1996 that "[a]t the end of 1995, Guyana's external debt stock amounted to U.S.$2.06 billion, or a 3 percent rise over the previous year."[4]

I do not suggest that no progress has been made in the region; notable progress has been made in life expectancy, general health care, education, and real per capita income in some countries, among other things. Yet, as one Trinidadian economist has observed, the achievements do not mask the reality that the region is in crisis, that poverty is rising in several states, and that Caribbean economies remain fragile and vulnerable.[5] My assessment of the region's economic security in *The Quest for Security in the Caribbean* shows that the vulnerability is not only functional but also structural, in that economies suffer from heavy reliance on foreign trade, limited production and export diversification, low savings, heavy dependence on foreign capital, and a dearth of capable economic and management skills, among other things.

All of these circumstances make credible the statement by one

3. Guyana, Parliament, *Budget Speech* (1995), 38.
4. Guyana, Parliament, *Budget Speech* (1996), 25.
5. Ramsaran, "Challenges to Caribbean Economic Development in the 1990s," 123, 125.

Table 14 Caribbean Socioeconomic Indicators

Country	Population ('000, 1994)	GNP per Capita (US$)	GNP Real Growth (%)	Debt (US&M)	FIDR	Unemployment (%)	HDIR (1992)
Antigua-Barbuda	65	5,800[h]	NA	236[h]	83	5.0[b]	55
Bahamas	273	16,500[h]	2.0[g]	452.7[h]	64	5.7[g]	36
Barbados	256	8,700[h]	−3.0[g]	449.1[h]	72	23.0[g]	20
Belize	209	2,700[h]	5.3[g]	143.7[f]	40	15.0[g]	88
Cuba	11,064	1,300[h]	−10.0[h]	6,800[d]	NA	NA	89
Dominica	88	2,100[g]	2.6[g]	90.3[h]	64	15.0[g]	64
Dominican Republic	7,826	3,100[h]	3.0[h]	4,700[h]	38	30.0[h]	96
French Guiana	139	4,400[a]	NA	1,200[c]	NA	13.0[e]	NA
Grenada	94	3,000[g]	−0.4[g]	76.9[h]	78	25.0[g]	78
Guadeloupe	429	8,400[f]	NA	NA	NA	31.3[e]	NA
Guyana	729	1,900[h]	8.3[h]	1,906[h]	23	22.0[g]	107
Haiti	6,491	800[h]	−13.0[g]	838[e]	26	25.0–50.0[f]	137
Jamaica	2,555	3,200[g]	1.2[g]	3,647.2[h]	26	15.4[g]	65
Martinique	392	9,500[f]	NA	NA	NA	32.1[e]	NA
Netherlands Antilles	186	9,700[h]	2.0[h]	701[b]	NA	16.4[f]	NA

Montserrat	13	4,300[g]	4.3[g]	10.0[h]	NA	3.0[c]	NA
Puerto Rico	3,802	7,100[g]	NA	NA	NA	18.0[h]	NA
St. Kitts–Nevis	41	4,000[g]	4.1[g]	38.7[h]	86	12.2[e]	69
St. Lucia	145	3,000[h]	6.6[g]	100.8[h]	76	NA	77
St. Vincent & the Grenadines	115	2,000[g]	6.5[g]	75.4[h]	113	35.0–40.0[g]	69
Suriname	423	2,800[h]	–0.3[h]	180[h]	40	16.5[e]	85
Trinidad & Tobago	1,328	8,000[h]	–1.0[h]	2,000[h]	81	18.5[f]	35

SOURCES: *Human Development Report, 1994; The World Factbook, 1994;* Caribbean Development Bank, *Annual Report, 1994* (1995).

FIDR = food import dependency ratio.
HDIR = human development index rank, on a scale of 1–173, where 1 is the highest.

[a] 1986.
[b] 1987.
[c] 1988.
[d] 1989.
[e] 1990.
[f] 1991.
[g] 1992.
[h] 1993.

ECLAC (Economic Commission for Latin America and the Caribbean) analyst, that people in Cuba, the Dominican Republic, Haiti, Jamaica, Suriname (and I would add Guyana)—the biggest Caribbean countries—have become poorer over the last decade.[6] In Guyana, for example, the 1994 budget report indicated that some 70 percent of the population lives below the poverty line. The decline in the countries concerned has been affected by reduced government services, a reduction meant to cope with budgetary difficulties generally but also to service debt. Currency depreciation has also aggravated the situation, affecting prices, purchasing power, savings, and investment. Reduced production and exports, economic mismanagement, and adverse global economic and financial conditions are also relevant factors.

The circumstances described above have led to several developments. For one thing, they have increased the importance of foreign remittances, both cash and in-kind, and both for the survival of individual families and the buoyancy of economies. According to Jamaica's minister of state for finance, Errol Ennis, between January and November 1994, Jamaicans resident in the United States alone remitted some U.S.$278 million to the Jamaican economy.[7] And, said Deputy Prime Minister and Minister of Foreign Trade Seymour Mullings, the two and a half million Jamaicans living in New York, Miami, Hartford, Washington, D.C., Toronto, London, and Philadelphia remitted U.S.$600 million to Jamaica during 1994.[8] According to the September 27–October 2, 1996, edition of the *Santo Domingo News,* remittances to the Dominican Republic by Dominicans living abroad reach U.S.$1.2 billion per year, the second largest source of foreign exchange after tourism. Moreover, the growth of the informal economy has been stimulated, such that to most citizens in places like the Dominican Republic, Guyana, Haiti, and Suriname it has become relatively more important than the formal economy.

The combined effect of the debt crisis, depressed exports, mismanagement, and other factors has been such that Caribbean countries have been forced to seek foreign economic and financial

6. Harker, "Caribbean Economic Performance in the 1990s," 10–12.
7. *New York Carib News,* "US$278 Million to Local Economy."
8. *New York Carib News,* "Jamaicans Remitted US$600 Million."

support. One consequence of this has been the prescription by the World Bank and the International Monetary Fund (IMF) of strong doses of structural adjustment, central to which are privatization and deregulation. Structural-adjustment programs have been presented as beneficial to Caribbean countries in the long term, but they have some deleterious short-term social and economic effects. One study of the Jamaica situation with regionwide relevance shows that the state's role in providing welfare has diminished as social justice has been subordinated to market considerations. Both the quantity and quality of social services have been affected by cuts in public-sector spending, and reduced or removed subsidies for food, education, and health services, as well as other cutbacks, have increased economic deprivation. Wages have lost the battle with persistent inflation, and prices have risen continually, partly because of the free market emphasis.[9]

What, then, given this economic profile, are some of the economic positives and negatives of drugs?

The Balance Sheet: The Credit Side

There are at least three areas of actual and potential economic benefits from Caribbean drug operations: employment, income regeneration, and revenue enhancement. The operations that provide these plus-side outputs are drug production, trafficking, and money laundering.

For obvious reasons, it is impossible to quantify the benefits from employment—or from any of the other areas for that matter—in terms of the numbers of people doing direct and indirect, and full-time and part-time work related to drugs. Categories and numbers of people employed vary from place to place and operation to operation, but, generally, several different occupational areas are involved, including farmers, pilots, laborers, engineers, drivers, accountants, lookouts, and guards. This list does not include the variety of people in different public- and private-sector roles who

9. See Grant-Wisdom, "Globalization, Structural Adjustment, and Democracy in Jamaica."

are bribed to facilitate production, trafficking, and other operations. Moreover, in thinking of employment, account must be taken of the fact that narcotics countermeasures by governments also often boost employment in police, customs, and other agencies.

A look at one area of operation—production—suggests that given marijuana production and eradication levels noted in Chapter 1, especially in Jamaica, Guyana, Belize, and the eastern Caribbean, the number of people throughout the region "employed" directly and indirectly in this area would run into the tens of thousands. In relation to Jamaica, production is said to have generated employment and income for small farmers and wage workers in the context of declining jobs and income from traditional agricultural exports such as sugar and bananas.[10] Indeed, some six thousand Jamaican farmers are said to have been involved in marijuana production during the 1980s.[11]

Regarding income generation, production, trafficking, sales, and money-laundering transactions do generate income. For some of the people involved, the income is primary income; for others it is supplementary earnings. One Jamaican government study established clear linkages between marijuana production and income generation:

> A number of farmers and young people have turned to the farming of marijuana to earn a living. The Government's anti-drug eradication program has succeeded in destroying vast areas planted in marijuana, but the socio-economic problems remain. The small growers in these target communities have been experiencing a worsened situation in generating income or finding suitable employment. Information from a study done prior to the eradication program indicated that the average disposable income was 84 percent above the national level, but since the program it fell to 18 percent above the per capita disposable income.[12]

For many people the relative economic deprivation and poverty in the region are justification for engagement in drug activities. As a

10. Stone, "Crime and Violence," 44.
11. See MacDonald, *Dancing on a Volcano*, 90.
12. Jamaica, Ministry of Agriculture, *Alternative Systems for an Illegal Crop*, 8.

matter of fact some analysts see clear linkages between drug activities and contributors to the deprivation, particularly debt and structural adjustment. Jamaican economist and diplomat Richard Bernal, for instance, asserts: "The debt burden serves to encourage indulgence in the illicit drug industry."[13] One University of the West Indies economics professor argues: "Amelioration of the drug trade is, [however,] impossible without a reduced burden of the so-called structural adjustment, which creates the fertile environment for drug activity."[14] Apart from poverty and deprivation, people are motivated by greed and acquisitive materialism. And given the "big money" involved in drugs and the poor salaries for a wide cross section of jobs in most places, one can understand the susceptibility to corruption, which itself generates income.

While it is true that drug operators do not pay income, corporate, or other taxes into the formal economy, some of the income they generate does interface with the formal economy, contributing to government revenue. This happens, for example, when income generated by drug transactions is used in a legal context where value-added, property, sales, and other taxes are paid. Moreover, countries that place a premium on offshore banking and financial services do benefit from licensing and relicensing fees both for companies that are created expressly to launder drug money and for those that undertake legitimate business but are also used for narcotics money laundering. Revenue enhancement is also a by-product of seizures of drug-related assets, fines levied by courts against people convicted of drug offenses, and fines imposed by regulatory agencies, such as central banks and customs departments, against companies that violate anti-trafficking and anti-money-laundering mandates.

Understandably, much of the economic activity generated by drug operations becomes a part of the informal economy. However, as noted above, the informal economy is crucial to economic survival in some countries. Moreover, there is always some interface between formal and informal economies in all countries, which means that formal economies in the Caribbean benefit from drug operations. Undoubtedly, employment, income generation, and rev-

13. Bernal, "Debt, Drugs, and Development in the Caribbean," 91.
14. Pantin, "The Colombian Nightmare," 145.

enue enhancement due to drugs affect the formal economy, and in both positive and negative ways.

The impact of drugs is also felt more indirectly—for example, in the area of savings. Although conspicuous consumption by and large characterizes those who profit from drug operations, they also save and invest, and in and through formal financial institutions. This not only adds to the stock of savings, but it affects, often positively, such things as investment capital and interest rates.[15] In relation to Jamaica, Carl Stone observed: "The drug trade provided access to capital and capital accumulation in an economy dominated by a closely knit network of local white, Jewish, Lebanese, and brown entrepreneurs, and [by] foreign capital. [It] served to open up opportunities for wealth accumulation for black middle class interests who found themselves unable to break into the big business sector dominated by the ethnic minorities."[16]

Drugs also have a direct impact on the availability of foreign currency. The stark reality is that given demand-supply dynamics and the strength of the currency of the world's most significant market, drug operations generate U.S. dollars, and these are used in both the formal and informal economies. As was seen in Chapter 3, drug operations in Guyana are said to have so influenced foreign-currency dealings as to affect not only the quantity of U.S. dollars available but also the official exchange rate with the local currency. In the case of Jamaica, Stone noted that in their highly dependent economy imports represent some 50 percent of GDP. However, the foreign-exchange crisis of the 1970s reduced the formal economy's ability to pay for imports, affecting negatively both production and consumption. The government's response to the crisis involved tight foreign-exchange controls and import restrictions.

Drug production and trafficking were, however, immensely helpful to Jamaica.

> The illegal marijuana trade emerged as the way business interests attempted to fill the growing gaps between their demand for foreign exchange and the declining supply through

15. Some of these relationships were noted by a Trinidad and Tobago Central Bank official, who requested anonymity, in an interview in Port of Spain on July 8, 1994.

16. Stone, "Crime and Violence," 45.

legitimate channels. In other words, the marijuana trade helped to sustain the flow of imports into this highly import dependent economy by providing a supplementary source of foreign exchange to importers, by way of a rapidly growing black market in U.S. dollars which was supplied mainly from the drug trade.[17]

Over and above all this, as is done in Latin America and elsewhere, Caribbean drug operators often engage in a form of social investment—Robin Hoodism—by doing what governments are sometimes unable to do: they fulfill social welfare needs, either on an individual or a communal basis. They provide medical and school supplies or funds for people to secure specialist medical care, sporting equipment and facilities, and church relief, among other things. They also bring business and work to some areas, and sometimes in a noticeable way. Understandably, the beneficiaries of this benevolence do not see the drug operators as moral or legal reprobates; often they see them as heroes. This partly explains why some communities not only fail to aid in the apprehension or conviction of drug operators, but sometimes actually protect those operators from the law. This was stressed by law-enforcement officials in relation to the Family Islands in the Bahamas and several parts of Jamaica. It also is the reality in Guyana, Belize, Puerto Rico, and the Dominican Republic.

The Balance Sheet: The Debit Side

Like the credit entries, the debit entries that need to be accounted for defy quantification. Notable here are the impact on certain industries, fines imposed by foreign countries, and resource use.

Tourism, which, as noted above, is critical to several countries, is vulnerable to drug operations. The impact is largely indirect, and relates to crime. As a matter of fact, Gordon "Butch" Stewart, one of the region's leading tourism entrepreneurs, has called crime "the evil of tourism."[18] There is evidence to suggest a negative effect of

17. Ibid., 44.
18. Bohning, "For Resorts, Crime = Crisis," BM 43.

drugs on tourism due to (a) media reports that scare potential tourists away and (b) the high incidence of drug-related crime in some places. Caribbean observers have known for some time what the *New York Times* reported in April 1994: that drug-related crime has transformed the "paradise" character of the U.S. Virgin Islands and other Caribbean vacation spots, driving fear into locals and tourists alike and depressing tourism.[19]

In the case of Jamaica, where tourism accounts for about 45 percent of the foreign-exchange earnings, in July 1994 the Jamaica Tourist Board reported a decline in tourist arrivals of 5.8 percent in April 1994 and 15.1 percent the following month. Carlyle Dunkley, then the tourism minister, attributed the decline to Jamaica's "image problem," caused by the alarmingly high rate of violent crime. There were over 653 murders in Jamaica in 1993 alone. By June 1994 some 360 people had been killed, and by the end of the year the figure had risen to 690, many of the cases involving drug-related issues. Indeed, crime is said to be a major factor in the 3 percent decline in tourism in 1994—U.S.$30 million less than the U.S.$943 million earned in 1993.[20]

The impact of drugs-driven crime on tourism is also of concern in Belize, Puerto Rico, Trinidad and Tobago, Barbados, and elsewhere in the region. While the Barbados situation is not as serious as that in Jamaica or Trinidad and Tobago, according to the Barbados police commissioner, "we have been challenged."[21] It is also a matter of concern in the Bahamas, where the 1994 crime rate was the highest in five years, and, as noted in Chapter 4, in Puerto Rico, which had 868 homicides in 1996, and Jamaica, which had 780 murders in 1995, 13 percent above the 1994 figure. The 1996 murder figure for Jamaica was 921, 17 percent more than in 1995.

The garment industry, which is used for trafficking, especially in Jamaica, the Dominican Republic, and the eastern Caribbean, is

19. Rohter, "Slaying in St. Thomas Stains Image."

20. *Trinidad Guardian*, "Alarm at Downturn in Jamaican Tourism"; Browne, "Multinationals Have No Plans to Leave"; and *Miami Herald*, "Jamaica Tourism Declines."

21. Interviews in Port of Spain on July 8, 1994, with a top Trinidad Central Bank official, who requested anonymity; Yvonne Gittens-Joseph, director of the Political Division of Trinidad's Ministry of External Affairs and International Trade; and Keith Kerwood, foreign service officer in the same division. The interview with Commissioner Durant was also done in July 1994.

also affected. In one Jamaican situation, Hanes, the country's largest garment manufacturer, suspended for many months all shipments of cut goods for assembly in Jamaica, following the discovery in June 1994, in a Florida warehouse, of two hundred pounds of marijuana in a shipment of apparel from Jamaica. One can well imagine the potential impact on Jamaica's economy when one recognizes that directly and through subcontracting Hanes produces about U.S.$200 million worth of garments annually.[22] The garment industry is critical to Jamaica's economy. It generated U.S.$570 million in exports in 1995, with a net value added of 20 percent. It is estimated to have provided direct employment for some 50,000 people, 14,000 working for the domestic market and 36,000 for the export market. There are 221 apparel plants, 110 of which are registered exporters. Garment manufacturers employ 35 percent of the workers in Jamaica's manufacturing sector. In some parishes, such as Hanover and St. Mary, it employs between 70 and 80 percent of the labor force.[23]

In addressing the implications of drugs for the industry, Lucien Rattray, president of the Jamaica Promotions Corporation, noted that for the period 1993–94 drugs were found in the shipments of eighteen garment companies. Such finds not only affect the integrity of products, but they also result in prohibitive fines against local and foreign contractors,[24] thereby affecting the solvency of companies and the performance of the industry overall. Ambassador Peter King explained in an interview that security measures by the apparel industry add 8 percent to its operating costs. Because of drugs, some shipping companies that transport garments or garment material have threatened to withdraw their services from Jamaica.

The second minus-side entry is fines, which, as just seen, have a bearing on the tourism and garment industries; but their effect goes beyond these areas. Heavy fines are often levied by U.S. Customs against the owners of carriers on which drugs are found in U.S. ports. Under U.S. legislation—19 U.S.C. 1584, amended by PL 99-

22. *New York Carib News,* "Ganja Found in Clothing Shipment."
23. Interview with Ambassador Peter King, August 1996, and Caribbean Textile and Apparel Institute, *The Jamaica Garment Industry.*
24. *Virgin Islands Daily News,* "Hats, Blouses,—and a Few Kilos," and *New York Carib News,* "Drug Traffickers Targeting Garment Exports."

570—if a vessel found with drugs is not seized, officials may levy a fine of $1,000 per ounce for cocaine, heroin, morphine, and opiate. The fine for marijuana or opium used for smoking is $500 per ounce.[25]

In January 1992, for example, a U.S.$1.2 million fine was imposed on the Guyana Airways Corporation (GAC) after a GAC flight arrived in New York with about 100 pounds of marijuana. On November 7 of the same year another GAC plane arrived in New York with 17 pounds of cocaine in an unaddressed mailbag, triggering a fine of U.S.$273,600 by U.S. Customs.[26] The most dramatic episode for GAC was on March 15, 1993, when flight GY 714 arrived in New York from Guyana with 117 pounds of cocaine in the plane's paneling. There was a U.S.$1.8 million fine for this infraction, which led the GAC to offer a million-dollar reward (in Guyana dollars) for information that would lead to the arrest and successful prosecution of the people involved in the affair.[27] Figure 7 shows the advertisement that was carried in the local press. That was the first time a Caribbean airline was forced to resort to such desperate and dramatic action to deal with air trafficking. The case is yet to be solved.

Of all the countries have been affected by fines, notably Guyana, the Dominican Republic, Haiti, the Bahamas, Trinidad and Tobago, the Cayman Islands, and Jamaica, the last has suffered the heaviest toll. There are several noteworthy instances:

- In 1986, two Air Jamaica planes were impounded in Miami and New York, and the fines totaled U.S.$657,000.
- Also in 1986, the now defunct Eastern Airlines was fined U.S.$900,000 after marijuana was found on a cargo flight. Three weeks later it was fined U.S.$1.6 million for a similar infraction. Cargo flights from Jamaica were suspended.
- In 1987, Evergreen, a Korean-owned shipping line, paid U.S.$135 million in fines to the U.S. Customs.
- In 1988, Sea-Land Services paid a fine of U.S.$85 million.

25. I am grateful to Lieutenant Commander J. Chris Sinnett of the U.S. Coast Guard for this information, provided in September 1996.
26. *Guyana Chronicle*, "GAC Fined 1.2M (US) for Transporting Ganja," and *Stabroek News*, "GAC Faces Further US$273,600 Fine for Cocaine Mail Bag."
27. See Persaud, "117 Pounds of Cocaine Found on GAC Plane," and *Stabroek News*, "GAC Offering G1M Reward for Cocaine Find Leads."

Fig. 7   GAC Million-Dollar Reward Advertisement

Guyana Airways

GUYANA AIRWAYS CORPORATION is offering a reward of **ONE MILLION GUYANA DOLLARS (GY\$1,000,000.00)** for any information that leads to the arrest and conviction of the person or persons who is/are responsible for the placement of Cocaine which was discovered in New York on flight GY 714 on the 15th March, '93.

Any person or persons supplying information in future which can lead to seizure of narcotics intended for smuggling on GAC flights will be suitably rewarded.

All information received will be dealt with in strictest confidence.

Contact Public Relations Department or Tel. Nos. 67563/61827.

- In 1989, the U.S. Customs imposed another U.S.$96 million charge against Sea-Land Services, following the discovery of 12,000 pounds of marijuana shipped from Jamaica. Sea-Land subsequently withdrew its service from Jamaica.
- In April 1989, an Air Jamaica plane was impounded in Miami, and a U.S.$28.8 million fine was imposed.
- Two boats belonging to the Jamaica Banana Cooperative Association were impounded for most of spring 1989, unable to pay the heavy fines imposed following the discovery of marijuana aboard them.[28]

The fines have been devastating to Air Jamaica, a state-owned corporation until November 1994, when, as noted in the July–August 1995 edition of *Caribbean Affairs,* it was acquired by Gordon "Butch" Stewart and a consortium of private businessmen. The fines contributed to Air Jamaica's 1988–89 losses of U.S.$14 million, which was 20 percent above the previous year's loss. In all, between 1989 and 1991, Air Jamaica was fined about U.S.$37 million for illegal drugs found on its planes entering the United States. The fines were, however, reduced to U.S.$3 million, with agreement that the remaining money be used to upgrade security at Jamaica's international airports.[29] Hence both state and commercial enterprises have felt the fines crunch. For private companies they directly affect the viability of the companies, but they also indirectly affect the economies concerned. In the case of state corporations, both impacts are direct. Hence, whether the fines are against private or public companies, they exact a toll against already weak Caribbean economies.

As will be seen in the next chapter, governments (and nongovernmental agencies) have been forced to adopt a wide range of narcotics countermeasures. Generally, the measures are costly. And even where there is external support, countermeasures have multiple

---

28. U.S. House, Select Committee on Narcotics Abuse and Control, *Drugs and Latin American,* 12–13, and Cumberbatch and Duncan, "Illegal Drugs, USA Policies, and Caribbean Responses," 166–68.

29. U.S. House, Select Committee on Narcotics Abuse and Control, *Drugs and Latin America,* 12–13; Cumberbatch and Duncan, "Illegal Drugs, USA Policies, and Caribbean Responses," 168; and *Jamaican Weekly Gleaner,* "US Customs, Air Jamaica Sign Anti-Drug Pact."

economic effects. First, they require governments to devote considerable portions of already scarce financial resources to combat drugs. A look at Table 15, for example, reveals that in recent times most of the Bahamas Defense Force expenditures have been devoted to counternarcotics measures. In 1990 they accounted for 85 percent of total expenditures. The seriousness of the situation is more readily appreciated when it is realized that such measures are undertaken not only by defense and police forces; they extend beyond interdiction and law enforcement.

Mention was made in the previous chapter of the extradition proceedings instituted by the United States in May 1996 in the St. Kitts–Nevis drugs-murder saga. That action involved astronomical costs for St. Kitts–Nevis. The extradition proceedings were estimated to cost at least U.S.$250,000 in legal fees, since the St. Kitts–Nevis attorney general's office has no lawyer on its staff with expertise in that area and has had to seek outside counsel. The magnitude of the sum involved becomes all the more obvious when it is recognized that the attorney general's entire budget for 1996 was U.S.$340,000.[30] Fortunately, from a budgetary standpoint, there was some "relief" with the denial of the extradition request in October 1996, as noted in the previous chapter.

Because of economic difficulties generally and budgetary constraints specifically, governments are obliged to reallocate resources, taking funds away from health, education, housing, and other areas to meet the drug threat. Jamaica is one dramatic case in point. As the Secretary to the Cabinet explained, for the last several years Jamaica's budgetary allocations to national security have been the second largest, after education and ahead of health, housing, and other critical social areas. For the 1994–97 budgets, the top three allocations have been as follows (figures in Jamaica dollars):

- 1994–95: education, $5.6 billion; national security, $3.92 billion; health, $3.24 billion;
- 1995–96: education, $8.2 billion; national security, $4.6 billion; health, $3.2 billion;

30. Rohter, "Storm Is Unleashed in St. Kitts, As a Cocaine Case Churns Politics."

Table 15 Bahamas Defense Force Expenditures, 1989 and 1990 ($ Bahamas)

Budget Item	1989 Overall	1989 D.R.	% D.R.	1990 Overall	1990 D.R.	% D.R.
Transportation within the Bahamas	7,580	3,790	50	5,514	2,757	50
Gas (cooking)	7,271	3,635	50	7,003	3,502	50
Insurance, equipment	174,238	139,390	80	742,865	594,292	80
Spare parts, marine equipment	608,452	486,761	85	391,208	332,527	85
Spare parts, air equipment	18,210	15,478	85	78,446	66,679	85
Provisions (food)	678,504	610,652	90	621,378	559,240	90
Fuels	1,165,226	1,048,702	95	1,119,753	1,063,766	95
Household & cleaning supplies	78,394	39,197	50	76,440	38,220	50
Clothing supplies	373,640	224,184	60	311,328	186,797	60
Military supplies	79,102	67,236	85	48,032	40,827	85
Sea craft (upkeep)	156,318	125,054	80	585,640	468,512	80
Air craft (upkeep)	215,170	172,136	80	45,530	36,424	80
Subsistence within the Bahamas	7,967	3,983	50	4,823	2,416	50
Personal emoluments	12,203,050	10,372,592	85	14,496,569	12,322,084	85
TOTAL	15,773,122	13,312,790	84	18,534,529	15,718,043	85

SOURCES: Ministry of National Security, *Summary Report on the Traffic in Narcotic Drugs Affecting the Bahamas* (Nassau, March 1990; March 1991).

D.R. = Drug related.

- 1996–97: education, $10.18 billion; national security, $4.71 billion; health, 4.42 billion.[31]

Apart from the three main economic costs of drugs discussed above, other, less significant but noteworthy implications exist. One relates to foreign aid. Although the gravity of the global drug threat offers the prospect of increasing certain bilateral and multilateral aid flows into the region, the potential for the denial of more significant aid is real. At the bilateral level, U.S. foreign aid, which is important to many Caribbean countries for substantive and symbolic reasons, has often been jeopardized by drug operations. One example will suffice.

Under the 1986 U.S. Anti–Drug Abuse Act (PL 99-570), the U.S. president is allowed to impose sanctions, including duties, withdrawal of tariff benefits, a 50 percent withholding of bilateral aid, and suspension of air services, against "offending countries"—countries the U.S. considers to be taking insufficient action to combat drug production, trafficking, or money laundering that affects it. The Congress can reverse presidential action to grant aid or impose sanctions by passing a joint resolution within forty-five days of the president's determination on the matter, which is due on March 1 of each year.[32]

Ever since the passage of PL 99-570 Caribbean countries concerned have managed to receive certification. But Congress has not always agreed with the president's assessment and certification. In both 1988 and 1989, for example, Congress attempted to overturn the certification for the Bahamas. In the 1989 case, Senator John Kerry (Democrat from Massachusetts), then chairman of the powerful Subcommittee on Terrorism, Narcotics, and International Operations, led the decertification effort. However, the president (and the Bahamas) won by a 57–40 vote. During fall 1996, veiled decertification threats were leveled against Jamaica as the U.S.-Jamaican shiprider dispute unfolded. As noted in the Introduction, the controversy was initially over the extent of U.S. maritime "hot pursuit" in Jamaican (and Barbadian) territorial waters. But it assumed added dimensions as Jamaica (and Barbados) called for compre-

31. Interview with Dr. Carlton Davies, August 1996.
32. U.S. Senate, Committee on Foreign Relations, *International Narcotics Control and Foreign Assistance Certification*, 1–2.

hensive agreements to include arms trafficking, deportees, and banana-market guarantees and as U.S. officials accused Jamaica of
foot-dragging in the fight against drugs and of harboring traffickers.

The debit-side entries discussed above are largely direct economic costs. But as noted earlier, drugs also carry indirect economic costs and social costs not amenable to easy economic
estimation. For instance, providing public and private health care
for drug users, for children exposed to drugs before and after birth,
and for victims of drug-related crime also exacts high social and
economic costs. Moreover, lost or lower labor productivity follows
from (a) absenteeism, (b) the use of illegal drugs, (c) imprisonment
for drug crimes, and (d) deaths from drug-related violence and
drug-related workplace and traffic accidents. Further, there is also
a cost attached to having legitimate industrial production diverted
to the production and distribution of illegal drugs. In addition, one
has to factor into this social and economic matrix the diminished
quality of life caused by illegal drug use, such as pain and suffering
of families, friends, and crime victims.[33]

One also gets a sense of the impact on social dynamics from observations made in reference to Jamaica in 1987 but now relevant,
in varying degrees, to the entire Caribbean: the persistent specter
of violent crime has transformed physical and social landscapes;
burglar bars and barbed-wire-topped metal fences have become a
normal part of the urban architecture; armed guards and attack
dogs are among the visible effects of the escalation of crime. The
point is also made that probably more pernicious than the above-
mentioned developments has been the impact on popular attitudes
and culture, given the emergence, as ghetto heroes, of men and
women who live by and with the gun but are esteemed and protected by their communities of origin.[34]

Conclusion

Partly because of the nonquantifiable nature of these social costs
and the imprecision of economic costs that are both direct and indi-

33. For a discussion of these issues in a general context, see Tonry and Wilson,
Drugs and Crime, and U.S. Department of Justice, *Drugs, Crime, and the Justice
System*.
34. Phillips, introduction to *Crime and Violence*, ed. Phillips and Wedderburn, vii.

rect, settling the balance sheet is not an easy task. Yet, it is difficult not to sense that, in national and regional terms, although not always in individual terms, the costs involved far outweigh the benefits. This chapter validates for drugs in the Caribbean an assertion made elsewhere about drugs internationally: they constitute a dilemma partly because there are both negative and positive aspects involved.[35] It is precisely this duality that places Caribbean policy makers between a rock and a hard place. Many of them recognize the duality. But they are all caught in a political matrix with some elements that are irreconcilable: the reality of their own resource and political limitations; the demands both for vengeance and tolerance by local constituencies; the necessity for expediency politics to placate their constituencies; and demands by the United States for aggressive countermeasures, which require not only resource allocation and reallocation but also political and bureaucratic adaptation. Hence, most Caribbean political elites take what public-policy analysts call the "satisficing" approach to the economic and public-policy implications of drugs, although there is also considerable "muddling through" in how they design and implement countermeasures, the subject to which I turn next.

35. See Griffith, "From Cold War Geopolitics," esp. 26–29.

7

National, Regional, and International Countermeasures

The fight against illicit trafficking in narcotic drugs and psychotropic substances has to comprise effective measures aimed, *inter alia,* at eliminating illicit consumption, cultivation and production of narcotic drugs and psychotropic substances; preventing the diversion from legitimate uses of precursor chemicals, specific substances, materials and equipment frequently used in the illicit manufacture of narcotic drugs and psychotropic substances; and preventing the use of the banking system and other financial institutions for the laundering of proceeds derived from illicit drug trafficking by making such activities criminal offenses.
—UN General Assembly, 17th Special Session, 1990

There are two strategies that prove effective—sustained efforts over time and flexible surprise tactics. Although our enemies are smart, well equipped, and elusive, they will opt for the path of least resistance. We must find ways to capitalize on that. —Vice Admiral James M. Loy, USCG

The preceding six chapters have analyzed the nature and scope of drug operations in the Caribbean and the nature and gravity of their security implications. However, a full assessment of the region's drug dilemma requires one final task: examination of countermeasures adopted to meet the threats and challenges. Some countermeasures have already been considered, especially in Chapter 4. This chapter goes beyond the discussion there, but it also places that discussion in the larger geonarcotics context outlined in the Introduction.

The context is one of multidimensional, multilevel, and multi-actor countermeasures, a reflection of the nature and scope of the drug phenomenon. Responses need to be multidimensional because drug operations and their impact are multidimensional; they need to be multilevel—national, regional, and international—because drug operations and many of the problems they precipitate are both national and transnational; and they have to be multiactor for the last two reasons and because countries in the region lack the necessary capabilities to meet the threats and challenges on their own. Hence, responses come not only from governments but also from national nongovernmental organizations (NGOs), international governmental organizations (IGOs), and international nongovernmental organizations (INGOs). Both state and nonstate actors recognize that the scope and gravity of the matter demand the collective effort of all sectors and actors. Of course, when non-Caribbean states contribute to Caribbean countermeasures, they invariably work also in their own interests in mitigating direct or indirect threats to themselves.

National Countermeasures

National countermeasures are, understandably, wide-ranging in scope, if not sufficiently substantive in nature. They include law enforcement, education, interdiction, demand reduction, rehabilitation, intelligence, crop substitution, airport and seaport management, financial-services regulation, and legislation. There is no regionwide standard for most of the countermeasures, although countries emulate successful models elsewhere and common practices do exist. The kind and impact of countermeasures introduced depend essentially on three things: perceptions of the predicament, national capability, and foreign support.

There is universal recognition that public-sector resources are insufficient for the design and implementation of narcotics countermeasures, especially because countermeasures need to be both multidimensional and simultaneous. In other words, circumstances are such that one cannot serially apply education and then rehabilitation and then interdiction, and expect noticeable results. As a matter of fact, no set of measures can really be undertaken only sequentially. Education, rehabilitation, interdiction, and other measures have to be applied at the same time. Indeed, in many places a failure to adopt simultaneous measures, based on misperception of the situation, has contributed to its deterioration.

Most countries have, therefore, adopted an inclusive approach, actively reaching out locally to NGOs and corporate agencies for partnership in countermeasures. In Grenada, for example, the following NGOs have been invited into the partnership: the Grenada Medical Association, the Grenada Trades Union Association, the Mental Health Association, the Grenada Bar Association, the Council of Churches, the Popular Theater Organization, the Private Sector Organization, the Grenada Farmers Organization, the Group of Concerned Women, the National Youth Council, the Parish Development Organization, Alcoholics Anonymous, Partners for the Americas, Students Against Drugs, the Christian Anti–Drug Abuse Committee, and the Catholic Youth Organization.[1] As might be expected, in countries bigger than Grenada, such as the Dominican Republic, Jamaica, and Trinidad and Tobago, the NGO part of the partnership is much larger.

Generally, however, even the combined available resources of governments and NGOs are insufficient, making foreign state and nonstate assistance not just desirable, but necessary. In some cases the foreign support is so critical that programs run the real risk of collapsing if that support is withdrawn. A case in point is Operation Buccaneer in Jamaica. That program began in 1974 with some very ambitious aims: eradication of all marijuana cultivation; arrest of all persons and impoundment of all equipment, aircraft, and marine vessels engaged in trafficking; and destruction of all illegal airstrips. It involved joint army-police operations heavily supported by the United States. The U.S. obligations were usually for salaries for twenty-five to thirty people to cut and burn marijuana fields; for fuel for the helicopters, boats, and vessels used in operations; for chemicals, equipment, and supplies to cut and spray fields; and for the lease of Bell 205 helicopters for use by the Jamaica Defense Force (JDF) air wing. The United States also provided vessels for the JDF Coast Guard and helped with intelligence gathering.

---

1. See Grenada, Ministry of Education, *National Policy and Program of Action Against the Illicit Use, Production, and Trafficking in Narcotics, Drugs, and Psychotropic Substances*, 10.

Operation Buccaneer was interrupted for eleven years largely because of the sour political relations between the United States and Jamaica, which themselves were due to U.S. antipathy toward the democratic socialist posture of Prime Minister Michael Manley and his government. It recommenced in 1985 and continues as an annual exercise, interrupted only in 1988 when Hurricane Gilbert hit Jamaica and destroyed most of the island's marijuana fields. Because of budget constraints, the United States reduced its support for Operation Buccaneer in 1993, dramatically affecting the program. Nevertheless, both U.S. and Jamaican officials expect the operations to continue, and both countries take pride in what has been achieved so far.[2]

Foreign assistance is not only bilateral, but multilateral. Assistance spans all areas. Aid sometimes comes from places generally with little interest in the Caribbean, which suggests that the rationale behind the assistance is often not the specific country getting the aid but the issue concerned; the fact that drugs constitute an interdependence issue is what really matters. In one case, Germany gave DM 4,500 (J$75,000) toward drug rehabilitation in Jamaica. The money was given in December 1993 for Patricia House, a rehabilitation facility for recovering addicts that had been established in 1991 with support from the European Community, the Jamaican government, and Richmond Fellowship, a Jamaican NGO.[3]

Virtually all Caribbean countries have national drug councils that are supposed to set policy on countermeasures. They usually are composed of officials from various government bodies as well as NGOs and the private sector. The National Council on Drug Abuse (NCDA) of Jamaica, the Programa Para la Prevención del Uso Indebido de Drogas (PROPUID) of the Dominican Republic, the National Advisory Council on Drugs (NACD) of Guyana, the National Council for Drug Abuse Prevention (NaCoDAP) of the Netherlands Antilles, and the National Drug Council (NDC) of the Bahamas are a few of these bodies. Understandably, their structure varies from country to country.

National master plans are considered the ideal tools for establishing strategies and mechanisms for combating drugs. Up to fall 1996

---

2. Interviews with Rear Admiral Brady and Captain Edwards, December 1994.
3. See *Jamaica Herald*, "Drug Rehab Program Gets German Aid."

there were master plans in twenty-one places: Anguilla, Antigua-Barbuda, Aruba, Bahamas, Barbados, Belize, Bermuda, the British Virgin Islands, the Cayman Islands, Dominica, the Dominican Republic, Grenada, Guyana, Jamaica, Montserrat, Netherlands Antilles, St. Lucia, St. Vincent and the Grenadines, Suriname, Trinidad and Tobago, and Turks and Caicos.[4] Some of the master plans are preliminary; others are complete.

However, there are several problems with the master plans. One United Nations International Drug Control Program (UNDCP) report, for example, noted: "A severe lack of consistent, pertinent, reliable, and comprehensive data on drug abuse and trafficking seriously inhibits proper assessment of the actual situation, and precludes planning of appropriate counter-measures."[5] UNDCP and European Union (EU) officials also have lamented the fact that some master plans are not comprehensive, concrete, or realistic. Also, some master plans often are products of one person's or one agency's designs or wishes, rather than reflections of broad-based governmental and nongovernmental consultation and planning.[6] Moreover, for a variety of resource and other reasons, the implementation record in many places is poor.

Drug-prevention programs have been undertaken in several countries. Generally, they include school curricula for drug education and teacher training, media-awareness campaigns aimed at school children and young adults, and sports-related activities. Several Caribbean countries have also mounted demand-reduction programs, and at least one has pursued crop substitution.

Trinidad and Tobago's demand-reduction program is actually one strand of a two-pronged national drug-control strategy. The second aspect is supply control. The overall plan attempts to develop a comprehensive and integrated response to ensure that the problems are addressed from all fronts simultaneously. The hope is to modify behavior through public education and positive influences on attitudes and values. Prevention through education is seen as a

4. United Nations International Drug Control Program, *Status of Master Plans in the Caribbean*, 9.

5. United Nations International Drug Control Program, *Subregional Program Framework for the Caribbean, 1994–1995*, 12.

6. Interviews in October 1996 with Michel Amiot of the EU and Muki Daniel of the UNDCP.

continuous process involving the psychological development of children, the training of teachers, the participation of professional and community leaders in delivering programs, and the treatment, rehabilitation, and social reintegration of the addicted population. Recognizing the need for multidimensional, multiactor efforts, the Trinidad plan also invites interagency and international cooperation, both state and nonstate.

The demand-reduction project began in October 1994 and runs through October 1997. It has four main components: research and information, community prevention, school prevention, and treatment and rehabilitation. Several target beneficiaries have been identified: among them, 150,000 people in five communities; students, teachers, and administrators in select schools; addicts and their families; and governmental and nongovernmental agency workers involved in counternarcotics work. The project is proceeding on two main tracks. The objective of the first is to improve the ability to design and implement demand-reduction programs. The focus here is on enhancing national research capabilities, public drug education, school prevention, treatment and rehabilitation, and training government and NGO officials.

The second track emphasizes the development and implementation of intensive demand-reduction activities in five communities, as mentioned above. The communities are San Fernando, in southwest Trinidad; Arima, in northern Trinidad; Chaguanas, the northwest section of the island; Scarborough, in southern Tobago; and Laventille, in northwest Trinidad. These five communities were selected based on several considerations. First, they are representative of different types of drug problems affecting Trinidad and Tobago. Second, they offer a fairly wide geographic spread, allowing models to be tested in a diverse selection of the country's population. Moreover, they are places where the social infrastructure and community and political organizations are sufficiently developed to give the project a reasonable chance of success.

The project is being implemented by the National Alcohol and Drug Abuse Prevention Program (NADAPP), under the aegis of the Ministry of Social Development. NADAPP itself has four institutional elements. The first is the Ministerial Committee, comprising ministers of social development, education, health, community development, youth and sports, and finance. This committee has overall responsibility for setting government policy on demand reduction. Responsible to the Ministerial Committee for developing, monitoring, and overseeing the implementation of programs is the Technical Advisory Council on Alcohol and Drug Abuse (TACADA), which is composed of people from various elements of the program. The project's third component is the NADAPP secretariat, and the fourth, which is still not fully in place, will include policy units within relevant government ministries.

The project is estimated to cost U.S.$1.9 million: U.S.$462,469 from local sources and the remainder from the UNDCP. This project is actually the second phase of a longer-term initiative, the first part of which ran from October 1992 to October 1994. Several things were accomplished during the first phase, including the training of 161 community leaders in basic drug-abuse prevention, preparation of educational materials, and establishment of the NADAPP secretariat. Given what officials in Trinidad and Tobago consider as current and projected drug-consumption practices, the expectation is that several other phases will be necessary after the current one is completed.[7]

The crop-substitution program in Jamaica has three aims: assisting growers who are experiencing economic hardships because of marijuana eradication countermeasures; encouraging potential marijuana growers to grow alternative crops and raise livestock; and assisting growers and their dependents to adapt to the pursuit of income-substitution activities. In specific terms, the plan is to establish 1,520 acres of permanent and semipermanent crops and 700 acres of cash crops, and to provide 1,890 farmers with chicken broilers for poultry rearing.

The project area covers farms in the parishes of St. Ann, St. Catherine, St. Elizabeth, and Westmoreland. As noted in Chapter 1, these are among the parishes with the highest marijuana production. Based on soil, land use, climate, and market considerations, three models have been developed. The first consists of one-acre units divided into sections for cash crops, permanent or semipermanent crops, and poultry farms, each with a hundred birds initially. The second involves two-acre units to be used for the same

---

7. United Nations International Drug Control Program, *Assistance to the [Trinidad and Tobago] National Drug Abuse Demand Reduction Program*, 5–22.

purposes but with different apportionment. The third model consists of three-acre units divided as follows: one acre for permanent or semipermanent crops; a half acre for cash crops; and the remainder for a two-hundred-bird poultry house.

The number of farmers expected to benefit from the program is to increase by a thousand in the second and third years. Substitute crops include yams, carrots, coffee, citrus, papaya, and sugar cane. Training will be offered to farmers, as will basic farm tools such as pitchforks, machetes, and files. The nonagricultural aspect of the program includes creation of cottage industries for processing agricultural produce, and dressmaking, embroidery, and needlecraft. Women are the principal target for these activities, but men are not excluded. The program began in late 1994 and is expected to cost J$234 million over its three-year duration. Funding comes from the Jamaican government and grants from local NGOs, IGOs, and foreign governments. This program builds on a 1988 pilot project in southwest St. Ann, where farmers were given J$1,700 worth of seeds, fertilizers, and pesticides each in an effort to encourage a shift away from marijuana cultivation. The St. Ann experiment had considerable problems, but was judged fairly successful. Notable in this regard has been the commitment of many farmers to reinvest part of their profit to extend the substitute acreage initially cultivated.[8]

Like crop-substitution initiatives in Latin America, the efforts in Jamaica raise the issue of the comparative economic advantage, from the standpoint of the farmers, of cultivating marijuana as opposed to the alternative crops. The planners in Jamaica are realistic but hopeful in this regard, noting that "[w]hile it is not realistic to expect this plan to generate [the same] income capacities as marijuana production, a sufficient level of income will be generated devoid of the risk and negative social impact [that comes] with production of the illegal crop."[9]

One troubling area in the region's antidrug efforts is rehabilitation. Some countries have several clinics and hospitals with rehabilitation programs. In the Bahamas, for example, rehabilitation is

8. Jamaica, Ministry of Agriculture, *Alternative Systems for an Illegal Crop*, 1–11.
    9. Ibid., 2.

offered at the Sandilands Rehabilitation Center, Doctors Hospital, and elsewhere. In Jamaica, it is provided at Bellvue Hospital, the University of the West Indies Hospital, and through NGOs such as Addiction Alert Organization. In Trinidad and Tobago, it is undertaken at New Life Ministries, Mount St. Benedict, Caura, Rebirth House, and elsewhere. But some countries, notably in the eastern Caribbean, have absolutely no rehabilitation capability. What is worse, in some places without facilities addiction is worsening because of the fallout from increased trafficking. Guyana is one of these places.[10] In Guyana and other places that lack rehabilitation facilities addicts are usually treated at mental institutions.

Regional and International Countermeasures

For reasons explained earlier, the response to the drug dilemma requires countermeasures at the regional and international levels. As Table 16 shows, Caribbean countries participate in a variety of regional and international networks. Some of them, like the Inter-American Drug Abuse Control Commission (CICAD), the Caribbean Financial Action Task Force (CFATF), and the UNDCP, are devoted solely to combating drugs. For some of them, like the Association of Caribbean Commissioners of Police (ACCP), INTERPOL, and the Regional Security System (RSS), drugs are part of a wider mandate. Like national efforts, regional and international initiatives are multidimensional, covering the very areas dealt with nationally. But unlike those at the national level, regional and international operations see less NGO and INGO involvement, and more from states and IGOs.

One regional plan resulted in the establishment of a Regional Drug Training Center. Jamaica initially made the proposal in 1989 at a meeting of CARICOM ministers responsible for drug-law enforcement. It was later endorsed by the CARICOM leaders at the 1991 summit in St. Kitts–Nevis. The authors of the proposal saw the center as a resource base for technical advice to Caribbean gov-

10. See Naraine, "A Drug Rehab Clinic—When?" and Khan, "Prison Boss Calls for Drug Rehab Clinic."

Table 16 Caribbean Participation in Multilateral Antidrug Organizations

Country	AACP	CCLEC	CICAD	CFATF	INTERPOL	RSS	UNDCP
Anguilla	X	X		X	X		X
Aruba	X	X		X	X		X
Antigua-Barbuda	X	X	X	X	X	X	X
Bahamas	X	X	X	X	X		X
Barbados	X	X	X	X	X	X	X
British Virgin Islands	X	X		X	X		X
Belize	X	X	X	X	X		X
Cayman Islands	X	X	X	X	X		X
Cuba		X			X		X
Dominica	X	X	X	X	X	X	X
Dominican Republic		X	X	X	X		X
French Guiana[a]		X		X	X		X
Grenada	X	X	X	X	X	X	X
Guadeloupe[a]		X			X		X
Guyana	X	X	X	X	X		X
Haiti		X	X		X		X
Jamaica	X	X	X	X	X		X
Martinique[a]		X			X		X
Montserrat	X	X		X	X		X
Netherlands Antilles	X	X		X	X		X
St. Kitts–Nevis	X	X	X	X	X	X	X
St. Lucia	X	X	X	X	X	X	X
St. Vincent and the Grenadines	X	X	X	X	X	X	X
Suriname		X	X	X	X		X
Trinidad and Tobago	X	X		X	X		X
Turks & Caicos	X	X		X	X		X

SOURCES: Ivelaw L. Griffith, *The Quest for Security in the Caribbean* (Armonk, N.Y.: M. E. Sharpe, 1993); United Nations International Drug Control Program, October 1996.

[a]France's FATF membership covers this French department.

ernments and as a mechanism to systematize the region's drug-law-enforcement training. The center, funded by Jamaica, the United States, the UNDCP, and CICAD, was initially to be ready by the end of 1993. However, its opening was delayed by incomplete needs assessment and delayed funding. It was finally opened on September 27, 1996, in Twickenham Park, St. Catherine, Jamaica. It offers a variety of training programs—for magistrates, police, army and customs personnel, drug-control officers, and private security operators. It serves the entire English-speaking Caribbean, and from 1999 its training programs will be made available to personnel from the Spanish-, French-, and Dutch-speaking Caribbean.[11]

Internationally, one critical agency is the UNDCP. The United Nations itself has been involved in antidrug work in the Caribbean since the mid-1980s, first through the United Nations Fund for Drug Abuse Control (UNFDAC), which opened its Caribbean office in 1988 in Barbados. The UNDCP was created in 1989 as a successor to the UNFDAC, after which the United Nation's counterdrug operations were shifted to the UNDCP, which retained the Barbados base. The UNDCP Caribbean regional office covers twenty-nine countries and dependent territories. And, as Table 17 shows, its work covers several areas, notably demand reduction, education, rehabilitation, and alternative programs.[12]

The EU, which has been involved in supporting antidrug programs in the region for some time, recently enhanced its presence and contribution in the antidrug area. The EU action followed an appeal from Barbados prime minister Owen Arthur to British prime minister John Major in 1995 for special counternarcotics assistance. Prime Minister Major invited the French president, Jacques Chirac, to join him in signing a letter of committal to increase drug assistance. The initiative was then broadened to include the Dutch prime minister and other EU leaders. In order to facilitate its enhanced presence and contribution, the EU established a drug-control office in Barbados and named the former UNDCP Caribbean director, Michel Amiot, as the EU drug-control adviser in the Caribbean. The EU drug office began functioning in April 1996, but was officially opened in June 1996. It is responsible for advising the ten EU delegations in the Caribbean on drug-control matters, liaising with EU member states and other donors, and helping to coordinate donor programs in the region.

Intelligence is fundamental in combating drug operations. As some European Union experts declared, "Efficient information and

11. Griffith, "Drugs and World Politics," 428; conversation with Michel Amiot, September 22, 1995; interview with Commissioner Macmillan of Jamaica, August 1996; and Jamaica, Office of the Prime Minister, *Speaking Notes for the Hon. P. J. Patterson.*

12. United Nations International Drug Control Program, *A Global Alliance for a Drug-Free Caribbean*, 3–5.

Table 17 UNDCP Ongoing Counternarcotics Projects

Country	Type of Project	Title of Project	Duration	Budget (US $)
Regional Projects				
	Law enforcement/prevention	Establishment of a Regional Anti-Narcotics Law Enforcement Training Center in Jamaica (REDTRAC)	1995–98	879,750
	Prevention	Caribbean Customs Enhanced Drug Program—Phase II	1993–97	280,000
	Coordination	Regional Meeting on Drug Control Cooperation in the Caribbean	1996–97	372,700
	Research/prevention	Regional/Certificate Program in Addiction Studies	1995–98	1,038,346
	Coordination	Establishment of a Coordination Mechanism in the Caribbean	1996–99	500,000
	Law enforcement/legal	Prosecution and Adjudication of Drug Offences—Phase II	1996–99	1,700,000
	Law enforcement/legal	Regional Strategy for Countering Narcotics Money Laundering in the Caribbean	1996–99	3,000,000
	Prevention	Health/Family Life Education (HFLE)[a]	1996–98	400,000
	Prevention	Preparatory Assistance for a Caribbean Drug Control Advocacy Program	1996	19,500

	Coordination/prevention			
		Strengthening of National Drug Councils	1996–99	2,754,000
	Prevention	Sub-regional Treatment and Rehabilitation	1996–98	250,000
Country Projects				
Bahamas	Prevention	Support to the National Drug Demand Reduction Program	1994–97	579,002
Barbados	Prevention	Integrated Demand Reduction	1995–97	395,000
Belize	Prevention	Integrated Prevention Program	1996–98	398,500
Cuba	Prevention	Reduction of HIV Through Drug Abuse Control[a]	1996–98	400,000
Dominican Republic	Prevention	National Integrated Prevention Program on Drug Abuse	1993–97	848,268
Guyana	Prevention	Interagency Project (with UNDP UNICEF, and PAHO)	1996–98	400,000
Haiti	Prevention	Demand Reduction and Institution-Building	1996–98	400,000
Jamaica	Prevention	Poverty Eradication	1996–98	500,000
Suriname	Prevention	Integrated Demand Reduction	1996–98	350,000
Trinidad & Tobado	Prevention	Assistance to the National Drug Abuse Demand Reduction Program	1996–99	1,419,678

SOURCE: UNDCP, October 1996.

[a]multiagency project.

intelligence sharing remain the key to effective drug interdiction. They are the blood supply for anti-drugs cooperation and coordination."[13] Recognizing the critical role of intelligence, the ACCP adopted a Barbados proposal and agreed in May 1994 to pursue the creation of a regional drug-intelligence system, to be called the Regional Organized Crime Intelligence Sharing System (ROCISS).[14] Up to fall 1996 the system was still in the planning stage.

Many Caribbean countries, including Jamaica, Trinidad and Tobago, Barbados, the Dominican Republic, Belize, Grenada, and Guyana, already have U.S.-sponsored Joint Information Coordinating Centers (JICCs) that are linked electronically with an operational and analysis center in Texas called EPIC—El Paso Intelligence Center. However, several Caribbean officials have expressed displeasure with the JICC-EPIC operations, since most of the intelligence-data flows are unidirectional: from JICCs to EPIC. They have stressed the importance of having a system within the region to serve the region. ROCISS is intended to do this.

Notwithstanding the disgruntlement of some Caribbean military and law-enforcement officials about the one-sidedness of the intelligence-sharing relationship with the United States, Caribbean countries benefit from U.S. intelligence exchanges through several mechanisms, including the Caribbean Law Enforcement and Intelligence Committee (CLEIC), which brings together several Caribbean, French, British, Dutch, and U.S. law-enforcement officials monthly in Puerto Rico.[15] It is important to observe that the reluctance of U.S. and other authorities to share intelligence is often based on justifiable concerns about the integrity of Caribbean military and law-enforcement agents and agencies, because of corruption, suspected corruption, operational constraints, and, sometimes, inefficiency.

Caribbean countries are also part of several international counternarcotics regimes, as Table 18 indicates. Among these are the 1961 Single Convention on Narcotic Drugs, the 1971 Convention

13. European Union, *The Caribbean and the Drugs Problem*, 19.

14. Interview with Commissioner Durant, July 1994; Hassim, "Regional Crime Data Exchange System Agreed"; and interview with Commissioner Macmillan, August 1996.

15. I had the opportunity to attend the May 19, 1996, meeting at GANTSEC headquarters in San Juan.

Table 18   The Caribbean in Internationl Drug Regimes

State	1988 U.N. Convention Signature/ Accession	Ratification	Other Agreements 1961	1972
Antigua-Barbuda	Accession	Apr. 5, 1993	X	X
Bahamas	Dec. 20, 1988	Jan. 30, 1989	X	X
Barbados	Accession	Oct. 15, 1992	X	X
Belize	Accession	July 24, 1996	X	X
Cuba	April 7, 1989	June 12, 1996	X	X
Dominica	Accession	June 30, 1993	X	X
Dominican Republic	Accession	Sept. 21, 1993	X	X
Grenada	Accession	Dec. 10, 1990		
Guyana	Accession	March 19, 1993	X	X
Haiti	Accession	Sept. 18, 1995	X	X
Jamaica	Oct. 2, 1989	Dec. 29, 1995	X	X
St. Kitts–Nevis	Accession	Apr. 19, 1995	X	X
St. Lucia	Accession	Aug. 21, 1995	X	X
St. Vincent & Grenadines	Accession	May 17, 1994		
Suriname	Dec. 20, 1988	Oct. 28, 1992	X	X
Trinidad & Tobago	Dec. 7, 1989	Feb. 17, 1995	X	X

SOURCE: United Nations Secretariat, 1995, 1996.

NOTE: Ratification of all three conventions by Britain covers Anguilla, Bermuda, British Virgin Islands, Montserrat, and Turks and Caicos Islands; France's ratification covers French Guiana, Guadeloupe, and Martinique; and that of the United States extends to Puerto Rico and the U.S. Virgin Islands.

X = party to agreement.

on Psychotropic Substances, the 1972 protocol amending the 1961 convention, and the 1988 Convention Against Illicit Traffic in Narcotic Drugs and Psychotropic Substances. Indeed, one Caribbean country—the Bahamas—has the distinction of being the first country to ratify the 1988 convention. The convention includes provisions on drug trafficking, money laundering, organized crime, and related issues, such as arms trafficking. It requires states that are party to it—139 as of January 1997—to strengthen laws concerning financial reporting, extradition, asset forfeiture, and other subjects. It also urges adherents to improve cooperation in intelligence, interdiction, eradication, and other areas.

Table 18 implies that Caribbean countries are good international citizens insofar as they have signed or acceded to and ratified the major international antinarcotics treaties. Yet this is only part of the reality. Beyond ratification most Caribbean countries are found wanting. More critical than ratification of treaties is execution of their provisions. All Caribbean countries are delinquent, in this respect, in different areas and for various reasons, including administrative lethargy and technical, financial, and other resource limitations. Of course, the extent of delinquency varies among countries.

About 90 percent of the regional and international countermeasures involve foreign support—by states, IGOs, and INGOs, in various combinations. Because the regional and international agencies involved recognize the importance of coordinating their assistance, several of them formed a coordinating mechanism in 1990. Called the Bridgetown Group because it is centered in the Barbados capital, it includes representatives from the American, British, Canadian, Dutch, and French diplomatic missions in Barbados (and in Trinidad and Tobago in the case of the Dutch and French missions), the OAS, and the UNDCP. The group meets every six to eight weeks to coordinate programs. The success of the Bridgetown Group has led to the creation of five other groups: the Georgetown Group (in Guyana), the Port of Spain Group (in Trinidad and Tobago), the Santo Domingo Group (in the Dominican Republic), the Kingston Group (in Jamaica), and the Paramaraibo Group (in Suriname). Moreover, there are plans to establish groups in Haiti and possibly Belize and Cuba.[16]

As might be expected, efficiency and coordination vary among groups. But the functioning of donor-coordination groups—often called Mini Dublin Groups—has left much to be desired. According to donor officials, except for the Bridgetown Group, for various reasons, coordination generally is less than commendable.[17] The poor performance of the Mini Dublin Groups has been a reflection of poor donor coordination generally. Recognition of this—by both donors and recipients—led to the convening of a coordination conference in Barbados in May 1996. The May 15–17 meeting was attended by 291 participants: 115 from Dublin Group member countries, 104

16. Interview with Michel Amiot, July 1994; European Union, *The Caribbean and the Drugs Problem*, 57; and interviews with Michel Amiot and Muki Daniel, October 1996.

17. Interviews in October 1996 with Muki Daniel of the UNDCP and Michel Amiot of the EU.

from twenty-nine Caribbean countries and territories, and 72 from NGOs, IGOs, and INGOs. That meeting was of signal importance. In the pursuit of better regional and international coordination and cooperation it was able to rationalize the role and contributions of the various state and nonstate donor actors, including the United States, the EU, the UNDCP, CARICOM, and the OAS. The meeting adopted a plan of action, which outlines the critical needs and identifies four priority action areas: legislation, law enforcement, demand reduction, and maritime cooperation.[18]

Most Caribbean countries have signed mutual-legal-assistance treaties (MLATs) with the United States, including Antigua-Barbuda, Jamaica, the Bahamas, Belize, the Dominican Republic, Grenada, Suriname, St. Kitts–Nevis, and Trinidad and Tobago. These treaties provide for training, asset sharing, intelligence, material and technical support, and interdiction. The interdiction area itself has different kinds of joint and other mechanisms, including ship boarding, ship riding, and overflight, as Table 19 shows.

Although no formal agreement exists between Cuba and the United States, occasionally there is meaningful antidrug cooperation between the two. One example of this occurred in September 1993. Cuba granted permission for U.S. aircraft to enter Cuban airspace in hot pursuit of suspected traffickers aboard a speedboat, *The Thief of Hearts*. Following the chase, Cuban maritime authorities detained the vessel and two suspects—Jorge Roberto Lam Rojas and Jose Angel Clemente Alvarez. They delivered the narcotics—720 pounds of cocaine—and the suspects to U.S. officials.[19] The suspects were later convicted on a variety of charges in Miami. More recently, in October 1996, Cuban authorities seized 6,000 kilos of cocaine and a ship and arrested the twelve crew members and handed them all over to U.S. law-enforcement authorities in Miami. According to Francisco Osorio Williams-May, the captain of the MV *Limerick*—a 219-foot freighter—the cocaine journey began in Barranquilla, Colombia. The Bahamas was the Limerick's in-

18. Interviews with Muki Daniel of the UNDCP and Michel Amiot of the EU, October 1996. For more on the donor-coordination conference, see United Nations International Drug Control Program, *Report of the Regional Meeting on Dog Control Cooperation in the Caribbean.*

19. French, "Cuba Gives Over Two Drug Suspects," and Gerstenzang, "Cuba, U.S. Join Forces to Catch Drug Suspects."

Table 19   U.S.-Caribbean Bilateral Interdiction Agreements

Country	Entry to Investigate	Order to Land	Overflight	Pursuit	Ship Boarding	Ship Riding
Antigua-Barbuda	X	X	X	X	X	X
Bahamas			X			X
Barbados						
Belize	X			X	X	X
Dominica	X			X	X	X
Dominican Republic	X			X	X	X
Grenada	X			X	X	X
Guyana			X			X
Haiti	X			X		
Jamaica						
Netherlands Antilles	X		X	X		X
St. Kitts–Nevis	X	X	X	X	X	X
St. Lucia	X	X	X	X	X	X
St. Vincent & Grenadines	X			X	X	X
Trinidad & Tobago	X	X	X	X	X	X
Turks & Caicos Islands						X
United Kingdom[a]					X	X

SOURCE: U.S. Department of State, December 1996.

NOTES:

"Entry to Investigate": Standing authority for U.S. law-enforcement assets to enter foreign waters or airspace to investigate vessels or aircraft located therein suspected of illicit traffic. May also include authority to stop, board, and search such vessels.

"Order to Land": Standing authority for U.S. law-enforcement assets to order to land in the host nation aircraft suspected of illicit traffic.

"Overflight": Standing authority for U.S. law-enforcement assets to fly in foreign airspace when in support of antidrug operations.

"Pursuit": Standing authority for U.S. law-enforcement assets to pursue into foreign waters or airspace fleeing vessels or aircraft suspected of illicit traffic.

"Ship Boarding": Standing authority for the U.S. Coast Guard to stop, board, and search foreign vessels suspected of illicit traffic that are located seaward of the territorial sea of any nation.

"Ship Riding": Standing authority to embark law-enforcement officials on platforms of the parties, from which officials may then authorize certain law-enforcement actions.

[a]Extends to British dependencies in the Caribbean other than Turks and Caicos Islands.

tended destination, the ultimate destination of the drugs being Florida. However, the ship ran aground off Guantánamo. It began to sink, was abandoned, and drifted into Cuban waters, where the Cubans took control of it. The ship had several secret compartments. Thus, only 1,725 kilos of cocaine was initially discovered. It took several close inspections to reveal the total cargo. The drugs were handed over to the United States in batches between October and December 1996.[20]

Other bilateral narcotics treaties include those between Suriname and Colombia, Cuba and Guyana, Suriname and Guyana, Venezuela and Guyana, Cuba and Jamaica, Trinidad and Tobago and Venezuela, Jamaica and Mexico, and others.[21] Belize, for example, has agreements with Mexico for improved narcotics cooperation, including intelligence exchange, and for Mexican assistance with demand reduction and rehabilitation. These treaties cover a range of joint and individual initiatives. In one unique intra-Caribbean case, Trinidad and Tobago and Venezuela signed a pact that provided for joint air patrols,[22] a program that unfortunately was not fully implemented.

However, one initiative involving aircraft that has been successful is Operation Prop Lock: a U.S.-Jamaican operation that targets the assets of Bahamian and Jamaican trafficking organizations that use U.S. registered aircraft to smuggle drugs into the United States. It began in January 1995, after the U.S. Federal Aviation Administration had furnished evidence to the Jamaican government that several Jamaican air traffic controllers were aiding smuggling operations by permitting aircraft to land legally at the country's two international airports, yet allowing the aircraft six to seven hours to overfly the country. Up to May 1996, Operation Prop Lock had led to the seizure of five airplanes. These were sold, and close to U.S.$400,000 was placed in an international assets-sharing program.[23]

20. Lyons, "Havana Helps U.S. Investigate Drug Case."

21. For a full country-by-country listing of bilateral and multilateral agreements, see United Nations International Drug Control Program, *Background Paper for Working Group II: Legislation,* 19–24.

22. *Trinidad Express,* "T&T, Venezuela Consider Joint Air Patrols."

23. U.S. Department of Justice, National Drug Intelligence Center, *The Caribbean Connection,* 4.

Intelligence and interdiction measures are among the most costly of countermeasures, and they involve considerable technology, which Caribbean countries lack. Mention is made later of several multinational interdiction operations conducted during 1996. The cost of operating one of the ships involved in one of those operations—Caribe Venture 3-96—was $30,000 per day.[24] Cost and technology considerations help explain the sustained and significant role of the United States. At one point during the 1980s there were ground-based air radar systems in Providenciales, Turks and Caicos Islands; Guantánamo Bay, Cuba; and Borinquen, Puerto Rico; and five sea-based aerostat radar systems in the Bahamas, some with both maritime and air detection capabilities. An aerostat radar system is an airborne surveillance system that consists of unmanned, tethered, helium-filled balloons that carry radar. Each aerostat cost about U.S.$10 million to establish and some U.S.$4 million to operate annually during the 1980s.[25] Radar was also used at Lovers Leap on the Jamaican south coast from August 1991 to December 1994 as part of the Caribbean Basin Radar Network (CBRN).[26]

Between December 1994 and November 1995, the U.S. Department of Defense deactivated three of the aerostats in the Bahamas due to budget constraints and questions about their technical efficiency. U.S. drug officials in the Bahamas regretted the decision, but felt that the combined effect of the decreased use of the Bahamas by traffickers and the operational limitations of the aerostats did not make their removal a major handicap in counternarcotics efforts.[27] Bahamian officials, however, fumed at the decision, pointing to evidence of increased trafficking since the removal of the aerostats, which U.S. officials conceded. They also saw the U.S. action as sending mixed signals about its commitment to sustaining antidrug measures in the Bahamas. Moreover, for them, even if the

24. This figure was provided by Captain Paul Zukunft, commanding officer of USCG cutter *Harriet Lane* for his ship, a 270-footer with an HH-65 helicopter and a crew of 109, in interview aboard the *Harriet Lane* on May 19, 1996.

25. U.S. General Accounting Office, *Drug Control: Anti-Drug Efforts in the Bahamas,* 17, 22.

26. Interview with Rear Admiral Brady, December 1994.

27. Interviews in August 1996 with Lieutenant Commander Michael Tosatto, USCG liaison officer in the Bahamas, and with Lieutenant Commander Steven Lilly, U.S. naval liaison officer in the Bahamas.

aerostats were not 100 percent technically efficient, their mere presence served to deter traffickers.[28]

One U.S.-Caribbean intelligence and interdiction countermeasure of some distinction is Operation Bahamas and the Turks and Caicos (OPBAT). It uses some of the technology mentioned above. OPBAT was started in 1982 as a U.S.-Bahamian operation dedicated to apprehending airborne smugglers in the Bahamas. U.S. equipment, primarily helicopters, and personnel have been used to transport and assist Bahamian law-enforcement officials, and later those of the Turks and Caicos Islands, in apprehending suspected smugglers. OPBAT uses DEA, U.S. Coast Guard, and U.S. Army personnel and equipment at the OPBAT sites in the Bahamas. In addition, DEA and U.S. Coast Guard personnel direct OPBAT helicopter maneuvers and coordinate all interdiction operations from the OPBAT headquarters in the U.S. embassy in Nassau.

Over the years supplementary operations have been mounted. For instance, in September 1986 Operation Bandit was initiated by the U.S. Customs to improve response time. Use was made of helicopters based in Florida, with Bahamian police and military aboard to authorize arrests and seizures in the Bahamas. In October 1986, SEABAT—Sea Based Apprehension Tactics—was launched to provide ship-based launch platforms for helicopters with Bahamian law-enforcement personnel aboard. OPBAT has been credited with securing hundreds of arrests and the seizure of thousands of tons of cocaine and marijuana, as well as hashish and other drugs. Indeed, it was considered so vital that a multilateral treaty involving the Bahamas, Britain (for the Turks and Caicos Islands), and the United States was signed on July 12, 1990, extending the OPBAT basing network from three bases to four, the fourth being at Great Inagua, the southernmost island of the Bahamas.[29]

Also of importance is CBRN, mentioned above. At its operational peak, it drew signals from seventeen radar sites in ten countries. However, CBRN has been plagued with problems. Each site covers

28. Interviews in August 1996 with Idris Reid, permanent secretary, Ministry of Public Safety and Immigration; Basil O'Brien, secretary to the cabinet; and Captain Anthony Allens of the Royal Bahamas Defense Force.

29. U.S. General Accounting Office, *Drug Control: Anti-Drug Efforts in the Bahamas*, 14–16; *INCSR* (1991), 180–81; and *INCSR* (1995), 160. The 1995 *INCSR* reported erroneously that OPBAT has been terminated.

only 180 miles, and sites are often nonfunctional because of bad weather or poor maintenance. In June 1995 the Cayman Islands site was closed; this followed earlier site closures in Honduras, Costa Rica, and Panama. CBRN is being replaced with a system that is more sophisticated.

The system that will replace CBRN is ROTHR—Relocatable Over-the-Horizon Radar. Originally designed to track Soviet bombers, it can scan many times further than conventional radar. A prototype ROTHR system was established in Virginia in April 1993, and a second system in Texas underwent final testing during September 1995. The Pentagon explained that the first two sites can scan 2,000 miles on a clear day, and 1,600 miles on a day with atmospheric disturbances. Thus, they can sweep most of the Caribbean, Central America, and northern Colombia and Venezuela.[30] Puerto Rico is to be the site of the third ROTHR system. However, there has been considerable opposition to the plan from a variety of political parties and interest groups in Puerto Rico. That opposition plus the 1996 elections climate made it inexpedient for U.S. authorities to pursue the establishment of the Puerto Rican site during 1996.[31] The opposition continued beyond 1996. On January 12, 1997, for example, some four hundred protesters held demonstrations against the plan outside the Roosevelt Roads Naval Base on Vieques Island.

ROTHR uses a technology different from conventional line-of-sight microwave radar. It works by bouncing signals off the ionosphere, the outer region of the atmosphere that begins about thirty miles from the earth. The fully functional system in Virginia consists of two installations, about seventy miles apart. One is in New Kent, and consists of thirty-two antennas; the other is in Chesapeake. The latter is the receiver site, with 372 pairs of nineteen-foot-tall aluminum poles arranged in two parallel rows stretching one and a half miles. As might be expected, ROTHR is even more expensive that CBRN: U.S.$12 million each, with annual operating costs of between U.S.$12 million and U.S.$14 million per facility.[32]

30. *New York Carib News*, "Radar Station to Close," and Johnson, "Cold War Tools Turned on Narcos."

31. *New York Times*, "Puerto Ricans Fight U.S. Radar Plan to Curb Drug Traffic," and interview with Captain Thomas Bernard, commanding officer, GANTSEC, May 1996.

32. Graham, "Drug Flights Cross Pentagon's Super Radar Screen."

As Table 20 indicates, some counterdrug operations are truly multinational, even though on most occasions U.S. involvement is the most significant. Indeed, as with some bilateral programs, such as Operation Buccaneer, the U.S. contribution is critical to the credibility and success of the mission. Most of the multinational operations shown in Table 20 have been successes, measured in terms of seizures. Caribe Venture 3-96, for example, resulted in the seizure of 889 kilos of cocaine, 182 kilos of marijuana, and six vessels. Yet, multinational operations are subject to several cooperation challenges because of the various sovereignties, law-enforcement methods, and bureaucracies involved. (Several cooperation challenges are examined in the Conclusion.)

Notwithstanding the cost and sophistication involved in intelligence and interdiction countermeasures, whether bilateral or multinational, there is a certain futility in efforts to halt drug operations completely. One writer expressed this in very practical terms: "Even if the United States can increase the risk of capture and conviction for traffickers, drug smuggling's tremendous profitability guarantees that there will be thousands of willing replacements for the traffickers that are successfully prosecuted. A payment of $50,000 per trip to the masters of these ships is common. The engineers make about $25,000, and each of the crewmen receives between $5,000 and $10,000."[33] Incidentally, the figures cited here are 1988 rates. They certainly have increased since then.

The manner in which the United States pursues some of its unilateral and joint countermeasures, especially ones related to eradication and interdiction, has often been a problem for some Caribbean countries. U.S. law-enforcement officials have often pursued suspects into the territorial waters of Caribbean countries, making arrests in those countries' jurisdictions, sometimes without even courtesy notification of the local authorities, either before of after the arrests. There has often been virtual coercion by U.S. agencies in the selection of personnel for local drug-enforcement operations and in the design and implementation of countermeasures. As was noted in the Introduction, Caribbean leaders have often protested such affronts to their sovereign authority.

In July 1988, for instance, writing on behalf of CARICOM, its

---

33. Meason, "War at Sea," 8.

Table 20 Multinational Interdiction Operations in the Caribbean

Name of Operation	Dates	Participating Nations	Naval and Air Assets
Caribe Storm 1-96	Jan. 9–18, 1996	U.S., Netherlands, U.K., St. Kitts–Nevis, Anguilla, France	USCGC Forward, HNLHM Abraham Crijnssen, USCGC Attu, USCGC Nunivak, USCGC Ocracoke, USCGC Port Huron, Stalwart (St. Kitts–Nevis), Dolpin (Anguilla), NL P-3/F-27 Aircraft, PRANG (UC-26), French Customs Aircraft
Caribe Storm 2-96	Jan. 29–Feb. 6, 1996	U.S., U.K., France, Netherlands, St. Kitts–Nevis, Anguilla, St. Lucia, Barbados	HNLHM Abraham Crijnssen, HMS Brave, FRA Oakleaf, USCGC Mohawk, USCGC Vashon, USCGC Forward, USCGC Harriet Lane, USCGC Ocracoke, USCGC Nunivak, USCGC Attu, USS Obannon, USN/NL P-3S/F-27S, British Virgin Islands Police Aircraft, French Customs Aircraft, PRANG (UC-2b), USCS Air Branch embarked HH-65 and Lynx helicopters

Caribe Venture 3-96	May 12–26, 1996	U.S., Netherlands, France, Grenada, St. Kitts–Nevis, Anguilla, St. Lucia, Barbados	USCGC Harriet Lane, USCGC Attu, USCGC Nunivak, HNLHM Abraham Crijnssen, HMS Argyll, RFA Oakleaf, Canot (France), Pinas (France), Doris (France), Tyrrel Bay (Grenada), Stalwart (St. Kitts–Nevis), Dolphin (Anguilla), Defender (St. Lucia), Trident (Barbados)
Caribe Venture 4-96	Aug. 30–Sept. 20, 1996	U.S., Netherlands, France, Grenada, St. Kitts–Nevis, Anguilla, St. Lucia, Barbados	U.S. Coast Guard cutters Thetis, Forward, Bear, Escanaba, Ocracoke, Nunivak, and Vashon, HNLHM Willem Van Der Zaan, Canot (France), Pinas (France), Doris (France), Tyrrel Bay (Grenada), Stalwart (St. Kitts–Nevis), Dolphin (Anguilla), Defender (St. Lucia), Trident (Barbados)

SOURCE: U.S. Coast Guard, October 1996.

NOTES:
FRA   Fleet Reserve Oiler.
HMS   Her Majesty's Ship.
HNLHM Her (Netherlands) Majesty's Ship.
NL   Netherlands.
PRANG Puerto Rico Air National Guard.
USCGC U.S. Coast Guard cutter.
USCS   United States Customs Service.
USN   United States Navy.
USS   United States ship.

chairman, Antigua-Barbuda prime minister Vere Bird Sr., wrote to President Ronald Reagan protesting "attempts to extend domestic United States authority into neighboring countries of the region without regard to the sovereignty and independent legal systems of those countries."[34] And in a December 23, 1996, letter to President Bill Clinton on the shiprider dispute discussed earlier, CARICOM chairman Lester Bird, prime minister of Antigua-Barbuda, noted: "Our Governments are troubled by what appears to us to be the tactics of certain U.S. agencies to try to pressure Caribbean Governments to accede to Treaties and Agreements, without sufficiently taking into account our deep concern regarding important issues such as the sovereignty of our States and respect of our Institutions."

This is part of the drugs dilemma for Caribbean countries. Michael Morris puts it aptly: "The policy dilemma posed by the drug trade for small Caribbean states is that individually [and even collectively] they cannot control the drug trade, but that a U.S.-controlled, anti-drug strategy for the region may impinge on national sovereignty."[35] This impact on sovereignty affects the conception and pursuit of "the national interest." As James Rosenau states in a general context, politicians may still resort to the rhetoric of exclusionary nationalism, patriotism, and national interest in order to mobilize support on behalf of issues involving the integrity of the polity, but their actions will likely offset their verbal pronouncements and involve efforts to coordinate policies with foreign counterparts.[36]

As shown in earlier chapters, the threats that the national, regional, and international countermeasures are meant to address are interrelated, and hence all the more problematic. However, some issues stand out in the extent of complication, and thus require special mention when it comes to countermeasures. One such issue is money laundering.

---

34. Sanders, "The Drug Problem: Policy Options for Caribbean Countries," 232, and West Indian Commission, *Time for Action*, 348–49. See also Cox, "Patterson Against Drugs, for Sovereignty," and Becker, "Sovereignty or Survival."

35. Morris, *Caribbean Maritime Security*, 141.

36. Rosenau, *Multilateral Governance and the Nation-State System*, 16.

Money-Laundering Countermeasures

Combating money laundering is both costly and complicated. Countermeasures have been adopted at all levels. One dramatic measure at the national level was the revocation in March 1991 of 311 banking licenses in Montserrat. Changes were also made in the island's constitution, with responsibility for the financial sector shifted from local politicians to the governor of the dependency.[37]

Some countries have improved management of customs and excise departments, and of airports and seaports. Some have also sought to reduce invoicing abuses.[38] There have also been both voluntary and induced changes in banking and nonbanking business practices. In 1989, for instance, the Caymans ceased granting private banking licenses to individuals. The following year bankers there agreed to a code of conduct that calls for banks to refuse cash deposits of over U.S.$10,000. And the Bahamas, Trinidad and Tobago, and other countries have introduced "Know Your Customer" practices. Moreover, during 1996 Aruba, Belize, the Cayman Islands, and Jamaica passed legislation to tighten financial operations that are vulnerable to money laundering.

Countries also have MLATs with the United States dealing with intelligence sharing, technical assistance, and asset sharing. In 1996 these countries were the Bahamas and the United Kingdom, on behalf of Anguilla, the British Virgin Islands, the Cayman Islands, and the Turks and Caicos Islands. With regard to asset sharing, during 1994 several Caribbean countries received portions of assets from the United States: the Bahamas, U.S.$56,323; the Cayman Islands, U.S.$422,388; and the Netherlands Antilles, U.S.$22,500. Some of the bilateral countermeasures with the United States are also executed through special information-exchange agreements, such as that involving Guyana, signed in August 1992.[39]

---

37. Treaster, "On Tiny Isle of 300 Banks," and *Economist*, "Oh, My Brass Plate in the Sun."

38. See, for example, *Stabroek News*, "Drug Trafficking for Scrutiny in Customs Training Sessions," and *Trinidad and Tobago Mirror*, "US Customs Here to Weed out Smuggling."

39. Lohr, "Where the Money Washes Up," 52, and *INCSR* (1995), 486, 509.

Several countries have introduced new legislation that, ancillary to its primary focus on financial crimes or drugs, covers money laundering; others have revised extant legislation to deal with money laundering. For example, the Proceeds of Crime Act of Antigua-Barbuda, which was adopted in May 1993, declares at section 61(2):

> A person, who, after the commencement of this Act, engages in money laundering commits an indictable offense and is liable, on conviction, to
> > (a) a fine of $200,000 or imprisonment for a period of twenty years, or both, if he is a natural born person; or
> > (b) a fine of $500,000, if it is a body corporate.

As part of the criminalization of money laundering, section 61(3) of the same law specifies that a person will be considered as having engaged in money laundering if that person engages directly or indirectly in a transaction that involves money or property that is the proceeds of crime; or if the person receives, owns, conceals, disposes of, or brings into Antigua and Barbuda any money or other property that is the proceeds of crime, knowing that the money or other property was derived from some illegal act.

Part of the difficulty for all Caribbean countries in combating money laundering is the complicated nature of the subject, a complication magnified by the paucity of technical expertise and tangible resources to deal with the challenge. Agencies in many countries are learning of the need to rise above turf concerns and bureaucratic politics because combating money laundering requires collective, interagency, multisector action. Among agencies that would be involved in a typical national money-laundering task force are the customs and excise department, the tax or revenue department, the central bank, commercial and other banks, the postal administration, the attorney general's chambers, the police, the finance and foreign affairs ministries, and interest groups representing insurance, securities, real estate, and other nonbanking financial companies.

The subject of money laundering involves issues of banking, economics, finance, trade, management, and law, among other things. The legal area is usually the first line of defense, and largely for two reasons: because the rule of law is central to governance and because of mandates from the United Nations and the OAS, especially by the 1988 United Nations drug convention. However, for reasons mentioned earlier, making legal headway is easier said than done.

In explaining Trinidad and Tobago's difficulties with legal countermeasures, one banker there cited the number of laws that required revision: the Central Bank Act, the Banking Act, the Non-Banking Financial Institutions Act, the Credit Union and Cooperatives Act, the Insurance Act, the Agricultural Development Bank Act, the Exchange Control Act, the National Insurance Act, the Relative Pension Benefits Act, the Stock Exchange Act, the Unit Trust and Deposit Insurance Act, the Industrial Deposit Act, the Industrial Corporation Act, the Money Lending Act, the Post Office Act, and the Evidence Act. Added to this, action was needed to develop the legal and administrative framework to bring the Board of Inland Revenue and the courts into the picture.[40] Given the similarities in legal systems and administrative structures among Anglophone Caribbean countries, the requirements elsewhere in that subregion would be similar to Trinidad's. If this is part of the task for Trinidad and Tobago, a relatively sound country in economic, educational, and technological terms, one could well imagine the Herculean tasks that face countries such as Antigua-Barbuda, Belize, Guyana, and St. Kitts–Nevis.

The complex, transnational nature of money laundering, coupled with the financial, technical, and other limitations of Caribbean countries, necessitates regional countermeasures. Yet, while regional efforts are necessary, they are, for some of these very reasons, not sufficient. International action is also required. One important initiative that demonstrates the regional-international linkages is the CFATF.

The origins of the CFATF are traceable to the work of the Financial Action Task Force (FATF), formed following the summit of the European Community and the G-7 industrialized nations—Britain, Canada, Germany, France, Italy, Japan, and the United States—in Paris in July 1989. Apart from North America, the efforts of the FATF were to be concentrated on three regions: the Caribbean, cen-

---

40. Thompson, "Strategies to Combat Money Laundering and Predicate Crimes," 51.

tral and eastern Europe, and Asia. In April 1990, the FATF issued a report with forty recommendations for legal, financial, and other cooperation to combat money laundering. Generally, the recommendations dealt with weakening bank secrecy laws, criminalizing money laundering, expanding confiscation powers, monitoring and sharing transaction information, and strengthening bank supervision and law enforcement.

Shortly after the FATF report was issued, a conference was held in Aruba in June 1990 to examine money laundering in the Caribbean. That meeting was attended by fifteen countries from the Caribbean Basin, plus FATF countries with an interest in the Caribbean: Aruba, the Bahamas, Barbados, Bermuda, the British Virgin Islands, the Cayman Islands, Colombia, the Dominican Republic, Honduras, Jamaica, Mexico, the Netherlands Antilles, Panama, Venezuela, and Trinidad and Tobago, plus Britain, Canada, France, the Netherlands, and the United States. The Aruba meeting examined the forty FATF recommendations and produced nineteen that were applicable to the Caribbean. They pertained to expanding the scope of the crime of narcotics money laundering and predicate offenses, enlarging confiscation powers, supervising banks, record keeping and reporting, and technical and other assistance. The CFATF was created out of the Aruba meeting.

The work of the CFATF progressed with a May 1992 technical workshop held in Jamaica and a ministerial meeting the following November in the same country. The November 1992 meeting produced the Kingston Declaration on Money Laundering, which endorsed the 1988 United Nations Convention, the FATF and CFATF recommendations, and the OAS Model Regulations, which had been adopted on May 23, 1992, at the OAS General Assembly session in the Bahamas. Two key aspects of the Kingston Declaration were creation of a regional secretariat to coordinate the implementation of the various recommendations, and establishment of a CFATF steering committee to oversee the secretariat. The steering committee was installed the same year, and the secretariat was established in 1994 in Trinidad. Britain provided the first executive director for the secretariat, Tim Wren, a former financial intelligence officer with London's National Crime Intelligence Service.[41]

41. Coopers and Lybrand, *Narcotics Money Laundering in the Caribbean Region,*

Wren served until the end of January 1997, when he was succeeded by his deputy, Carlos Correa from the U.S. Department of Treasury. Correa was a senior attorney in the U.S. Department of Justice from 1980 to 1989, when he went to the Department of Treasury as director of international relations in the Enforcement Division. Between 1992 and 1994, he was director of regulations and rulings in the same division.

As a reflection of the increased scope of the money-laundering issue, the work of the CFATF has grown to include the participation of twenty-nine countries and territories in 1996: the original fifteen plus Anguilla, Belize, Dominica, Grenada, Guatemala, Guyana, Montserrat, Nicaragua, St. Kitts–Nevis, St. Vincent and the Grenadines, Suriname, and the Turks and Caicos. Cuba and Haiti are the only countries not participating, as Table 16 reveals.[42]

The CFATF secretariat concentrates on three sets of activities: self-assessment, mutual evaluation, and technical assistance and training. The self-assessment is done periodically through questionnaires and is intended to ascertain progress made in regard to recommendations and mandates, and to identify further needs. Mutual evaluation provides a more detailed examination of developments and identifies strengths and weaknesses. As one FATF official explained, the procedures (used by both the FATF and the CFATF) are modeled on the surveillance mechanisms used by the International Monetary Fund and the Organization for Economic Cooperation and Development—on-site visits by teams of examiners, followed by reports that are discussed at meetings of the teams.[43]

As of December 1996 mutual evaluation has been done in the Cayman Islands (January 1995) and Trinidad and Tobago (April 1995). The Netherlands Antilles and Aruba were evaluated during March 1995 by the FATF, with CFATF participation, as an extension of the report on the Netherlands. Antigua-Barbuda, the Bahamas,

4–6; Wren, "Multilateral Cooperation," 1–3; and telephone conversation with Wren on July 11, 1995. For the texts of the FATF and the CFATF recommendations, the May 1992 Kingston Workshop Report, the Kingston Declaration, and the OAS Model Regulations, see *Narcotics Money Laundering in the Caribbean Region.*

42. U.S. membership in the FATF covers Puerto Rico and the U.S. Virgin Islands, and France's covers French Guiana, Guadeloupe, and Martinique.

43. Griffiths, "The Financial Action Task Force Mutual Evaluation Procedure," 1.

Barbados, Costa Rica, the Dominican Republic, Jamaica, St. Kitts–Nevis, St. Lucia, and St. Vincent and the Grenadines were scheduled for evaluation during 1997 and 1998. Regarding technical assistance and training, the secretariat helps to coordinate programs sponsored by hemispheric and international bodies such as the OAS, the UNDCP, and the Commonwealth of Nations.

The work of the CFATF was initially funded by five FATF members: Britain, Canada, France, the Netherlands, and the United States. However, CFATF members agreed in November 1994 to assume this responsibility from 1996. This has been done. The financial difficulties of some member states have often constrained the fulfillment of these financial obligations. In an effort to have CFATF better execute its mandate, a new structure has been designed. It involves creating national anti-money-laundering committees to liaise with the secretariat, a monitoring group to oversee the CFATF work program, and two sets of meetings—a technical one to meet twice yearly and a ministerial one to meet annually to examine policy.

The CFATF's legal standing was transformed in October 1996, when twenty-one member states signed a Memorandum of Understanding in an effort to strengthen the organization's institutional capacity. The signing took place in Costa Rica at the October 9–10 ministerial meeting. Under the memorandum, CFATF member states agree to adopt and implement wide-ranging measures for the prevention and control of money laundering, taking antilaundering efforts beyond the declaratory standing of the Kingston Declaration mentioned earlier.[44]

Countermeasures have also been adopted within CARICOM. Following a mandate from the 1994 Barbados CARICOM summit, Trinidad and Tobago designed CARICOM's Guidelines on Money Laundering, which CARICOM central-bank governors began implementing from June 1995. As a matter of fact, some countries, including the Bahamas and the Cayman Islands, had already been adopting some of the measures outlined in the guidelines. The guidelines pertain to both banking and nonbanking financial institutions, making them and their employees liable when they conceal, dispose, disguise, transfer, or bring into the country money or

---

44. Interview with Tim Wren, October 1996. The CFATF membership was also increased, with the admission of Belize, Guatemala, and Nicaragua.

other property knowing, or having reasonable grounds for knowing, that the property is derived directly or indirectly from drug trafficking.

In issuing the guidelines each country is expected to identify the major laws applicable and the sanctions associated with conviction for violations of them. The guidelines deal with "Know Your Customer" procedures, record keeping, suspicious transactions, compliance, and training and education, among other things. Some of the provisions are as follows:

- Policies and procedures should be established for verifying the identity of all customers (i.e. both new and existing customers) of licensees—institutions that are granted banking or other licenses. Licensees shall request from new customers documentary evidence of identity that includes a photograph and signature. Documents should be retained on file for a minimum of five years after the banker-customer relationship ends. Obtain from all customers including signatories to corporate accounts, their full name, date of birth (or Certificate of Registration in the case of a company), nationality, and occupation (or the Memorandum and Articles of Association in the case of a company). Where practical, confirmation of identity for opening accounts should be sought from other financial institutions.
- Occupational income should be verified by the customer's employer or by audited financial statements for the previous three years in the case of self-employed persons and companies. Of corporate customers, obtain information concerning principal shareholders. This information should be verified through the registers of the company. For non-resident customers, secure references from their foreign bankers. A licensee should not enter into a relationship with a customer or provide any services to any person who refuses to provide evidence of identity.
- Licensees shall not keep anonymous accounts. Where accounts are opened or services provided by a licensee and there is suspicion that the customers are acting as intermediaries, the licensee should verify the true identity of the persons on whose behalf the account is opened or the transaction is conducted. If the licensee is not satisfied with the response of the customer it shall terminate all relations with that customer forthwith. Where licensees

provide nominee services or numbered accounts, steps must be taken to verify the true identity of the beneficiaries of such services or the holders of such accounts.

- Maintain for a minimum of five years all necessary records on transactions, both domestic and international, to facilitate compliance with requests for information from law enforcement authorities. These records should be made available to law enforcement authorities for criminal investigations and prosecutions. Licensees should properly document the background and purpose of all large, complex, and unusual transactions or patterns of transactions with no apparent economic or visibly lawful purpose.

- Where it is suspected that any transaction executed or to be executed by a licensee on behalf of a customer may form part of or constitute a suspicious transaction, the procedures established by the licensee for reporting such matters to the law enforcement authorities shall be instituted promptly. A suspicious transaction is one that is inconsistent with a customer's known legitimate business or personal activities, or with the normal business for that type of account.

- Licensees should designate one or more senior officials within their organization to carry out the functions of Compliance Officers. These officers will have responsibility for reviewing the initial findings of suspicious or unusual transactions. Where Compliance Officers consider the suspicions to be justified they shall report those suspicions to the law enforcement authorities. Compliance Officers shall operate as the liaison officers where the licensee is required to cooperate with law enforcement authorities. Their identity must be treated with the strictest confidence by employees.

- Licensees shall make all efforts to ensure that they hire and retain staff of the highest levels of integrity and competence, and continually update their staff records for this purpose. They should exercise extreme caution in their business dealings with persons including financial institutions from other countries, especially those countries with no legal provisions or insufficient legal provisions to counter money laundering.

- The internal and external auditors of licensees should test their policies, procedures, and systems for compliance with these guidelines. Semi-annual reports by the internal auditors should be submitted to the Board of Directors of the licensee and to the relevant central bank during the first two years of the operation of these guidelines. The report of the external auditors is to be submitted to the central bank annually.[45]

Some government officials are skeptical about some of the new surveillance and other practices being introduced. One top central-bank official voiced concern about central banks becoming investigative agencies over and above regular regulatory measures, and about the possible negative effects of some anti-money-laundering regimes on the solvency of financial institutions and, ultimately, on the economic health of countries. With regard to people making large deposits, he worried about casting veils of suspicion indiscriminately, since, for cultural and other reasons, some ethnic groups in the region interface infrequently with official banks, and when they do, they tend to make large deposits or withdrawals. Apart from concern that some countermeasures compromise revenue collection, a top customs official also flagged the issue of the physical security of customs agents. Several agents have been subjected to physical assault and death threats in Guyana following the introduction of some countermeasures there.[46]

Conclusion

Close observers of the Caribbean know that there is considerable "muddling through" in the design and implementation of narcotics countermeasures in the region. Various factors account for this: capability limitations, administrative lethargy, the rock-and-the-hard-place dilemma mentioned in Chapter 6, and the fact that decisions about many national programs, not to mention the regional

45. I am grateful for a copy of the Guidelines provided by Henry Jeffers, inspector of banks, Central Bank of Trinidad and Tobago, and for information provided by John Carrington on July 12, 1995.

46. Interviews with Assistant Comptroller Hubbard, July 1994, and a top official at the Trinidad and Tobago Central Bank, who requested anonymity, Port of Spain, July 8, 1994.

and international ones, do not lie with local elites (not that the deci-sion-making abilities of local elites are all superb). What is worse is the sense of fatalism in some places, expressed by several officials through assertions like "We can't win this War!" This is dangerous for several reasons: it adversely affects the psychological buoyancy of people involved in countermeasures; it contributes to greater cynicism in the general population of countries; and it emboldens drug operators, with the possibility that they might increase the scope of their operations in the region.

This chapter does not examine each and every narcotics counter-measure.[47] But it offers evidence that much is being done to combat drugs in the region. Of course, some possible options are "too hot to handle." For reasons not appropriately examined here, decrimi-nalization is one such option. All the policy makers interviewed op-posed this option, although some people on the front line of the drug fight felt that it warrants consideration. For all that is being done to combat drugs, given the magnitude of the problems and the vulnerability of the Caribbean to continued involvement, much more needs to be done. More needs to be done in *all* respects, in *all* countries, though some more than others in some areas. But for many people and governments, the spirit is willing, but the body is weak.

---

47. Other initiatives and operations not examined include Carpro+, an intelli-gence operation linking the Netherlands and the Dutch Caribbean, Centre Intermin-istériel de Formation Anti-Drogues (CIFAD, or Inter-Ministerial Drug Control Training Center), and the Joint Inter-Agency Task Force–East (JIATF-E), a U.S. orga-nization based in Key West, Florida.

Conclusion:
Prospects for Ending the Siege

The tension between the traditional role of national sovereignty and the need to move expeditiously against high-
level narcotics traffickers as well as other criminals will
preoccupy legislators, administrators, courts, academi-
cians, and economists for the foreseeable future.
                      —*International Handbook on Drug Control*

Caribbean countries would be better prepared for the future by strengthening international procedures and procedures to combat drug trafficking, protect states under
military assault from drug trafficking, help to remove government officials who cooperate with drug traffickers, and
more generally protect constitutional government.
                                      —Jorge Domínguez

In applying the geonarcotics framework developed in the Introduction the preceding seven chapters demonstrate that the narcotics
phenomenon involves a dynamic interplay among four factors:
drugs, geography, power, and politics. The chapters also illustrate
that

- understanding the Caribbean drug dilemma requires going beyond a single level of analysis;
- there is no uniformity in drug operations and their consequences;
- the dilemma is multifaceted, with internal and external aspects;
- both state and nonstate actors are involved in the drug phenomenon, and they engage in both conflict and cooperation;

- the security implications are varied, with military, political, economic, and social dimensions; and
- all the threats and challenges presented by drugs are not amenable to military countermeasures.

The only aspect of the Introduction's framework not developed and validated in the preceding chapters is that pertaining to environmental security. This is because the environmental security threat exists at a very low level of significance in the Caribbean. Two reasons explain this: one, the environmental drug threat is linked primarily with cocaine and heroin production; two, neither of these drugs is produced in the Caribbean. But this is not to suggest that Caribbean drug production has no environmental consequences. Deforestation is the most important of these. As noted in the Introduction, its consequences include soil loss through erosion, extinction of genetic sources, wood and lumber shortage, and wildlife reduction.

Deforestation is problematic for Jamaica, Grenada, Guyana, St. Vincent and the Grenadines, and other countries with high levels of marijuana production. It is perhaps no coincidence that the Food and Agricultural Organization has found that seven of the ten countries with the highest deforestation rates in the world are in Latin America and the Caribbean. Three of the seven are in the Caribbean: Jamaica, with an annual average loss of 7.2 percent between 1981 and 1990; St. Lucia, with a 5.2 percent annual decline; and Haiti, where the decrease is 4.8 percent per year.[1] Of course, deforestation in these and other Caribbean countries is not solely attributable to marijuana cultivation.

Two general conclusions can be offered at this point. First, the security impact of drugs is multidimensional and variable. Notwithstanding the scope and gravity of drug operations—production, consumption-abuse, trafficking, and money laundering—it is not these things alone that explain the threat related to drugs. The implications and consequences extend to arms trafficking, corruption, crime, garment exports, tourism, and resource allocation, among other things. In other words, the drug phenomenon has an impact

    1. Silva, "Trees in Trouble."

not only on things military but also on things political, economic, and social—on security in the nontraditional sense. Moreover, drug operations and the problems they precipitate are regionwide, but not uniform; and they are problematic for the entire region, but not manifested the same way throughout the region.

The multidimensionality of drug operations and their consequences is itself a reason for countermeasures to be commensurately multidimensional. Yet, as was shown in Chapter 7, the countermeasures need to be more than just multidimensional. They also have to be multilevel—national, regional, and international—because drug operations and many of the problems they precipitate are both national and transnational. Countermeasures also require multiactor responses, for the additional reason that no single Caribbean nation has the necessary resources to meet the threats and challenges involved. Hence the need for partnerships involving non-Caribbean states as well as nongovernmental organizations (NGOs), international governmental organizations (IGOs) and international nongovernmental organizations (INGOs).

The second general conclusion is that the nature, scope, and dynamics of drugs undermine the sovereignty of Caribbean countries. Sovereignty, however, is under siege not only because of the pursuits of drug operators. It is also compromised by the dynamics of interaction of Caribbean states with powerful states, and with IGOs and INGOs, some of which are more powerful than some Caribbean countries. These dynamics have a deleterious effect largely because the critical needs of Caribbean states and their subordinate status in the international arena hinder their capacity to bargain meaningfully in the design and implementation of many countermeasures. Often they go through the motions of bargaining, in effect making a pretense to sovereignty.

Sovereignty is, nevertheless, a prized element of nationhood, partly because the Caribbean is a region still largely in the infancy of independent statehood. Sovereignty is also part of the schema for dealing with drugs and other issues. Prime Minister Patterson of Jamaica stated this clearly: "We will work with other law enforcement agencies in a manner consistent with our own constitution, international conventions, and treaty obligations. We are spearheading the combat against drug trafficking because our own enlightened self-interest clearly dictates that we should. *But we have to do so compatible with our sovereignty as a nation.*"[2] Barbados foreign minister Billie Miller was even more pointed in her remarks before the United Nations General Assembly in fall 1996: "We will not stand accused of not cooperating with our partners, but neither will we allow our hard-fought sovereignty to be sacrificed in the tug-of-war between the moral and societal imperative to curtail [drug] demand and the need to reduce [drug] supply."[3] This is a sentiment held throughout the region.

Yet, as an interdependence issue, the matter of drugs is one that spans national boundaries and cannot be resolved merely through national- or local-level action. There is abundant evidence that the traditional approach to sovereignty cannot cope with interdependence issues, especially if the absolute, "chunk" approach to sovereignty is adopted. As two scholars have rightly asserted: "Whether the power structure of sovereign states ever accurately reflected textbook characteristics, sovereignty is no longer sovereign; the world has outgrown it. The exclusivity and inviolability of state sovereignty are increasingly mocked by global interdependence."[4]

James Rosenau makes an important point on this matter:

> If the authority and competence of states have undergone diminution, it follows that their sovereignty is decreasingly a protector of boundaries and a source of swagger. . . . Most countries have moved too far down the interdependence road to reinstate effective border controls over the movement of people, goods, ideas, and currencies without incurring costs deemed too high to bear. . . . Their voices claiming sovereignty are largely mute, having been replaced by those calling for accommodation and cooperation with counterparts abroad. In the words of the UN's secretary general, "the time of absolute sovereignty has long passed."[5]

2. Jamaica, Office of the Prime Minister, *Speaking Notes for the Hon. P. J. Patterson*, 9–10.

3. Bohning, "Anti-Drug Pacts Founder Between U.S., Caribbean."

4. Chopra and Weiss, "Sovereignty Is No Longer Sacrosanct," 6.

5. Rosenau, *Multilateral Governance and the Nation-State System*, 14.

Critical Considerations

The above reasons make it important to consider the prospects for salvaging sovereignty in the Caribbean. Hence, it is appropriate to ask the question, What can be done to end the drug siege?

A preliminary observation is warranted: ending the drug siege will not bring full restoration of "lost sovereignty." This is partly because there are other interdependence issues, including migration, that have already altered the correlates of power held by domestic elites in ways that affect both formal-legal and positive sovereignty. Moreover, the resolution of the drug dilemma will not lead to the acquisition by governments of the means fully to enjoy positive sovereignty—the economic, technical, military, and other capabilities to declare, implement, and enforce meaningful public policy.

The prospects for ending the drug siege rest on several factors. These are not presented here in any strict order of importance. As a matter of fact, it is better to view them as part of a matrix rather than as a hierarchical list. One factor pertains to capabilities— money, manpower, training, and technology. As noted in Chapter 7 and earlier, because of the multidimensionality of drugs, counter-measures also need to be multidimensional. However, the economic difficulties of Caribbean countries inhibit the independent fulfill-ment of their needs, which brings us to the second factor: external support.

External support is needed from two basic sources: from other countries, both within and outside the Americas, and from nonstate actors—IGOs, INGOs, and MNCs. The latter support is required particularly to compensate for reduced aid from states. One of the realities of the post–Cold War world is policy reevaluation by big and middle powers once deeply engaged in the region either be-cause they considered the Caribbean to be important to them or because the Caribbean states placed importance on them. The noteworthy countries are the United States, Britain, the Nether-lands, and Venezuela. The reprioritizing by these countries is the result of several factors, sometimes acting in combination. These include leadership changes that cause policy reevaluation, budget-ary constraints, economic recession, the demand by domestic con-stituencies for more attention to the "home front," aid reallocation, and shifting foreign-policy focus. In tangible terms, these mean reduced aid, readjustments in preferential trading arrangements, reduction in foreign-investment guarantees, and diplomatic downgrading of Caribbean countries.

For example, the British withdrawal of their military garrison in Belize between 1993 and 1995 has been prompted by both budgetary difficulties and a review of British foreign and security policy toward Central America and the Caribbean. This has had a dual effect: increased Belizean vulnerability to territorial and political sovereignty violation by Guatemala, and reduced Belizean capacity to offer credible responses to drug operations. When the United States slashed its 1990 aid package to Jamaica to augment its aid to Poland, more important than the sum of money involved— U.S.$20 million—was the symbolism of the action. Moreover, in May 1994 the U.S. State Department explained that it planned to close embassies in Antigua-Barbuda and Grenada because of the strategic insignificance of those countries and partly "to shift resources to Eastern Europe and the former Soviet Union." It took congressional pressure, especially from the Black Caucus, for a reversal of the decision in relation to Grenada. The embassy there will remain open—for the time being.[6]

The third factor, directly related to the second, is the continued nurture of political relations with states that are critical bilateral partners for countermeasures in the Caribbean, including the United States, Britain, Canada, France, and the Netherlands. These countries are important in bilateral terms, but they are also the largest contributors to IGO assistance to the region, especially by the United Nations International Drug Control Program (UNDCP), the Caribbean Financial Action Task Force (CFATF) and the Inter-American Drug Abuse Control Commission (CICAD). Thus, especially in light of the second factor, Caribbean states will have to bend over backward to accommodate the interests of these states in both bilateral and multilateral dealings.

The tactics and strategy of drug operators amount to a fourth factor that would influence the lifting of the siege. Decisions by South American cocaine producers about the use of the Caribbean for

---

6. See Holmes, "Less Strategic Now, Grenada Is to Lose American Embassy," and idem, "U.S. Embassy for Grenada."

trafficking would be important. Such decisions themselves would be influenced by North American and European demand, cocaine- and heroin-production levels, and the success of eradication and interdiction countermeasures, among other things. Decisions about marijuana production and trafficking, by both Caribbean and South American operators, would also be part of the picture. An allied factor—number five—is demand reduction. Though it re- quires no belaboring, it needs to be stated that ending the drug siege is tied to demand reduction—within the Caribbean, in North America, and in Europe.

A sixth factor is the political will of Caribbean political elites to make tough decisions about strategies and tactics for coping with the dilemma. One can hardly disagree with the suggestion that "[t]he cornerstone of any successful antidrug strategy is political will. A country can have state-of-the-art antidrug hardware and en- forcement units and still not cripple the drug trade—unless its gov- ernment is willing to weather the short-term political backlash that effective antidrug measures inevitably trigger."[7] The issue of politi- cal will is tied to a seventh factor: the nature and gravity of other socioeconomic problems that compete for already scarce resources. As shown in Chapter 6, there are links between drugs and these matters. Poverty, production, exports, and other socioeconomic headaches have both domestic and international dimensions. Thus, whether and how decisions about them affect narcotics coun- termeasures involve not only domestic decisions and developments but also international ones.

International economic developments would, therefore, form an important, although indirect, factor—factor number eight. The im- pact of the global recession on Caribbean exports like bananas, sugar, and bauxite matters. Increased marijuana production and export could very well result as a way to cope with depressed ex- ports in the formal economy and the consequent increase in relative economic deprivation. Herein lie some of the implications of the United States' joining South and Central American banana produc- ers in seeking an end to the European Union's banana-market guarantees to the Caribbean.[8]

---

7. *INCSR* (1996), 4.
8. See Whitefield, "Caribbean Ripe for a Banana War."

Cooperation Challenges

The point has been made elsewhere that an underlying assumption of regional security cooperation in the Caribbean is the commonality of regional threats, or at least the perception of such threats by the relevant political and military elites.[9] Countries also cooperate because of capability limitations. Money, manpower, weapons, technology, and training and other resources are short everywhere in the Caribbean. However, the assessment of common threats and the existence of capability limitations should not mask the reality that there are challenges to cooperation. One challenge relates to capability. This challenge does not arise merely because of the actual constraints and limitations with regard to money, equipment, training, and the like. It does so because inherent in the capability disparities of cooperating states is the need for those with fewer deficiencies to give relatively more to the collective effort.

This is not always easily achieved. Sometimes the political elites of countries are unwilling to commit resources to the cooperative effort when it is unclear that there will be commensurate returns. Many times political leaders are unable to see the national-interest value in participating in some ventures. Paradoxically, however, those ventures themselves may be jeopardized because of capability dilemmas that are resolvable only by the reluctant or recalcitrant partners. And often domestic considerations, such as changes in the national leadership, public opinion, and timing, may make it difficult for the country with the least deficiency to honor earlier pledges.

Beyond the capability challenge is a sovereignty challenge. Few scholars (or statesmen) would deny that for reasons related to power deficiencies and the nature and scope of some of the threats involved, the traditional notion of sovereignty in the Caribbean is untenable. Yet, as was noted earlier, sovereignty is cherished by Caribbean states. The larger states in the antidrug partnerships therefore need to be mindful of sovereignty sensibilities, in relation to both the decision-making and the execution sides of cooperation. One further challenge that is a perennial bugbear in some places pertains to bureaucratic politics. Whether liked or not, jurisdic-

9. Griffith, *Caribbean Security on the Eve of the 21st Century*, 61–63.

tional turf battles and coordination difficulties will continue between army and coast guard/navy, army and police, army
intelligence units and police intelligence outfits, and so forth. Some
of these battles and difficulties can undermine security initiatives
within a single country. Thus, the potential dangers when several
countries and agencies are involved are even greater. All countries
and agencies involved should be constantly mindful of these dangers. Difficult though it is, line and staff operators should work to
subordinate the ego and interest of an individual bureaucracy or
service to the larger interest: combating drugs.

Conclusion

This book provides ample evidence that the drug phenomenon in
the Caribbean does not constitute a security matter for the region
simply because there is drug production, consumption-abuse, trafficking, and money laundering, no matter how these have grown in
scope and volume. It does so essentially for four reasons:

- these operations have multiple consequences and implications,
  including increased crime, systemic and institutionalized corruption, arms trafficking, and multiple economic effects;
- the operations and their consequences have increased in scope
  and gravity over the last decade;
- they have dramatic impact on agents and agencies of national security and good governance, in military, political, and economic
  ways; and
- both the formal-legal and positive sovereignty of Caribbean countries have been tested and infringed, by both state and nonstate
  actors, because of drugs.

The problems, travails, and challenges presented by drugs in the
Caribbean highlight the geographic, economic, political, and military vulnerability of the region. It is evident that ending the drug
siege is easier said than done. Indeed, many people, including Raymond Kendall, head of INTERPOL, feel that efforts to eliminate the

global drug threat completely are futile.[10] However, ending the siege in the Caribbean is something that people and governments both within and outside the region can ill afford not to pursue continuously. The "war on drugs" will be a long "war." And it has to be a "total war" and a "collective war." The words of Caribbean poet Martin Carter, first written in 1954 in *Poems of Resistance,* capture the exigency of the situation:

> Like a jig
> Shakes the loom
> Like a web
> is spun the pattern
> All are involved!
> All are consumed!

---

10. See *Stabroek News,* "Interpol Chief Says Drugs Trade Can't Be Stopped."

Appendix A: Model Caribbean-U.S. Counternarcotics Treaty

AGREEMENT BETWEEN
THE GOVERNMENT OF THE UNITED STATES OF AMERICA
AND
THE GOVERNMENT OF
THE REPUBLIC OF TRINIDAD AND TOBAGO
CONCERNING MARITIME COUNTER-DRUG OPERATIONS

Preamble

The Government of the United States of America and the Government of the Republic of Trinidad and Tobago (hereinafter, the "Parties");

Bearing in mind the special nature of the problem of illicit maritime drug traffic;

Having regard to the urgent need for international cooperation in suppressing illicit maritime drug traffic, which is recognized in the 1961 Single Convention on Narcotic Drugs and its 1972 Protocol, in the 1971 Convention on Psychotropic Substances, and in the 1988 United Nations Convention Against Illicit Traffic in Narcotic Drugs and Psychotropic Substances; and

Desiring to promote greater cooperation between the Parties in combating illicit maritime drug traffic;

Have agreed as follows:

Nature and Scope of Agreement

1.   The Parties shall cooperate in combating illicit maritime drug traffic to the fullest extent possible, consistent with available law-enforcement resources and related priorities.

2.   Maritime counter-drug operations in Trinidad and Tobago waters are the responsibility of, and subject to the authority of, the Government of the Republic of Trinidad and Tobago.

3.   In the Agreement, unless the context otherwise requires:

a. Trinidad and Tobago waters means the territorial sea, archipelagic waters, and internal waters of Trinidad and Tobago, and the air space over such waters; and

b. Law-enforcement vessels include any embarked aircraft.

Shiprider Program and Enforcement in and over
Trinidad and Tobago Waters

4.   The parties shall establish a joint law-enforcement shiprider program between Trinidad and Tobago law-enforcement authorities and the United States Coast Guard (hereafter "Coast Guard"). Each Party may designate a coordinator to organize its program activities and to identify the vessels and officials involved in the program to the other Party.

5.   The Government of the Republic of Trinidad and Tobago may designate qualified law-enforcement shipriders. Subject to Trinidad and Tobago law, these shipriders may, in appropriate circumstances:

a. Embark on United States Coast Guard and Navy vessels with Coast Guard law-enforcement detachments embarked (hereafter, "U.S. vessels");

b. Authorize the pursuit, by the U.S. vessels on which they are embarked, of suspect vessels fleeing into Trinidad and Tobago waters;

c. Authorize the U.S. vessels on which they are embarked to conduct counter-drug patrols in Trinidad and Tobago waters;

d. Enforce the laws of Trinidad and Tobago in Trinidad and Tobago waters, or seaward therefrom in the exercise of the right of hot pursuit or otherwise in accordance with international law; and

e. Authorize the Coast Guard to assist in the enforcement of the laws of Trinidad and Tobago.

6.   The Government of the United States of America may designate qualified Coast Guard law-enforcement officials to act as law-enforcement shipriders. Subject to United States law, these shipriders may, in appropriate circumstances:

a. Embark on Government of the Republic of Trinidad and Tobago vessels;

b. Advise and assist Trinidad and Tobago law-enforcement officials in the conduct of boardings of vessels to enforce the laws of Trinidad and Tobago;

c. Enforce, seaward of the territorial sea of Trinidad and Tobago, the laws of the United States where authorized to do so; and

d. Authorize the Trinidad and Tobago vessels on which they are embarked to assist in the enforcement of the laws of the United States seaward of the territorial sea of Trinidad and Tobago.

7.   When a shiprider is embarked on the other Party's vessel, and the enforcement action being carried out is pursuant to the shiprider's authority, any search or seizure of property, any detention of a person, and any use of force pursuant to this Agreement, whether or not involving weapons, shall be carried out by the shiprider, except as follows:

a. Crew members of the other Party's vessel may assist in any such action if expressly requested to do so by the shiprider and only to the extent and in the manner requested. Such request may only be made, agreed to, and acted upon in accordance with the applicable laws and policies of both parties; and

b. Such crew members may use force in self-defense, in accordance with the applicable laws and policies of their Government.

8.   The Government of the United States of America shall not conduct counter-drug operations in Trinidad and Tobago waters without the permission of the Government of the Republic of Trinidad and Tobago, granted by this Agreement or otherwise. This Agreement constitutes permission by the Government of the Republic of Trinidad and Tobago for United States counter-drug operations in any of the following circumstances:

a. An embarked Trinidad and Tobago shiprider so authorizes;

b. A suspect vessel or aircraft, encountered seaward of the territorial sea of Trinidad and Tobago flees into Trinidad and Tobago waters and is pursued therein by a U.S. vessel with a Trinidad and Tobago shiprider embarked, in which case the suspect vessel may be boarded and searched, and, if the evidence warrants, detained pending disposition instructions from Trinidad and Tobago authorities; and

c. A Trinidad and Tobago shiprider is unavailable to embark on a U.S. vessel, in which case the U.S. vessel may enter Trinidad and Tobago waters in order to investigate any suspect aircraft or board and search any suspect vessel other than a Trinidad and Tobago flag vessel, and, if the evidence warrants, detain any such vessel pending disposition instructions from Trinidad and Tobago authorities.

Nothing in this Agreement precludes the Government of the Republic of Trinidad and Tobago from otherwise expressly authorizing United States counter-drug operations in Trinidad and Tobago waters or involving Trinidad and Tobago flag vessels or aircraft suspected of illicit traffic.

9.   The Government of the Republic of Trinidad and Tobago shall permit aircraft of the Government of the United States of America (hereafter, "U.S. aircraft") when engaged in law-enforcement operations or operations in support of law-enforcement agencies to:

a. Overfly the territory and waters of Trinidad and Tobago; and

b. Order aircraft suspected of trafficking in illegal drugs to land in Trinidad and Tobago.

The Parties shall, in the interest of flight safety, institute procedures for notifying appropriate Trinidad and Tobago authorities of such overflight activity by U.S. aircraft.

Operations Seaward of the Territorial Sea

10.   Except as expressly provided herein, this Agreement does not apply to or limit boardings of vessels conducted by either Party seaward of any nation's territorial sea, whether based on the right of visit, the rendering of assistance to persons, vessels, and property in distress or peril, the consent of the vessel master, or an authorization from the flag State to take law-enforcement action.

11.   Whenever Coast Guard officials encounter a Trinidad and Tobago flag vessel, located seaward of any nation's territorial sea and suspected of illicit traffic, this Agreement constitutes an authorization of the Government of the Republic of Trinidad and Tobago for the boarding and search of the suspect vessel and the persons found on board by such officials. If evidence of illicit traffic is found, Coast Guard officials may detain the vessel and persons on board pending expeditious disposition instructions from the Government of the Republic of Trinidad and Tobago.

Jurisdiction over Detained Vessels

12.   In all cases arising in Trinidad and Tobago waters, or concerning Trinidad and Tobago flag vessels seaward of any nation's territorial sea, the Government of the Republic of Trinidad and Tobago shall have the primary right to exercise jurisdiction over a detained vessel and/or persons on board (including seizure, forfeiture, arrest, and prosecution), provided, however, that the Government of the Republic of Trinidad and Tobago may, subject to its Constitution and the laws, waive its primary right to exercise jurisdiction and authorize the enforcement of United States law against the vessel and/or persons on board.

Implementation

13.   Counter-drug operations pursuant to this Agreement shall be carried out only against vessels and aircraft used for commercial or private purposes and suspected of illicit maritime drug traffic, including vessels and aircraft without nationality.

14.   A Party conducting a boarding and search pursuant to this Agreement shall promptly notify the other Party of the results thereof.

15.   Each party shall ensure that its law-enforcement officials, when conducting boardings and searches pursuant to this Agreement, act in accordance with its applicable national laws and policies and with international law and accepted international practices.

16.   Boardings and searches of vessels pursuant to this agreement shall be carried out by uniformed officials from ships or aircraft clearly marked and identified as being on Government service. The boarding and search team may carry personal arms.

17.   All use of force by a Party pursuant to this Agreement shall be in strict accordance with applicable laws and policies of the respective Government and shall in all cases be the minimum reasonably necessary under the circumstances. Nothing in this Agreement shall impair the exercise of the inherent right of self-defense by law-enforcement or other officials of either Party.

18.   To facilitate implementation of this Agreement, each Party shall ensure that the other Party is fully informed concerning its applicable laws and policies, particularly those pertaining to the use of force. Each Party has the corresponding responsibility to ensure that all of its officials engaging in law-enforcement operations pursuant to this Agreement are knowledgeable concerning the applicable laws and policies of both Parties.

19.   Assets seized in consequence of any operation undertaken in Trinidad and Tobago waters pursuant to this Agreement shall be disposed of in accordance with the laws of Trinidad and Tobago. Assets seized in consequence of any operation undertaken seaward of the territorial sea of Trinidad and Tobago pursuant to this Agreement shall be disposed of in accordance with the laws of the seizing Party. To the extent permitted by its laws and upon such terms as it deems appropriate, a Party may, in any case, transfer forfeited assets or proceeds of their sale to the other Party.

20.   In case a questions arises in connection with implementation of this Agreement, either Party may request consultations to resolve the matter. If any loss or injury is suffered as a result of any action taken by the law-enforcement or other officials of one Party in contravention of this Agreement, or any improper or unreasonable action is taken by a Party pursuant thereto, the Parties shall meet at the request of either Party to resolve the matter and decide any questions relating to compensation.

21.   Nothing in the Agreement is intended to alter the rights and privileges due any individual in any legal proceeding.

Entry into Force and Duration

22.   This Agreement shall enter into force upon signature by both Parties.

23.   This Agreement may be terminated at any time by either party upon written notification to the other Party through the diplomatic channel. Such termination shall take effect one year from the date of notification.

24.   This Agreement shall continue to apply after termination with respect to any administrative or judicial proceedings arising out of actions taken pursuant to this Agreement.

IN WITNESS WHEREOF, the undersigned, being duly authorized by their respective Governments, have signed this Agreement.

DONE at Port of Spain, this 4th day of March, 1996, in duplicate.

FOR THE GOVERNMENT OF THE   FOR THE GOVERNMENT OF THE
UNITED STATES OF AMERICA: REPUBLIC OF TRINIDAD AND TOBAGO:

Warren Christopher   Basdeo Panday
[Secretary of State]   [Prime Minister]

Appendix B:
Caribbean Counternarcotics
Who's Who

NATIONAL AGENCIES

Country	Agency	Agency Head	Contact Data
Anguilla	National Council on Drug Abuse	Mr. Stanley Mussington Chairman	Ministry of Social Services and Land The Valley, Anguilla TEL: (809) 497-2032 FAX: (809) 497-3761
Antigua-Barbuda	National Drug Awareness Committee	Hon. Sam Aymer Chairman	National Drug Council Ministry of Health & Home Affairs Cecil Charles Building Cross Street St. John's, Antigua TEL: (268) 462-4601 FAX: (268) 462-5003
		Mr. Wrenford Ferrance Special Adviser to the Prime Minister on Drugs and Money Laundering	Office of the Prime Minister Queen Elizabeth Highway St. John's, Antigua TEL: (268) 462-4956 FAX: (268) 462-3225
Aruba	Coordination Office for Drug Control	Mr. Eric Nassy National Drug Coordinator	Coordination Office for Drug Control Ministry of Justice J.E. Irausquinplein 2-A Oranjestad, Aruba TEL: (297) 8-34554 FAX: (297) 8-34101

Country	Agency	Agency Head	Contact Data
Bahamas	National Drug Council	Mr. William Weeks Chairman	National Drug Council Ministry of Health and the Environment PO Box N-3729 Nassau, The Bahamas TEL: (242) 325-4633 FAX: (242) 322-7788
Barbados	National Council of Substance Abuse	Mr. Danny Gill Acting Chairman	National Council on Substance Abuse National Drug Resource Center Trents St. James, Barbados TEL: (246) 432-0509/0590 FAX: (246) 432-0267
	National Drug Resource Center	Mrs. Tessa Chaderton-Shaw Manager	Same as above
Belize	National Drug Abuse Control Council	Hon. Elito Urbina Chairman	Belize National Drug Abuse Council 54 Freetown Road Belize City, Belize TEL: (501-2) 31-125/31-143 FAX: (501-2) 31-121
Bermuda	National Drug Commission	Ms. Eugenie Simmons Chief Executive Officer	National Drug Commission Global House 43 Church Street Hamilton HM 12, Bermuda TEL: (809) 292-3049 FAX: (809) 295-2066
British Virgin Islands	National Drug Advisory Council	Dr. Orlando Smith Chairman	National Drug Advisory Council Road Town, Tortola British Virgin Islands TEL: (809) 494-3743 FAX: (809) 494-3753
Cayman Islands	National Drug Council	Mr. Douglas Barzey Executive Director	Drug Abuse Prevention and Rehabilitation Government Administration Building Grand Cayman, Cayman Islands TEL: (809) 949-7900 ext 2319 FAX: (809) 949-7544

Country	Agency	Agency Head	Contact Data
Cuba	Ministerio de Justicia	Dra. Zenaida Osorio Zizcaino Vice-Ministra Primera	Ministerio de Justicia Calle O No. 216 entre 23 y 25 Vedado Ciudad Havana, Cuba TEL: (53) 32-4888/6319 FAX: (53) 33-3164
Dominica	Advisory Council on the Misuse of Drugs	Dr. Robert Nasiiro Chairman	Government Headquarters Kennedy Avenue Roseau Commonwealth of Dominica TEL: (809) 448-2401 ext. 260/357 FAX: (809) 448-6086
	National Drug Prevention Unit	Mr. Leo Casimir Director	
Dominican Republic	Dirección Nacional de Control de Drogas	Dr. Manuel Herrera Director	Dirección Nacional de Control de Drogas Programa de Prevención del Uso Indebido de Drogas Ave. Masimo Gomez #70 Santo Domingo Dominican Republic TEL: (809) 221-4166 FAX: (809) 221-6551
Grenada	Grenada National Drug Avoidance Committee	Mr. Evelyn Cenac Chairman Mr. Dave Alexander Drug Avoidance Officer	Grenada National Drug Avoidance Committee Drug Avoidance Secretariat Ministry of Education Young Street St. George's, Grenada TEL: (809) 440-2737/ 2738/7911 FAX: (809) 440-6650
Guadeloupe	Direction Regional des Douanes	M. Jean-Roger Foulon Directeur	Direction Regional des Douanes De la Guadeloupe Chemin du Stade Félix Eboué 97100 Basse-Terre, Guadeloupe TEL: (590) 81-1822 FAX: (590) 81-3392

Country	Agency	Agency Head	Contact Data
Guyana	National Anti-Narcotic Commission	H.E. Mr. Samuel A. Hinds Chairman Lt. Col. Fabian Liverpool Secretary	National Drug Law Enforcement Committee c/o Ministry of Home Affairs 6 Brickdam Georgetown, Guyana TEL: (592-2) 56-221/ 61-717 FAX: (592-2) 62-740
Haiti	Ministerie de la Justice	M. Max Antoine Ministerie de la Justice	Ministerie de la Justice Ave. Charles Sumner Boite Postale #15395, Petion Ville Port-au-Prince, Haiti TEL: (509) 450 0624/ 459 852 FAX: (509) 450 474
Jamaica	National Council on Drug Abuse	Dr. Charles Thesiger Chairman Mr. Michael Tucker Executive Director	National Council on Drug Abuse 2-6 Melmac Avenue Kingston, Jamaica TEL: (809) 926-9002/ 9004/3028 FAX: (809) 960-1820
Montserrat	National Drug Committee	Mr. Ronnie Cooper Chairman	National Drug Committee Ministry of Health Glendon Hospital PO Box 24 Plymouth, Montserrat TEL: (809) 491-2552/4 FAX: (809) 491-3131
Netherlands Antilles	National Office for National Coordination on Addiction Affairs	Mr. Siegfried Victorina Director	Trompstraat Willemstad Curaço Netherlands Antilles TEL: (5999) 650-555 FAX: (5999) 650-585
Puerto Rico	Department of Health	Dr. Carmen Feliciano Secretary of Health	Department of Health Call Box 7184 San Juan, Puerto Rico 09936 TEL: (787) 274-7600/7602 FAX: (787) 250-6547

Country	Agency	Agency Head	Contact Data
St. Kitts-Nevis	The Advisory Council on the Misuse of Drugs	Dr. Mervyn Laws Chairman	The Advisory Council on the Misuse of Drugs Church Street Basseterre, St. Kitts-Nevis TEL: (809) 465-2837
St. Lucia	National Committee for the Control and Prevention of Drug Abuse	Hon. Stevenson King Chairman	Drug Abuse Secretariat National Committee for the Control and Prevention of Drug Abuse Ministry of Health Waterfront Castries, Saint Lucia TEL: (758) 453-6316 FAX: (758) 453-7352
St. Vincent and the Grenadines	Advisory Council on the Misuse of Drugs	Mr. Carl Browne Chairman	The Advisory Council on the Misuse of Drugs Ministry of Health and The Environment Kingstown Saint Vincent and the Grenadines TEL: (809) 457-1745 FAX: (809) 457-2684
Suriname	National Council for Drugs Control	Mr. Prim Ritoe Chairman	National Council for Drugs Control Cultuurtuinlaan 1 Paramaribo, Suriname TEL: (597) 411-011/ 477-072
Trinidad and Tobago	Strategic Services Agency	Mr. Lancelot Selman Director	Strategic Services Agency 17 Richmond Street Port of Spain Trinidad and Tobago TEL: (809) 624-4416/627-0327 FAX: (809) 627-0326
	National Alcohol and Drug Abuse Prevention Program	Hon. Manohar Ramsaran Chairman	Ministry of Social Development National Alcohol and Drug Abuse Prevention Program Secretariat First Floor, Agostini Insurance Bldg.
	Technical Advisory Committee on	Dr. Peter Lewis Chairman	

Country	Agency	Agency Head	Contact Data
	Alcohol and Drug Abuse		No. 119 Henry Street Port of Spain Trinidad and Tobago TEL: (809) 627-3506/3527 FAX: (809) 627-4471
Turks and Caicos	National Drug Council	Rev. Desmond Coverley Chairman	Ministry of Education, Youth and Sports National Drug Council Grand Turk, Turks and Caicos TEL: (809) 946-1201 FAX: (809) 946-1202
U.S. Virgin Islands	Department of Health	Dr. Jose F. Poblete Commissioner of Health	Department of Health Commissioner of Health 3500 Richmond Christiansted, USVI 00821 TEL: (809) 774-0117 FAX: (809) 777-4001

REGIONAL, HEMISPHERIC, AND INTERNATIONAL AGENCIES

Agency	Agency Head	Contact Data
Caribbean Customs Law Enforcement Council (CCLEC)	Mr. Euan Stewart Permanent Secretary	Customs House Jeremie Street Castries, St. Lucia TEL: (758) 453-2556 FAX: (758) 453-2563
Caribbean Financial Action Task Force (CFATF)	Mr. A. Carlos Correa Executive Director	CFATF Secretariat 17 Richmond Street Port of Spain Trinidad and Tobago TEL: (809) 623-9667 FAX: (809) 624-1297 E-mail: Cfatf@opus.co.tt Home page: www.opus.co.tt/cfatf
Centre Interministériel de Formation Anti-drogue (CIFAD)	M. Christian Capdeville Directeur	Centre Interministériel de Formation Anti-drogue 31, Rue du Professeur Garcin 97200 Fort-de-France, Martinique TEL: (596) 636-600 FAX: (596) 638-518

Agency	Agency Head	Contact Data

European Union (EU)	Mr. Michel Amiot
	Drugs Control Adviser
	for the Caribbean
		European Union
		  Delegation
		P.O. Box 654C
		Hincks Street
		Bridgetown, Barbados
		TEL: (246) 228-8558
		FAX: (246) 228-8033
		E-mail:
		  Eurodrugs
		  @sunbeach.net

Inter-American Drug
Abuse Control
Commission (CICAD)
	Mr. David Beall
	Executive Director
		Organization of
		  American States
		1889 F Street, NW, Room
		  No. 845
		Washington, DC 20006
		TEL: (202) 458-3174
		FAX: (202) 485-3650
		E-mail:
		  Beall_David@OAS.org
		Home page:
		  www.oas.org/
		  EN/PROG/W3/EN/
		  cicad/htm

International Criminal
Police Organization
(INTERPOL)
	Mr. Jose Berrios
	Director
		Regional Station
		Special Investigations
		  Bureau
		Department of
		  Justice—Interpol
		San Juan, Puerto Rico
		TEL: (787) 724-4163/
		  729-2496
		FAX: (787) 722-0809

	Mr. Roland W. Peterson Chairman, Regional Committee for Caribbean and Central America	Caya Dick Cooper 11 San Nicolas, Aruba TEL: (2978) 44190 FAX: (2978) 43258
Regional Security System (RSS)	Brig. Rudyard Lewis Regional Security Coord.	Central Liaison Office Regional Security Paragon Base Christ Church, Barbados TEL: (246) 420-7110 FAX: (246) 420-7316
Regional Drug Law Enforcement Training	Mr. Bertram Millwood Director	Twickenham Park

Agency	Agency Head	Contact Data
Center (REDTRAC)		St. Catherine Jamaica TEL: (809) 943 9111; 907 3608 FAX: (809) 943 8987
United Nations International Drug Control Program (UNDCP)	Dr. Sandro Calvani Director	Regional Office for the Caribbean P.O. Box 625C Bridgetown, Barbados TEL: (246) 437-8732 FAX: (246) 437-8499 E-mail: Undcpbarbados @undcp.un.or.at Home page: www.undcp.org/ undcp.html

Bibliography

Books and Monographs

Bagley, Bruce M., and William O. Walker III, eds. *Drug Trafficking in the Americas.* Miami, Fla.: North-South Center, University of Miami, 1994.

Beaty, Jonathan, and S. C. Gwynne. *The Outlaw Bank.* New York: Random House, 1993.

Bergquist, Charles, Ricardo Peñaranda, and Gonzalo Sánchez, eds. *Violence in Colombia.* Wilmington, Del.: Scholarly Resources, 1992.

Buzan, Barry. *People, States, and Fear.* Boulder, Colo.: Lynne Rienner, 1991.

Campbell, Horace. *Rasta and Resistance: From Marcus Garvey to Walter Rodney.* Trenton, N.J.: Africa World Press, 1987.

Chevannes, Barry. *Background to Drug Use in Jamaica.* Institute of Social and Economic Research Working Paper No. 34, University of the West Indies, Jamaica, 1988.

Cornez, Arnold L. *The Offshore Money Book.* Chicago: International Publishing, 1996.

Dreher, Melanie Creagan. *Working Men and Ganja.* Philadelphia: Institute for the Study of Human Issues, 1982.

Fischer, Dietrich. *Nonmilitary Aspects of Security: A Systems Approach.* Aldershot: Dartmouth, 1993.

Fitzpatrick, Gary, and Marilyn Modelin. *Direct-Line Distances.* Int'l ed. Metuchen, N.J.: Scarecrow Press, 1986.

Flynn, Stephen E. *The Transnational Drug Challenge and the New World Order.* Washington, D.C.: Center for Strategic and International Studies, 1993.

Fowler, Michael Ross, and Julie Marie Bunck. *Law, Power, and the Sovereign State.* University Park: Pennsylvania State University Press, 1995.

Godson, Roy, and William J. Olson. *International Organized Crime: Emerging Threat to U.S. Security.* Washington, D.C.: National Strategy Information Center, 1993.

Griffith, Ivelaw L. *Caribbean Security on the Eve of the 21st Century.* McNair

Paper No. 54, Institute for National Security Studies, National Defense University, October 1996.

———. *The Money Laundering Dilemma in the Caribbean.* Working Paper No. 4, Institute of Caribbean Studies, University of Puerto Rico, September 1995.

———. *The Quest for Security in the Caribbean.* Armonk, N.Y.: M. E. Sharpe, 1993.

Headley, Bernard. *The Jamaican Crime Scene: A Perspective.* Washington, D.C.: Howard University Press, 1996.

Jackson, Robert H. *Quasi-States: Sovereignty, International Relations, and the Third World.* New York: Cambridge University Press, 1990.

Kleiman, Mark A. R. *Marijuana: Costs of Abuse, Costs of Control.* Westport, Conn.: Greenwood Press, 1989.

Lee, Rensselaer W., III. *The White Labyrinth.* New Brunswick, N.J.: Transaction, 1991.

Lyman, Michael D. *Gangland: Drug Trafficking by Organized Criminals.* Springfield, Ill.: Charles Thomas, 1989.

MacDonald, Scott B. *Dancing on a Volcano: The Latin American Drug Trade.* New York: Praeger, 1988.

MacDonald, Scott B., and Bruce Zagaris, eds. *International Handbook on Drug Control.* Westport, Conn.: Greenwood Press, 1992.

Maingot, Anthony P. *The United States and the Caribbean.* Boulder, Colo.: Westview Press, 1994.

Marby, Donald J., ed. *The Latin American Narcotics Trade and US National Security.* Westport, Conn.: Greenwood Press, 1989.

Merrill, Tim L., ed. *Guyana and Belize: Country Studies.* Washington, D.C.: Library of Congress, 1993.

Mills, James. *The Underground Empire.* Garden City, N.Y.: Doubleday, 1986.

Morris, Michael A. *Caribbean Maritime Security.* New York: St. Martin's Press, 1994.

Nadelmann, Ethan A. *Cops Across Borders.* University Park: Pennsylvania State University Press, 1993.

Oppenheimer, Andrés. *Castro's Final Hour.* New York: Simon & Schuster, 1992.

Phillips, Peter, and Judith Wedderburn, eds. *Crime and Violence: Causes and Solutions.* Department of Government Occasional Paper No. 2, University of the West Indies, Jamaica, September 1988.

Pollard, Duke. *The Problems of Drug Abuse in Commonwealth Caribbean Countries.* Georgetown, Guyana: CARICOM, 1987.

Rogozinski, Jan. *A Brief History of the Caribbean.* New York: Facts on File, 1992.

Romm, Joseph J. *Defining National Security.* New York: Council on Foreign Relations Press, 1993.

Rosenau, James N. *Multilateral Governance and the Nation-State System: A Post–Cold War Assessment.* Inter-American Dialogue Occasional Papers in Western Hemisphere Governance No. 1, Washington, D.C., September 1995.

————. *Turbulence in World Politics*. Princeton: Princeton University Press, 1990.

Rubin, Vera, and Lambros Comitas. *Ganja in Jamaica*. Garden City, N.Y.: Anchor Books, 1976.

Scherer, J. *Crack Cocaine*. Minneapolis, Minn.: Community Intervention, 1988.

Spitz, Barry, ed. *Tax Haven Encyclopedia*. London: Butterworth, 1991.

Sterling, Claire. *Octopus*. New York: W. W. Norton, 1990.

————. *Thieves' World*. New York: Simon & Schuster, 1994.

Sutton, Paul, ed. *Europe and the Caribbean*. London: Macmillan, 1991.

Thomas, Clive Y. *The Poor and the Powerless*. New York: Monthly Review Press, 1988.

Tonry, Michael, and James Q. Wilson, eds. *Drugs and Crime*. Chicago: University of Chicago Press, 1990.

Weisheit, Ralph A. *Domestic Marijuana: A Neglected Industry*. Westport, Conn.: Greenwood Press, 1992.

Articles and Book Chapters

Abbott, Michael H. "The Army and the Drug War: Politics or National Security?" *Parameters* 18 (December 1988): 95–112.

Adams, David. "Drug Prosecutions Difficult on Islands." *St. Petersburg Times*, May 6, 1996, 1A, 8A.

————. "Drug Runners Paradise." *St. Petersburg Times*, May 5, 1996, 1A, 4A.

Alexiou, Emanuel M. "The Bahamas." In *Tax Haven Encyclopedia*, edited by Spitz, 1–45.

Allen, Dudley. "Urban Crime and Violence in Jamaica." In *Crime and Punishment in the Caribbean*, edited by Rosemary Brana-Shute and Gary Brana-Shute, 29–51. Gainesville, Fla.: University of Florida, 1980.

Alonzo, Robert. "Third Antiguan Charged with Trafficking in 'Coke.'" *Trinidad Guardian*, June 14, 1994, 1.

Anderson, Kenneth. "$10M Coke Haul off St. Thomas." *St. Croix Avis*, August 27, 1994, 3, 23.

Andreas, Peter. "Profits, Poverty, and Illegality: The Logic of Drug Corruption." *NACLA Report on the Americas* 27 (November–December 1993): 22ff.

Anglin, M. Douglas, and George Speckart. "Narcotics Use and Crime: A Multisample, Multimethod Analysis." *Criminology* 26, no. 2 (1988): 197–231.

Armstead, L. "Illicit Narcotics Cultivation and Processing: The Ignored Environmental Drama." *Bulletin on Narcotics* 44, no. 2 (1992): 9–20.

Bagley, Bruce M. "Myths of Militarization: Enlisting Armed Forces in the War on Drugs." In *Drug Policy in the Americas*, edited by Peter H. Smith, 129–50. Boulder, Colo.: Westview Press, 1992.

————. "The New Hundred Year War? U.S. National Security and the War on Drugs in Latin America." *Journal of Interamerican Studies and World Affairs* 30 (Spring 1988): 161–82.

Beard, David. "Drug Money Laundering Puts Pressure on DEA." *Ft. Lauderdale Sun Sentinel,* July 30, 1995, 1G.

———. "Drug Planes Seen Using Cuba as a Shield." *Ft. Lauderdale Sun Sentinel,* April 26, 1996, 3A.

———. "When Drug Woes Hit Home, Caribbean Cooperates." *Ft. Lauderdale Sun Sentinel,* August 31, 1996, 1A, 12A.

Becker, Michael. "Sovereignty or Survival." *Caribbean Week* (Barbados), July 20–August 2, 1996, 2.

Benavente Urbina, Andrés. "Drug Traffic and State Stability." *North-South* 2 (August–September 1992): 34–37.

Bernal, Richard. "Debt, Drugs, and Development in the Caribbean." *Trans-Africa Forum* 9 (Summer 1992): 83–92.

Best, Tony. "Cupid's Arrow May Do More Than Pierce the Heart." *New York Carib News,* March 7, 1995, 6.

Bhattacharya, Anindya K. "Offshore Banking in the Caribbean by U.S. Commercial Banks: Implications for Government-Business Interaction." *Journal of International Business Studies* 11 (Winter 1980): 37–46.

Blackman, Courtney N. "Tourism and Other Services in the Anglophone Caribbean." In *Small Country Development and International Labor Flows: Experiences in the Caribbean,* edited by Anthony P. Maingot, 53–81. Boulder, Colo.: Westview Press, 1991.

Bohning, Don. "Anti-Drug Pacts Founder Between U.S., Caribbean." *Miami Herald,* November 29, 1996, 18A.

———. "For Resorts, Crime = Crisis." *Miami Herald,* April 10, 1995, BM43, BM44.

Booth, Cathy. "Caribbean Blizzard." *Time,* February 26, 1996, 46–48.

Boyne, Ian. "Crime, Corruption, and Civility." *Sunday Gleaner* (Jamaica), December 18, 1994, 8F.

Browne, Richard. "Drug Abuse Still a Major Problem Here." *Sunday Gleaner* (Jamaica), September 26, 1993.

———. "Multinationals Have No Plans to Leave." *Sunday Gleaner* (Jamaica), December 18, 1994, 1F.

Byron, Dawud. "RSS Troops Arrive to Help Search for Prison Escapees." *St. Croix Avis,* November 13–14, 1994, 4.

———. "Scotland Yard Blames Drugs for Vanishings from St. Kitts." *Virgin Islands Daily News,* October 31, 1994, 3.

———. "Son of St. Kitts Acting Prime Minister and Girlfriend Missing." *St. Croix Avis,* October 5, 1994.

———. "St. Kitts' Morris Resigns as Second-in-Command." *Virgin Islands Daily News,* November 16, 1994, 7.

Caribbean Daylight (U.S.). "Guyana: City Businessman on Drug Charge." June 3, 1996, 3.

———. "St. Vincent Top Cop Wants Legal Loopholes Tightened." January 24, 1993, 16.

———. "T'dad Govt Moves Against Small Armies." May 6, 1996, 1.

Caribbean Today (U.S.). "Bahamas." November 1996, 2.

Caribbean Week (Barbados). "Puerto Rico: 1650 Kilos of Cocaine." August 3–16, 1996, 18.

———. "Report on Cayman: The Largest Island Banking Center in the World." November 11–24, 1995, 38, 39.

Cawthorne, Andrew. "Cocaine Barons Threaten Suriname." *Stabroek News*, March 8, 1995, 1,12.

Chernik, Marc W. "Colombia's Fault Lines." *Current History* 95 (February 1996): 76–81.

Chopra, Jarat, and Thomas G. Weiss. "Sovereignty Is No Longer Sacrosanct: Codifying Humanitarian Intervention." *Ethics and International Affairs* 6 (1992): 95–117.

Cichon, Deborah. "British Dependencies: The Cayman Islands and the Turks and Caicos." In *Islands in the Commonwealth Caribbean*, edited by Sandra W. Meditz and Dennis W. Hanratty, 579–81. Washington, D.C.: Library of Congress, 1989.

Claxton, Melvin. "Virgin Islands Drugs Linked to Antigua." *Virgin Islands Daily News*, March 3, 1994, 1, 5.

Corr, Edwin G. "Rubik's Cube, Manwaring's Paradigm for Gray Area Phenomenon and a New Strategy for International Narcotics Control." In *Gray Area Phenomena: Confronting the New World Disorder*, edited by Max G. Manwaring, 171–94. Boulder, Colo.: Westview Press, 1993.

Cox, Richard. "Patterson Against Drugs, for Sovereignty." *Sunday Stabroek*, July 7, 1996, 5.

Cumberbatch, Janice A., and Neville C. Duncan. "Illegal Drugs, USA Policies, and Caribbean Responses: The Road to Disaster." *Caribbean Affairs* 3 (October–December 1990): 150–81.

Daily Observer (Antigua-Barbuda). "Constables in St. Kitts Arrested in Drug Bust." August 21, 1996, 1.

Daily Observer (Jamaica). "Crown Witness Murdered." August 13, 1996, 1, 4.

Davidson, Wendella. "Businessman Abrams Convicted on Illegal Ammunition Charges." *Guyana Chronicle*, February 1, 1995, 7.

de Leon, Sherrie Ann, and Ria Taitt. "T&T Biggest Drug Haul Seized at Sea." *Sunday Express* (Trinidad and Tobago), June 12, 1994, 4.

Domínguez, Jorge I. "The Caribbean in a New International Context: Are Freedom and Peace a New Threat to Its Prosperity?" In *The Caribbean: New Dynamics in Trade and Political Economy*, edited by Anthony T. Bryan, 1–23. Miami, Fla.: North-South Center, University of Miami, 1995.

Donnelly, Jack. "The United Nations and the Global Drug Control Regime." In *Drug Policy in the Americas*, edited by Peter H. Smith, 282–304. Boulder, Colo.: Westview Press, 1992.

Dutch Caribbean Gazette (Curaçao). "Authorities Seize Drugs Going to U.S., Coming from Spain." May 24, 1995, 9.

Earle, Sharon. "25% of Tourists Flock to J'ca for Drugs." *Gleaner* (Jamaica), February 27, 1992.

Earle, Sharon, and McPherse Thompson. "Cops Say Visitors Overdosed." *Gleaner* (Jamaica), March 23, 1994.

Economist. "Oh, My Brass Plate in the Sun." March 16, 1991, 84.

———. "Stormy Weather." December 9, 1989, 41.

Eggleston, David, and Noreen Flanagan. "Belize Civil Rights Could Be Victim in Fight Against Crime." *Miami Herald*, December 19, 1994, 10A.

Ehrenfeld, Rachel. "Narco-Terrorism and the Cuban Connection." *Strategic Review* 16 (Summer 1988): 55–63.

Falco, Mathea. "U.S. Drug Policy: Addicted to Failure." *Foreign Policy*, no. 102 (Spring 1996): 120–33.

Farah, Douglas. "Caribbean Key to US Drug Trade." *Washington Post*, September 23, 1996, A1, A9.

French, Howard. "Cuba Gives Over Two Drug Suspects." *New York Times*, September 20, 1993, A5.

———. "U.S. Says Haiti's Military Runs Cocaine." *New York Times*, June 8, 1994, A15.

Frost, Charles C. "Drug Trafficking, Organized Crime, and Terrorism." In *Hydra of Carnage*, edited by Uri Ra'anan et al., 189–98. Lexington, Mass.: Lexington Books, 1986.

Gayle, Dennis J. "The Evolving Caribbean Business Environment." In *The Caribbean: New Dynamics in Trade and Political Economy*, edited by Anthony T. Bryan, 135–56. Miami, Fla.: North-South Center, University of Miami, 1995.

Gerstenzang, James. "Cuba, U.S. Join Forces to catch Drug Suspects." *Los Angeles Times*, September 19, 1993, A1, A17.

Gilbert, Frederick. "Police Discover G$1 Billion of Ganja in Berbice." *Stabroek News*, May 23, 1992, 1.

Gleaner (Jamaica). "Cuba Not Trafficking in Drugs—Havana Official." August 12, 1996, 6A.

———. "Foreigners Languishing in Prison." April 25, 1996, 2A.

———. "Major Ganja Find in Manchester." March 8, 1995, 3A.

Goldfarb, Ronald. "Start the Clean-Up; in Puerto Rico, an Effective, Humane Response to Dope-Dealing." *Washington Post*, May 19, 1996, C3.

Graham, Bradley. "Drug Flights Cross Pentagon's Super Radar Screen." *Washington Post*, August 23, 1995, A1.

Grant-Wisdom, Dorith. "Globalization, Structural Adjustment, and Democracy in Jamaica." In *Democracy and Human Rights in the Caribbean*, edited by Ivelaw L. Griffith and Betty N. Sedoc-Dahlberg, 193–211. Boulder, Colo.: Westview Press, 1997.

Green, E. George. "The Role of Governments in Strengthening Human Rights Machinery." In *International Human Rights Law in the Commonwealth Caribbean*, edited by Angela D. Byre and Beverly Y. Byfield, 309–16. Dordrecht: Martinus Nijhoff, 1991.

Griffith, Ivelaw L. "Caribbean Manifestations of the International Narcotics Phenomenon." In *Security Problems and Policies in the Post–Cold War Caribbean*, edited by Jorge Rodríguez Beruff and Humberto García Muñiz, 181–200. London: Macmillan, 1996.

————. "Drugs and World Politics: The Caribbean Dimension." *Round Table* 332 (October 1994): 419–31.

————. "Drugs and Security in the Commonwealth Caribbean." *Journal of Commonwealth and Comparative Politics* 31 (July 1993): 70–102.

————. "Drugs in the Caribbean: An Economic Balance Sheet." *Caribbean Studies* 28, no. 2 (1995): 285–303.

————. "From Cold War Geopolitics to Post–Cold War Geonarcotics." *International Journal* 49 (Winter 1993–94): 1–36.

————. "Some Security Implications of Commonwealth Caribbean Narcotics Operations." *Conflict Quarterly* 13 (Spring 1993): 25–45.

Griffith, Ivelaw L., and Trevor Munroe. "Drugs and Democracy in the Caribbean." *Journal of Commonwealth and Comparative Politics* 33 (November 1995): 357–76.

————. "Drugs and Democratic Governance in the Caribbean." In *Democracy and Human Rights in the Caribbean*, edited by Ivelaw L. Griffith and Betty N. Sedoc-Dahlberg, 74–94. Boulder, Colo.: Westview Press, 1997.

Griffith, Janice. "$6M Ganja Haul." *Sunday Sun* (Barbados), July 5, 1992, 1.

Gunst, Laurie. "Jamaica Drug Gangs: Johnny-Too-Bad and the Sufferers." *Nation* (U.S.), November 13, 1989, 549ff.

Guyana Chronicle. "Cocaine Traffickers Jailed for Life." July 1, 1994, 4.

————. "GAC Fined 1.2M (US) for Transporting Ganja." January 29, 1992, 3.

————. "Illegal Airstrip Case: Three Colombians, One Guyanese Charged." January 29, 1989, 1, 4.

Guyana Review. "Gun Runnings." June 1995, 12.

————. "Prison Problems." October 1994, 16.

Hagley, Lystra. "Crime and Structural Adjustment in Trinidad and Tobago: On the Exercise of Judicial Discretion." *Caribbean Affairs* 6 (January–March 1993): 147–54.

Hancock, David, and Mary Beth Sheridan. "Requiem for a Drug Courier." *Miami Herald*, February 8, 1995, 1A, 6A.

Harker, Trevor. "Caribbean Economic Performance in the 1990s: Implications for Future Policy." In *The Caribbean in the Global Political Economy*, edited by Hilbourne A. Wason, 9–27. Boulder, Colo.: Lynne Rienner, 1994.

Harrison, Faye V. "Drug Trafficking in World Capitalism: A Perspective on Jamaican Posses in the U.S." *Social Justice* 16, no. 4 (1989): 115–31.

Hassim, Alim. "Marijuana Container Valued at US2M." *Stabroek News*, January 6, 1995, 1.

————. "Regional Crime Data Exchange System Agreed." *Stabroek News*, May 25, 1994, 12.

Headley, Bernard D. "War Ina 'Babylon': Dynamics of the Jamaican Informal Drug Economy." *Social Justice* 15, nos. 3–4 (1988): 61–86.

Henville, Marcia. "Procope: Cops Were Harassing Chadee." *Trinidad Express*, August 21, 1996, 7.

Hierso, Daniel. "Two Bodies Found in St. Martin." *Virgin Islands Daily News*, November 2, 1994, 7.

———. "Year's Biggest Drug Cache in French Islands Is Seized." *Virgin Islands Daily News*, June 5, 1996, 7.

Hinze, Paul B. "Organized Crime and Drug Linkages." In *Hydra of Carnage*, edited by Uri Ra'anan et al., 171–87. Lexington, Mass.: Lexington Books, 1986.

Holmes, Steven A. "Less Strategic Now, Grenada Is to Lose American Embassy." *New York Times*, May 2, 1994, A-1, A-6.

———. "U.S. Embassy for Grenada." *New York Times*, May 19, 1994, A-9.

Hutt, Katherine. "The DEA Opens Caribbean Office in Puerto Rico." *Virgin Islands Daily News*, November 16, 1995, 7.

———. "Drug Traffic Fuels Puerto Rico's Rising Murder Rate." *Miami Herald*, December 26, 1994, 26A.

Jamaica Herald. "Deportees on the Rise." September 29, 1996, 1A, 12A.

———. "Drug Rehab Program Gets German Aid." December 15, 1993.

———. "Security Industry Regulation Takes Hold." August 12, 1996, 3.

Jamaican Weekly Gleaner. "US Customs, Air Jamaica Sign Anti-Drug Pact." December 23, 1991, 5.

Jekel, James F., et al. "Nine Years of Freebase Cocaine Epidemic in the Bahamas." *American Journal on Addictions* 3, no. 1 (1994): 14–24.

John, Deborah. "A Bid to Police the Police." *Daily Express* (Trinidad and Tobago), February 2, 1993, 1, 10.

Johnson, Tim. "Cold War Tools Turned on Narcos." *Miami Herald*, September 14, 1995, 18A.

———. "Colombia, Peru Down Planes." *Miami Herald*, August 7, 1995, 6A.

———. "Hitting Rock Bottom." *Miami Herald*, April 2, 1995, 1A, 20A.

———. "Scary Liaison in Colombia: Traffickers Financing Guerrillas, says Samper." *Miami Herald*, February 5, 1997, 13A.

Jordan, Michael. "One Thousand Guyanese Deported in Past 18 Months." *Sunday Stabroek*, July 28, 1996, 1, 22.

Kassirer, Jerome P. "Federal Foolishness and Marijuana." *New England Journal of Medicine* 336 (January 30, 1997): 366.

Kawell, Jo Ann. "The Addict Economies." *NACLA Report on the Americas* 22 (March 1989): 33–40.

Khan, Mohamed. "Drugs Dropped by Mysterious Aircraft." *Stabroek News*, June 8, 1993, 1, 11.

———. "Four Held in $720M Mahaica Marijuana Bust." *Stabroek News*, July 28, 1994, 1, 24.

———. "Prison Boss Calls for Drug Rehab Clinic." *Stabroek News*, September 4, 1993, 1, 13.

———. "Serious Offenses on the Increase." *Stabroek News*, December 22, 1994, 1, 24.

Laguerre, Michel S. "National Security, Narcotics Control, and the Haitian Military." In *Security Problems and Policies in the Post–Cold War Caribbean*, edited by Jorge Rodríguez Beruff and Humberto García Muñiz, 99–120. London: Macmillan, 1996.

Lantigua, John. "Target: Offshore Scams." *Miami Herald,* March 21, 1996, 1A, 20A.

La-Ongsri, S. "Drug Abuse Control and the Environment in Northern Thailand." *Bulletin on Narcotics* 44, no. 2 (1992): 31–35.

Larrubia, Evelyn. "Man Charged with Smuggling Cocaine in Stomach." *Ft. Lauderdale Sun Sentinel,* March 6, 1996, 1B.

Lee, Rensselaer W., III. "Drugs: The Cuba Connection." *Current History* 95 (February 1996): 55–58.

———. "Global Reach: The Threat of International Drug Trafficking." *Current History* 94 (May 1995): 207–11.

Lee, Rensselaer W., III, and Scott B. MacDonald. "Drugs in the East." *Foreign Policy* 90 (Spring 1993): 89–107.

Leen, Jeff. "Castro Drugs Probe Collapses in Heap of Dead Ends, Lies." *Miami Herald,* November 24, 1996, 1A, 17A.

———. "Traffickers Tie Castro to Drug Run." *Miami Herald,* July 25, 1996, 1A, 14A.

Lindsay, Lynn. "Caribbean Offshore Banking." *North-South* 1 (February–March 1992): 40–43.

Lohr, Steve. "Where the Money Washes Up." *New York Times Magazine,* March 29, 1992, 27ff.

Lorch, Donatella. "In Zambia, a Legacy of Graft and a Drug Scandal Taint Democratic Reforms." *New York Times,* January 30, 1994, 30.

Lyons, David. "Couple Who Did 'Favor' Freed from Legal Tangle." *Miami Herald,* December 13, 1995, 1B, 4B.

———. "Ex-Prosecutors Charged with Aiding Drug Bosses." *Miami Herald,* June 6, 1995, 1A, 7A.

———. "Havana Helps U.S. Investigate Drug Case." *Miami Herald,* December 11, 1996, 1B, 4B.

———. "Smuggler Ties Cuba to Drugs." *Miami Herald,* October 10, 1996, 1B, 2B.

MacDonald, Scott B., and Bruce Zagaris. "Caribbean Offshore Financial Centers: The Bahamas, the British Dependencies, the Netherlands Antilles and Aruba." In *International Handbook on Drug Control,* edited by MacDonald and Zagaris, 137–56.

Mager, Andy. "Three Walk Free in St. Kitts." *Caribbean Week* (Barbados), November 9–22, 1996, 6.

Mahabir, Noor Kumar. "Marijuana in the Caribbean." *Caribbean Affairs* 7 (September–October 1994): 28–40.

Maingot, Anthony P. "Confronting Corruption in the Hemisphere: A Sociological Perspective." *Journal of Interamerican Studies and World Affairs* 36 (Fall 1994): 49–74.

———. "Laundering the Gains of the Drug Trade: Miami and Caribbean Tax Havens." *Journal of Interamerican Studies and World Affairs* 30 (Summer–Fall 1988): 167–87.

Marajh, Camini. "Operation Crack Attack Is Here." *Internet Express,* available at www.trinidad.net/express/home.htm, November 10, 1996.

———. "Police 'Drug Cartel' Charges Made in 1991—Murray Told NAR Government." *Sunday Guardian* (Trinidad and Tobago), April 12, 1992, 1, 5.

Markowitz, Arnold. "At Last, a Mean Season Ends." *Miami Herald*, November 30, 1995, 1A, 16A.

———. "Cash Cache: DEA, Customs Agents Find More Than $6 Million at Warehouse." *Miami Herald*, August 12, 1996, 1B, 2B.

———. "Drug Money Haul Puts Week's Total at $15 Million Plus." *Miami Herald*, August 23, 1996, 1B, 3B.

Marks, Alexandra. "Haiti's Military May Dig in Heels to Keep Lucrative Drug Trade." *Christian Science Monitor*, November 1, 1993, 1, 14.

Marotta, E. "Drug Abuse and Illicit Trafficking in Italy: Trends and Countermeasures." *Bulletin on Narcotics* 44, no. 1 (1992): 15–22.

Marquis, Christopher. "Bananas or Drugs, Caribbean Tells US." *Miami Herald*, June 6, 1996, 18A.

Massing, Michael. "Crack's Destructive Sprint Across America." *New York Times Magazine*, October 1, 1989, 38–41, 58–62.

May, Patrick. "Drug Trade Is 'Booming.'" *Miami Herald*, September 8, 1996, 1A, 10A.

McClelland, Charles A., and Gary D. Hoggard. "Conflict Patterns in the Interactions Among Nations." In *International Politics and Foreign Policy*, edited by James N. Rosenau, 711–24. New York: Free Press, 1969.

McClintick, David. "Capturing the Butterfly." *New York Times Magazine*, April 4, 1993, 32ff.

McGee, Jim. "Drug Smuggling Is Built on Franchises." *Washington Post*, March 26, 1995, A1, A20.

———. "US Set Up Fake Bank to Trick Drug Lords." *Miami Herald*, December 17, 1994, 1A, 14A.

Meason, James E. "War at Sea: Drug Interdiction in the Caribbean." *Journal of Defense and Diplomacy* 6, no. 6 (1988): 7–13.

Miami Herald. "Antigua." May 8, 1995, 7A.

———. "Antigua." May 18, 1995, 12A.

———. "Apparel Exports Soar Under U.S. Program." April 18, 1996, 18A.

———. "Belize Fast Turning into Offshore Financial Haven." November 20, 1994, 1K, 2K.

———. "Body Packers on the Increase." February 8, 1995, 6A.

———. "Cocaine Found on Coast Brings 29 Before Court." April 14, 1992, 13A.

———. "Coke Found in Crushed Aluminum." March 21, 1996, 3B.

———. "Colombia: Foreign Minister Leaves Post to Face Charges." March 20, 1996, 4A.

———. "Crack Cocaine Speeds Spread of AIDS." November 24, 1994, 9A.

———. "Dominican Republic: 2 Officials Dismissed in Drug-Related Scandal." November 2, 1995, 29A.

———. "Guyana Probes Scheme Tied to Gold Smuggling: Operation Involves Money Laundering." November 28, 1995, 8A.

———. "Jamaica Murder Rate Goes Up, Other Violence Drops." January 4, 1996, 13A.

———. "Jamaica Tourism Declines." January 17, 1995, 3C.

———. "Man Sentenced for Bid to Smuggle Coke in Dog." April 27, 1995, 3A.

———. "Many Drug Defendants Freed on Technicalities." February 18, 1995, 16A.

———. "NY Drug Agents Find 10 Cocaine-Filled Condoms Inside Dog." December 6, 1994, 3A.

———. "Puerto Rico." January 5, 1995, 14A.

———. "Puerto Rico." March 9, 1996, 12A.

———. "Stockbroker Is Charged with Laundering Drug Money." February 8, 1995, 6B.

———. "Three Guilty of Importing Marijuana." January 21, 1995, 2B.

———. "$22.3 Million in Cocaine Found." July 27, 1995, 12A.

———. "U.S., Haiti Cooperate on Drug Seizure." August 23, 1996, 2B.

Miami Times. "Security Now Big Business in Barbados." March 14, 1996, 8A.

Möbius, Gerald. "Money Laundering." *International Criminal Police Review* 440 (January–February 1993): 1–8.

Morris, Margaret. "Cocaine Knocking Tourists out West." *Gleaner* (Jamaica), March 24, 1994.

Morris, Roy. "Bajan Connection Arrested in London." *Daily Nation* (Barbados), May 16, 1990, 1.

Murray, John B. "Marijuana's Effects on Human Cognitive Functions, Psychomotor Functions, and Personality." *Journal of General Psychology* 113 (January 1986): 23–55.

Naraine, Ryan. "A Drug Rehab Clinic—When?" *Stabroek News,* September 6, 1993, 5.

———. "Plans for Corruption Court Moving Ahead." *Stabroek News,* July 20, 1993, 20.

Navarro, Mireya. "Puerto Rico Accepts Plans for Relocating Program Witnesses." *New York Times,* January 22, 1997, A15.

———. "Puerto Rico Is Sending Many Drug-Case Witnesses to Florida, Creating Tensions There." *New York Times,* October 20, 1996, 12Y.

———. "Puerto Rico Reeling Under Scourge of Drugs and Rising Gang Violence." *New York Times,* July 23, 1995, 11Y.

Neville, Michael, and Nelson Clark. "Drug Abuse in the Bahamas." *Journal of Substance Abuse Treatment* 2 (1985): 195–97.

New York Carib News. "Bahamas Crime Rate Highest in Five Years." January 3, 1995, 14.

———. "Barbados Offshore Market Secure." October 31, 1995, 10.

———. "Big Drugs Bust." May 14, 1996, 5.

———. "British Warship Makes Cocaine Haul." February 3, 1996, 4.

———. "Crackdown on Vigilantes." June 23, 1993, 8.

———. "[Dominica Prime Minister] Charles Says No to Drugs: Hang Them." July 29, 1992, 3.

———. "Drug Smugglers Link Castro." August 6, 1996, 5.

———. "Drug Traffickers Targeting Garment Exports." December 6, 1994, 7.

————. "Five Territories Sign Maritime Agreement." August 20, 1996, 10.

————. "GAC Official, Son on Cocaine Charge." August 27, 1996, 10.

————. "Ganja Found in Clothing Shipment." July 12, 1994, 7.

————. "Guyana Crime Wave Blamed on Deportees." September 17, 1996, 12.

————. "Jamaica: Appeal Dismissed in Bernal Drug Case." February 6, 1996, 4.

————. "Jamaica: 800-Pound Cocaine Haul." October 26, 1995, 7.

————. "Jamaicans Remitted US$600 Million." November 7, 1995, 13.

————. "Jamaica Under Drug Siege." May 2, 1989, 4.

————. "Police Seize Colombian Ganja." December 19, 1995, 6.

————. "Politicians United Against Drugs." May 16, 1989, 3.

————. "Questions Surround Air Jamaica Drug Find." May 16, 1989, 3.

————. "Radar Station to Close." April 4, 1995, 10.

————. "US$278 Million to Local Economy." November 28, 1994, 7.

New York Newsday. "Marijuana Floating off Caymans." January 5, 1995, 13.

New York Times. "Assets in Drug Inquiry Seized in Puerto Rico." March 1, 1996, A13.

————. "Puerto Ricans Fight U.S. Radar Plan to Cut Drug Traffic." October 9, 1995, A9.

Nwanyanwu, Okey C., et al. "Acquired Immune Deficiency Syndrome in the United States Associated with Injecting Drug Use, 1981–1991." *American Journal of Drug and Alcohol Abuse* 19, no. 4 (1993): 399–408.

Pantin, Dennis. "The Colombian Nightmare: Drugs and Structural Adjustment." *Caribbean Affairs* 2 (October–November 1989): 141–45.

Perl, Raphael. "International Narcopolicy and the Role of the U.S. Congress." In *The Latin American Narcotics Trade and U.S. National Security,* edited by Donald Marby, 89–102. Westport, Conn.: Greenwood Press, 1989.

Persaud, Anand. "117 Pounds of Cocaine Found on GAC Plane." *Stabroek News,* March 18, 1993, 1, 2.

Persaud, Gitanjali. "Police, Army Uncover Biggest Ganja Plot Yet." *Stabroek News,* March 15, 1992, 1.

Philadelphia, John. "Drug Wars: Can Guyana Win?" *Guyana Review* 3 (April 1993): 14, 16.

————. "Drug Wars: The Threat to Guyana." *Guyana Review* 2 (March 1993): 15–16.

————. "Drug Wars: What Is to Be Done." *Guyana Review* 4 (May 1993): 18–19.

Phillips, Peter. Introduction to *Crime and Violence: Causes and Solutions,* edited by Phillips and Wedderburn, vii–ix.

Pilarte, Doralisa. "A Latin Mecca for Laundering Drug Money." *Miami Herald,* June 16, 1995, 1A, 17A.

Ramsaran, Ramesh. "Challenges to Caribbean Economic Development in the 1990s." In *The Caribbean: New Dynamics in Trade and Political*

Economy, edited by Anthony T. Bryan, 111–34. Miami, Fla: North-South Center, University of Miami, 1995.

Roberts, Michael D. "Panday: Crime Is Number One." *New York Carib News,* October 8, 1996, 5.

Robles, Frances. "Alleged Smugglers Carried Lots of Cash—and Ex-Cops' IDs." *Miami Herald,* August 23, 1996, 1B, 2B.

Rohter, Larry. "New Drug Scandals in Panama Are Tainting Its Reform Leader." *New York Times,* June 12, 1996, A1, A8.

———. "Slaying in St. Thomas Stains Image of an American Paradise." *New York Times,* April 19, 1994, A17.

———. "Storm Is Unleashed in St. Kitts, As a Cocaine Case Churns Politics." *New York Times,* August 19, 1996, A4.

Rolley, Robin. "United Nations' Activities in International Drug Control." In *International Handbook on Drug Control,* edited by MacDonald and Zagaris, 415–31.

Ross, Karl. "Drug Shipments Under the Navy's Nose." *Miami Herald,* December 10, 1995, 10A.

Sanders, Ron. "The Drug Problem: Policy Options for Caribbean Countries." In *Democracy in the Caribbean,* edited by Jorge I. Dominguez, Robert A. Pastor, and R. Delisle Worrell, 229–37. Baltimore: Johns Hopkins University Press, 1993.

———. "Narcotics, Corruption, and Development: The Problems in the Smaller Islands." *Caribbean Affairs* 3 (January–March 1990): 79–92.

Schemo, Diana Jean. "A U.S. Slap on the Hand Brings Colombia Out Punching." *New York Times,* March 6, 1996, A5.

Schmitt, Eric. "Colorado Bunker Built for Cold War Shifts Focus to Drug Battle." *New York Times,* July 18, 1993, 18.

Sealey, Marilyn. " 'No' to Drugs Agreement." *Sunday Sun* (Barbados), July 7, 1996, 32A.

Sheridan, Mary Beth. "The Samper Scandal." *Hemisphere* 7, no. 2 (1996): 22–24.

Sheridan, Mary Beth, and Christopher Marquis. "Cartel's High-Tech Tools Confound Drug Agents." *Miami Herald,* June 18, 1995, 14A.

Silva, Samuel. "Trees in Trouble." *IDB,* April 1995, 9.

Sniffen, Michael J. "International Drug Sting in Anguilla Nets 88 Arrests." *Virgin Islands Daily News,* December 17, 1994, 8.

Spart, Jessica. "The New Drug Mules." *New York Times Magazine,* June 11, 1995, 44–45.

Stabroek News. "Bahamian Police Charged for Cocaine." March 18, 1992, 7.

———. "Cops in US $12M Cocaine Timehri Haul." September 12, 1992, 1.

———. "Cops Raid Mahaica Marijuana Fields." August 23, 1994, 1.

———. "Court Refuses Bail to Nine-Month Pregnant Accused." March 3, 1992, 16.

———. "Deportees to Come Under Close Scrutiny." November 6, 1994, 1.

———. "Drugs Accused Sentenced to Jail in Her Absence." April 14, 1992, 16.

———. "Drug Seizures Said to be a Factor in US\$ Rate Rise." July 7, 1993, 3.

———. "Drug Trafficking for Scrutiny in Customs Training Sessions." July 26, 1993, 16.

———. "GAC Faces Further US\$273,600 Fine for Cocaine Mail Bag." December 8, 1992, 20.

———. "GAC Offering G1M Reward for Cocaine Find Leads." March 19, 1993, 1.

———. "Interpol Chief Says Drugs Trade Can't Be Stopped." September 7, 1993, 2.

———. "Jamaica Police Sergeant Gets Seven Years for Cocaine." July 9, 1994, 5.

———. "Magistrate Calls for Parliamentary Revision of Drug Sentences." December 1, 1994, 3.

———. "Singh Brothers Fined \$150,000 in Drug Case." November 27, 1993, 5.

———. "10 Years in Jail for Honduran." November 1, 1993, 1.

———. "Three Charged for Trafficking." January 16, 1995, 1, 24.

———. "Trinidad and Tobago Police Make Big Cocaine Seizure." July 29, 1992, 7.

———. "Trinidad Senator Advocates Hanging for Drug Traffickers." August 29, 1991, 9.

———. "23 Held in Air-Dropped Cocaine Probe." June 9, 1993, 1, 11.

———. "U.S. Hands Over Drug Testing Field Kits, Vehicles." April 29, 1994, 24.

Stabroek News Online. "Number of Deportees Up by 40%." Available at www.trinidad.net/express/stabroektop.htm, January 23, 1997.

St. Croix Avis. "Drug Scandal Rocks St. Kitts." November 26, 1994.

Stone, Carl. "Crime and Violence: Socio-Political Implications." In *Crime and Violence: Causes and Solutions,* edited by Phillips and Wedderburn, 19–48.

Stuart-Young, Brian. "The Antiguan Advantage: International Financial Services." *Antigua-Barbuda Adventure* 6 (1996): 60, 62.

Sunday Advocate (Barbados). "Drug Convict Points to Top DLP Members in Scandal." October 2, 1994, 1, 4.

Sunday Gleaner (Jamaica). "Arms Shipment: Traffickers, Terrorists Involved." January 8, 1989, 1, 13B.

———. "Jamaica Makes Progress in Drug Fight." October 3, 1993.

———. "Text of Statement Made at a Press Conference at Up Park Camp Yesterday by Minister of National Security Errol Anderson." January 8, 1989, 16B.

Sutton, Paul, and Anthony Payne. "The Off-Limits Caribbean: The United States and the European Dependent Territories." *Annals of the American Academy of Political and Social Sciences* 533 (May 1994): 87–99.

Swarns, Rachel L. "At Huge Risk, Smugglers Swallow Drugs for Money." *Miami Herald,* February 8, 1995, 6A.

Tanner, Adam. "Helped by New Freedoms, Russian Drug Trade Is Booming." *Miami Herald,* December 25, 1994, 21A.

Taylor, R. T. "The Insurgent Economy: Black Market Guerrilla Organizations." *Crime, Law, and Social Change* 20 (July 1993): 13–51.

Thomas, Clive Y. "Foreign Currency Black Markets: Lessons from Guyana." *Social and Economic Studies* 38, no. 2 (1989): 137–84.

Thorndike, Tony. "Avarice in the Aviary." *Corruption and Reform* 6, no. 2 (1991): 171–83.

———. "Making Money in the Sun." *BWIA Caribbean Beat*, Autumn 1995, 69ff.

Treaster, Joseph B. "Fearing AIDS, Users of Heroin Shift to Inhaling Drugs." *New York Times*, November 17, 1991, L34.

———. "On Tiny Isle of 300 Banks, Enter Scotland Yard." *New York Times*, July 27, 1989, A4.

Trinidad and Tobago Mirror. "US Customs Here to Weed Out Smuggling." February 18, 1994, 2.

Trinidad Express. "Colombia Swamped by the High Cost of War." August 21, 1996, 15.

———. "5 Held; Ganja Field Destroyed." August 21, 1996, 7.

———. "T&T, Venezuela Consider Joint Air Patrols." July 24, 1991, 2.

Trinidad Guardian. "Alarm at Downturn in Jamaican Tourism." July 4, 1994, 9.

———. "Nation's Laws Must Be Enforced—Panday." July 15, 1994, 6.

Tulloch, Vincent. "Terrorism/Drugs Combination Threatens Security." *Sunday Gleaner* (Jamaica), January 15, 1989, 10A.

Viarruel, Alviva. "Police March in Historic Protest." *Daily Express* (Trinidad and Tobago), February 6, 1993, 1, 10.

Virgin Islands Daily News. "Hats, Blouses,—and a Few Kilos." November 25, 1994.

Waddell, Ronald. " 'Baby Arthur' Was a Crack Addict." *Stabroek News*, December 11, 1994, 1, 24.

———. "Deranged Man Murders Mother, Five Others." *Stabroek News*, December 10, 1994, 1.

Weekly Gleaner (U.S.). "Guyana Goes Ahead on Deportee Legislation." July 5–11, 1996, 14.

Weigand, Bruce, and Richard Bennett. "The Will to Win: Determinants of Public Support for the Drug War in Belize." *Crime, Law, and Social Change* 19 (March 1993): 203–20.

Weiner, Tim. "Colombian Drug Trafficker Implicates Haitian Police Chief." *New York Times*, April 22, 1994, A7.

Whitefield, Mimi. "Caribbean Ripe for a Banana War." *Miami Herald*, August 26, 1996, BM15.

Wilkinson, Bert. "Deportees Rattle Police." *New York Carib News*, September 24, 1996, 27.

Williams, Lloyd. "Envoy's Son Testifies He Unknowingly Smuggled Drugs to US." *St. Croix Avis*, November 4, 1994.

Wray, S. R., and L. E. Young. "Consequences of Substance Abuse." *West Indian Medical Journal* 41 (June 1992): 47–48.

Wren, Christopher S. "Big Cocaine Cache Is Found Stashed in Airliner Cockpit." *New York Times*, March 23, 1996, 6Y.

————. "Puerto Rico Joins U.S. in Plan to Fight Island Drug Runners." *New York Times*, April 17, 1996, A17.

Young, Alma H. "The Territorial Dimension of Caribbean Security: The Case of Belize." In *Strategy and Security in the Caribbean*, edited by Ivelaw L. Griffith, 124–48. New York: Praeger, 1991.

Unpublished Papers

Brana-Shute, Gary. "Jamaican Posse Gangs in the United States." Washington, D.C., 1993.

Crane-Scott, Maureen. "The Impact of International Narco-Trafficking on the Domestic Structures of Commonwealth Caribbean States." Paper prepared for the Conference on International Narco-Trafficking and the Security of Caribbean States, Institute of International Relations, St. Augustine, Trinidad, January 1995.

Davidson, Winston. "Integrated Demand Reduction Strategy: A Comprehensive Method." Paper prepared for the Third International Conference on Demand Reduction, Kingston, Jamaica, October 1991.

Flynn, Stephen E. "The Erosion of Sovereignty and the Emerging Global Drug Trade." Paper prepared for the annual convention of the International Studies Association, Chicago, February 1995.

Fox, Kristin. "Situation Analysis of Drug Abuse in Jamaica." Study prepared for USAID, January 1994.

Griffiths, Dilwyn. "The Financial Action Task Force Mutual Evaluation Procedure." Paper prepared for the Summit of the Americas Working Level Group Conference, Washington, D.C., June 23, 1995.

Lewis, Peter. "Overview of Cocaine Abuse in Trinidad and Tobago." Paper prepared for the joint meeting of the American Psychiatric Association and the Caribbean Psychiatric Association, Bridgetown, Barbados, May 1991.

Loy, Vice Admiral James M. "Trans-regional Cooperation." Paper prepared for the SOUTHCOM-NDU Latin American Strategy Symposium, Miami, Fla., April 1996.

McCaffrey, Gen. Barry. "Lessons of 1994: Prognosis for 1995 and Beyond." Paper prepared for the SOUTHCOM-NDU Latin American Annual Strategy Symposium, Miami, Fla., April 1995.

Monroe, Kirk W. "Surviving the Solution: The Extraterritorial Reach of the United States." Paper prepared for the Conference on International Narco-Trafficking and the Security of Caribbean States, Institute of International Relations, St. Augustine, Trinidad, January 1995.

Morley, Charles H. "The Impact of Money Laundering on State Security." Paper prepared for the Conference on International Narco-Trafficking and the Security of Caribbean States, Institute of International Relations, St. Augustine, Trinidad, January 1995.

Rider, Barry. "Taking the Profit out of Corruption." Paper prepared for the Conference on International Narco-Trafficking and the Security of

Caribbean States, Institute of International Relations, St. Augustine, Trinidad, January 1995.

Stone, Carl. "National Survey on the Use of Drugs in Jamaica." Study prepared for USAID, Jamaica, 1990.

Thompson, Eric A. "Strategies to Combat Money Laundering and Predicate Crimes." Paper prepared for the Money Laundering Symposium, Port of Spain, Trinidad, March 1993.

Wren, Tim. "Multilateral Cooperation with Reference to Financial Crime and International Narco-Trafficking." Paper prepared for the Conference on International Narco-Trafficking and the Security of Caribbean States, Institute of International Relations, St. Augustine, Trinidad, January 1995.

Government and Other Documents

Bahamas. *Bahamas Narcotics Control Report, 1991.* March 1992.

Bahamas. Ministry of Foreign Affairs. *Report of the Commission of Inquiry into the Illegal Use of the Bahamas for the Transshipment of Dangerous Drugs Destined for the United States.* Nassau, the Bahamas, 1984.

Bahamas. Ministry of National Security. *Summary Report on the Traffic in Narcotic Drugs Affecting the Bahamas in 1990.* Nassau, March 28, 1991.

Bahamas. Royal Bahamas Police Force. *Annual Report, 1993.* Nassau, 1995.

———. *Annual Report, 1994.* Nassau, 1996.

Barbados. Attorney General's Office. *Address of the Hon. David Simmons, Attorney General and Minister of Home Affairs, Delivered on Behalf of the States of the Caribbean Community to the Ministerial Hemispheric Conference on the Laundering of Proceeds of Crime, Held in Argentina, December 1, 2, 1995.*

Blom-Cooper, Louis. *Guns for Antigua: Report of the Commission of Inquiry into the Circumstances Surrounding the Shipment of Arms from Israel to Antigua and Transshipment on 24 April 1989 en Route to Colombia.* London: Duckworth, 1990.

Caribbean Development Bank. *Annual Report, 1994.* Bridgetown, Barbados, March 1995.

———. *Annual Report, 1995.* Bridgetown, Barbados, March 1996.

Caribbean Financial Action Task Force. *Annual Report, 1994–95.* Port of Spain, Trinidad, August 1995.

Caribbean Publishing Company. *1996 Caribbean Basin Commercial Profile.* Grand Cayman, 1996.

Caribbean Textile and Apparel Institute. *The Jamaican Garment Industry.* August 7, 1996.

CARICOM. *Communiqué, Fifth Special Meeting of the Conference of Heads* of Government of the Caribbean Community, No. 601. St. Michael, Barbados, December 16, 1996.

———. Report on Delays in the Administration of Justice. Georgetown, Guyana, July 26, 1994.

Cayman Islands. Royal Cayman Islands Police. Annual Report, 1995. February 1996.

Coopers and Lybrand. Narcotics Money Laundering in the Caribbean Region: A Vulnerability Assessment. May 23, 1993.

European Union. The Caribbean and the Drugs Problem: Report of the EU Experts Group. Brussels, April, 1996.

Grenada. Ministry of Education. National Policy and Program of Action Against the Illicit Use, Production, and Trafficking in Narcotics, Drugs, and Psychotropic Substances. May 1992.

Guyana. Ministry of Information. Guyana in Brief. Georgetown, Guyana: Government Information Service, 1979.

Guyana. Parliament. Budget Speech. Sessional Paper No. 1 of 1995, February 6, 1995.

———. Parliament. Budget Speech. Sessional Paper No. 1 of 1996, January 19, 1996.

International Monetary Fund. Government Finance Statistics Yearbook. Washington, D.C.: International Monetary Fund, 1994.

Jamaica Constabulary Force. Annual Report, 1995. June 1996.

Jamaica. Ministry of Agriculture. Alternative Systems for an Illegal Crop. September 1994.

Jamaica. Ministry of Justice. Crime and Justice in the Caribbean: Keynote Address by the Honorable R. Carl Rattray, Q.C., Minister of Justice and Attorney General of Jamaica. May 10, 1991.

Jamaica. National Task Force on Crime. Report of the National Task Force on Crime. Kingston, Jamaica. April 1993.

Jamaican National Export Corporation. Export Security Service Manual. Kingston, Jamaica, 1988.

Jamaica. Office of the Prime Minister. Speaking Notes for the Hon. P. J. Patterson, Q.C., M.P., at the Opening of the Regional Drug Training Center. Twickenham Park, St. Catherine, September 27, 1996.

Jamaica. Parliament. Presentation of the Hon. K. D. Knight, Minister of National Security and Justice. Budget Sectoral Debate, July 15, 1993.

———. Presentation of the Hon. K. D. Knight, Minister of National Security and Justice. Budget Sectoral Debate, June 7, 1994.

National Export Security Council, Jamaica. Statement by Amb. Peter King to the Meeting of the Maritime Security Council. San Antonio, Tex., May 1, 1996.

Official Airline Guides, Inc. Official Airline Guides. Oak Brook, Ill., June 1994.

Organization of American States. Addendum to the Report of the Drafting Group to the Fifteenth Regular Session of CICAD. OEA/Ser.L/XVI.2.15, CICAD/doc.570/94 add.1.

———. Inter-American Convention Against Corruption. OEA/Ser.K/XXXIV.1, CICOR/doc.14/96 rev. 2, March 29, 1996.

———. *Long-term Police and Training Strategies and International Coopera-tion and Coordination of Training on Control of Illicit Narcotics.* CICAD/doc.612/94, August 4, 1994.

———. *Report of the Inter-American Drug Abuse Control Commission on Measures to Implement the Strategies and Priorities of CICAD.* AG/doc.3185/95, May 4, 1995.

———. *Report of the Officer in Charge of CICAD to the Seventeenth Regular Session of the Inter-American Drug Abuse Control Commission.* CICAD/doc.683/95, February 13, 1995.

Planning Institute of Jamaica. *Economic and Social Survey, 1991.* Kingston, Jamaica, 1992.

———. *Economic and Social Survey, 1992.* Kingston, Jamaica, 1993.

———. *Economic and Social Survey, 1993.* Kingston, Jamaica, 1994.

———. *Economic and Social Survey, 1994.* Kingston, Jamaica, 1995.

———. *Economic and Social Survey, 1995.* Kingston, Jamaica, 1996.

Surrett, William Roy. *The International Narcotics Trade: An Overview of its Dimensions, Production Sources, and Organizations.* CRS Report for Congress 88–643, Oct. 3, 1988.

Trinidad and Tobago. Central Statistical Office. *Annual Statistical Digest, 1993.* 1996.

Trinidad and Tobago. Ministry of Consumer Affairs and Social Services. *Strategic Plan 1992–97.* January 1993.

Trinidad and Tobago. Ministry of National Security. *Final Report for the Government of Trinidad and Tobago on Investigations Carried out by Officers from New Scotland Yard in Respect of Allegations Made by Rodwell Murray and Others About Corruption in the Trinidad and Tobago Police Service.* July 20, 1993.

Trinidad and Tobago. Ministry of Social Development. *Report to the Cabinet Approved Committee to Examine the Juvenile Delinquency and Youth Crime Situation in Trinidad and Tobago.* January 1994.

Trinidad and Tobago. Parliament. *Report of the Commission of Inquiry into the Extent of the Problem of Drug Abuse in Trinidad and Tobago.* House Paper No. 2 of 1987.

Trinidad and Tobago. Prison Service. *Administration Report, 1993.* July 1994.

U.K. House of Commons. *Report of Mr. Rodney Gallagher of Coopers and Lybrand on the Survey of Offshore Financial Sectors in the Caribbean Dependent Territories.* London, January 19, 1990.

United Nations. *Report of the International Narcotics Control Board for 1992.* E/INCB/1992/1, 1992.

———. *Report of the International Narcotics Control Board for 1994.* E/INCB/1994/1, February 1995.

———. *Report of the International Narcotics Control Board for 1995.* E/INCB/1995/1, January 1996.

———. *Resolutions and Decisions Adopted by the General Assembly During Its Seventeenth Special Session.* February 20–23, 1990.

United Nations Development Program. *Human Development Report, 1994.* New York: Oxford University Press, 1994.

——. *Human Development Report, 1995.* New York: Oxford University Press, 1995.

United Nations International Drug Control Program. *Assistance to the [Trinidad and Tobago] National Drug Abuse Demand Reduction Program.* AD/TRI/94/910, 1994.

——. *Background Paper for Working Group I: Strengthening National Drug Control Councils.* UNDCP/CAR/1996/2, April 19, 1996.

——. *Background Paper for Working Group II: Legislation.* UNDCP/CAR/1996/3, April 17, 1996.

——. *Background Paper for Working Group III: Sub-regional Law Enforcement Cooperation.* UNDCP/CAR/1996/4, April 14, 1996.

——. *Background Paper for Working Group IV: Drug Demand Reduction.* UNDCP/CAR/1996/5, April 19, 1996.

——. *Background Paper for Working Group V: Sub-regional Maritime Cooperation.* UNDCP/CAR/1996/3, April 17, 1996.

——. *A Global Alliance for a Drug-Free Caribbean.* April 1996.

——. *Report of the Regional Meeting on Drug Control Cooperation in the Caribbean, Held at Bridgetown, Barbados, May 15–17, 1996.* UNDCP/CAR/1996/7, May 29, 1996.

——. *Status of Master Plans in the Caribbean.* September 9, 1996.

——. *Subregional Program Framework for the Caribbean, 1994–1995.* October 1994.

U.S. Central Intelligence Agency. *The World Factbook, 1994.* Washington, D.C., 1994.

——. *The World Factbook, 1995.* Washington, D.C., 1995.

U.S. Department of Justice. Drug Enforcement Administration. *Drugs of Abuse.* Washington, D.C., 1989.

——. *Illegal Price/Purity Report, January 1992–March 1995.* October 1995.

U.S. Department of Justice. National Drug Intelligence Center. *The Caribbean Connection.* May 1996.

——. *Drugs, Crime, and the Justice System.* December 1992.

——. *The Jamaica Intelligence Connection.* Report No. 95-E0117-001, January 1995.

——. *Jamaican Organized Crime: A Baseline Assessment.* May 1994.

U.S. Department of State. *International Narcotics Control Strategy Report.* Washington, D.C., March 1991.

——. *International Narcotics Control Strategy Report.* Washington, D.C., March 1992.

——. *International Narcotics Control Strategy Report.* Washington, D.C., April 1993.

——. *International Narcotics Control Strategy Report.* Washington, D.C., April 1994.

——. *International Narcotics Control Strategy Report.* Washington, D.C., March 1995.

——. *International Narcotics Control Strategy Report.* Washington, D.C., March 1996.

U.S. General Accounting Office. *Drug Control: Anti-Drug Efforts in the Baha-mas.* GAO/GGD-90-42, March 1990.

————. *Drug Control: U.S. Interdiction Efforts in the Caribbean Decline.* GAO/NSIAD-96-119, April 1996.

U.S. House. Select Committee on Narcotics Abuse and Control. *Drugs and Latin America: Economic and Political Impact, and U.S. Policy Options.* 101st Cong., 1st sess., April 26, 1989.

U.S. Office of the President. *National Drug Control Strategy.* Washington, D.C., February 1994.

————. *National Drug Control Strategy: 1996.* Washington, D.C., April 1996.

U.S. Senate. Committee on Foreign Relations. *Drug Money Laundering, Banks, and Foreign Policy.* Hearings before Subcommittee on Narcotics, Terrorism, and International Operations. 101st Cong., 2d sess., September 27, October 4, and November 1, 1989.

————. *Drugs, Law Enforcement, and Foreign Policy: The Cartel, Haiti, and Central America.* Hearings. Subcommittee on Terrorism, Narcotics, and International Operations. Pt. 4. 100th Cong., 2d sess., July 11, 12, 14, 1988.

————. *International Narcotics Control and Foreign Affairs Certification: Requirements, Procedures, Timetables, and Guidelines.* 100th Cong., 2d sess., March 1988.

————. *Recent Developments in Transnational Crime Affecting U.S. Law Enforcement and Foreign Policy; Mutual Legal Assistance Treaty in Criminal Matters with Panama, Treaty Doc. 102–15; and 1994 International Narcotics Control Strategy Report.* Hearings. Subcommittee on Terrorism, Narcotics, and International Operations. 103rd Cong., 2d sess., April 20 and 21, 1994.

U.S. Senate. Committee on Governmental Affairs. *Arms Trafficking, Mercenaries, and Drug Cartels.* Hearing. Permanent Subcommittee on Investigations. 102d Cong., 1st sess., February 27 and 28, 1991.

————. *Cocaine Production, Eradication, and the Environment: Policy, Impact, and Options.* 101st Cong., 2d sess., August 1990.

————. *Crime and Secrecy: The Use of Off-shore Banks and Companies.* Permanent Subcommittee on Investigations, 99th Cong., 1st sess., August 28, 1985.

————. *Current Trends in Money Laundering.* Report by the Permanent Subcommittee on Investigations. 102d Cong., 2d sess., December 1992.

————. *Illicit Narcotics: Recent Efforts to Control Chemical Diversion and Money Laundering.* December 1993.

UWI/UNDCP Drug Control Legal Training Program. *Drug Offenses Workshop for Magistrates, Held in Georgetown, Guyana, June 3–4, 1994.* 1994.

West Indian Commission. *Time for Action: The Report of the West Indian Commission.* Black Rock, Barbados, 1992.

Interviews and Conversations

Name	Title	Place	Date
Dave Alexander	Drug Avoidance Officer, Grenada	St. George's	July 11, 1994
Dr. Francis Alexis	Attorney General, Grenada	St. George's	July 12, 1994
Capt. Anthony Allens	Acting Chief of Staff, RBDF	Nassau	August 15, 1996
Comdr. Albert Ambrister	Commanding Officer, Commando Squadron, RBDF	Nassau	August 15, 1996
Michel Amiot	Regional Director for Caribbean, UNDCP;	Bridgetown telephone	July 15, 1994 various times in 1995
	Technical Adviser on Drugs, European Union	Bridgetown	October 23, 1996
Glen Andrade	Director of Public Prosecutions, Jamaica	Port of Spain telephone	January 20, 1995 various times in 1995
		Kingston	August 13, 1996
Comdr. Chris Annamunthodo	Chief of Military Intelligence, JDF	Kingston	August 12, 1996
Asst. Supt. George Antoinne	Head, Grenada Special Branch	St. George's	July 11, 1994
Linda Baboolall, M.D.	Minister of Social Development, Trinidad	Port of Spain	July 7, 1994
Cipriani Baptiste	Acting Comm. of Prisons, Trinidad	Port of Spain telephone	July 7, 1994 June 16, 1995
Jules Bernard	Commissioner of Police, Trinidad	Port of Spain	July 8, 1994
Capt. Thomas E. Bernard	Commanding Officer, GANTSEC	San Juan	May 17, 1996
Lt. Comdr. Gary Best	Acting Head, Guyana Coast Guard	Georgetown	July 1, 1994
Lt. Comdr. Matthew M. Blizzard	Chief of Law Enforcement, GANTSEC	San Juan	May 17, 1996
Roy Bouchier	CEO, International Trade & Investments, Ltd.	Nassau	August 15, 1996

Name	Title	Place	Date
Rear Adm. Peter Brady	Chief of Staff, JDF	Kingston Miami	December 19, 1994 April 25, 1996
Donald Brown	Asst. Commissioner, JCF	Kingston	August 13, 1996
Louis Bryan	Permanent Secretary, Ministry of Social Development	Port of Spain	July 7, 1994
Lewis Burchal	Asst. Superintendent, JCF	Kingston	August 13, 1996
Comdr. Neil Buschman	Operations Officer, GANTSEC	San Juan	May 17, 1996
Arlington Butler	Minister of Public Safety, Bahamas	Nassau	December 22, 1994
Leroy Cadore	Acting Asst. Commissioner of Police, Grenada	St. George's	July 11, 1994
John Carrington	Legal Officer, Trinidad and Tobago Central Bank	telephone	July 12, 1995
Asst. Supt. John Charles	Head, Grenada Coast Guard	St. George's	July 11, 1994
Nelson Clark, M.D.	Psychiatrist, Doctors Hospital	Nassau	December 21, 1994
Supt. James Clarkson	Head, Grenada Crime Prevention and Community Affairs	St. George's	July 11, 1994
Lt. Col. Edward Collins	Chief of Military Intelligence, GDF	Georgetown	June 30, 1994
Winston Courtney	Commissioner of Prisons, Grenada	St. George's	July 12, 1994
Edward Cumberbatch	General Secretary, CCC	Bridgetown	July 19, 1994
Muki Daniel	Asst. Regional Director for Caribbean, UNDCP	Bridgetown	October 23, 1996
Maurice Darius	Asst. Commissioner of Police, Grenada	St. George's	July 11, 1994
Dr. Carlton Davies	Secretary to the Cabinet, Jamaica	Kingston	August 12, 1996

Name	Title	Place	Date
Lt. Col. Allan Douglas	Staff Officer, Operations and Training, JDF	Kingston	December 19, 1994
Maj. Paul C. Dunn	Military Intelligence Officer, JDF	Kingston	August 12, 1996
Orville Durant	Commissioner of Police, Barbados	Bridgetown	July 19, 1994
Capt. Desmond Edwards	Military Intelligence Officer, JDF	Kingston Kingston	December 19, 1994 August 13, 1996*
Beverly Eighmy	Caribbean Program Officer, INL	telephone	various times in 1995
Errol Farquharson	Deputy Commissioner of Police, RBPF	Nassau	August 15, 1996
Calvin Farrier	Chief Secretary, Ministry of Home Affairs, St. Kitts–Nevis	Port of Spain	January 20, 1995
Asst. Comm. Winston Felix	Deputy Crime Chief, Guyana Police Force	Georgetown	June 28, 1994
Supt. Reginald Ferguson	Chief, Drug Enforcement Unit, RBPF	Nassau telephone	December 22, 1994 September 1995
Thelma Ferguson	Permanent Secretary, Ministry of Justice and Immigration, Bahamas	Nassau	December 21, 1994
Supt. Reynell Frazer	Brit. Virgin I. Police Force	Port of Spain	January 20, 1995
Ronald Frazier	Acting Permanent Secretary, Home Affairs, Guyana	Georgetown	July 1, 1994
Yvonne Gittens-Joseph	Head, Political Division, Ministry of External Affairs and Int'l Trade	Port of Spain	July 8, 1994
Alvin Goodwin	Deputy Commissioner of Police, RABPF	Port of Spain	January 21, 1995
David Granger	Publisher, *Guyana Review*	Georgetown telephone	various times in 1994 and 1995

Name	Title	Place	Date
Fred Hanna	Superintendent, RBPF	Nassau	August 15, 1996
William Harry	Deputy Commissioner, RSVGPF	Port of Spain	January 20, 1995
Joshua Hubbard	Asst. Comptroller of Customs, Guyana	Georgetown	July 1, 1994
Amb. Jeanette Hyde	U.S. Amb. to Barbados and Eastern Caribbean	Bridgetown	July 18, 1994
Maj. George Kates	Security Intelligence Officer, JDF	Kingston	August 12, 1996
Capt. Richard Kelshall	Acting Chief of Defense Staff, TTDF	Chaguaramas	July 5, 1994
Keith Kerwood	Foreign Service Officer, Ministry of External Affairs and Int'l Trade	Port of Spain	July 8, 1994
Amb. Peter King	Chair, National Export Security Council	Kingston	August 12, 1996
Richard King	Managing Director, PSC, Jamaica	Kingston	August 14, 1996
Rev. Dr. Kingsley Lewis	President, Caribbean Council of Churches	St. John's	August 20, 1996
Laurie Lewis	Commissioner of Police, Guyana	Georgetown	July 1, 1994
Peter Lewis, M.D.	Chair, TACADA	Port of Spain	July 5, 1994
Lt. Comdr. Steven R. Lilly	Naval Liaison Officer, U.S. Embassy, Bahamas	Nassau	August 16, 1996
Col. Trevor N. N. Macmillan	Commissioner of Police, Jamaica	Kingston	August 13, 1996
Feroze Mohammed	Minister of Home Affairs, Guyana	Georgetown	July 1, 1994
Judge Stanley Moore	Eastern Caribbean Supreme Court	St. George's	July 11, 12, 1994
Ezekiel Munning	Drug Program Coordinator, Bahamas	Nassau	December 22, 1994

Name	Title	Place	Date
Lt. Comdr. Wayne Mykoo	Commanding Officer, ABDF Coast Guard	St. John's	August 19, 1996
Paul Nolan	Legal Attaché, U.S. Embassy, Barbados	Bridgetown	July 15, 1994
Basil G. O'Brien	Secretary to the Cabinet, Bahamas	Nassau	August 16, 1996
Irmia Osoba, Ph.D.	Resident Tutor, UWI	St. John's	August 19, 1996
Asst. Supt. Rawlston Pompey	Staff Officer to Commissioner of Police	St. John's	August 20, 1996
Dr. Kenneth Rattray	Solicitor General of Jamaica	Kingston	August 12, 1996
Supt. Ray Raymond	Head, Grenada SSU	St. George's	July 11, 1994
Idris G. Reid	Permanent Secretary, Ministry of Public Safety and Immigration	Nassau	August 16, 1996
Vincent Richards	Drug Abuse Consultant	Georgetown	June 28, 1994
Nathanial Rolle	Asst. Commissioner of Police, Bahamas	Nassau	August 15, 1996
Alvin Rollins	Asst. Country Attaché, DEA, Barbados	Bridgetown	July 18, 1994
Lancelot Selman	Director, Strategic Services Agency, Trinidad and Tobago	Port of Spain telephone	July 4, 1994 various times in 1995
Brig. Joseph Singh	Chief of Staff, GDF	Georgetown	June 30, 1994
Trueheart O. M. Smith	Deputy Commissioner of Police, Antigua-Barbuda	St. John's	August 20, 1996
Hon. Baldwin Spencer	Leader, United Progressive Party	St. John's	August 19, 1996
Dawne Spicer	Legal Officer, Strategic Services Agency	Port of Spain	July 4, 1996

Name	Title	Place	Date
Wilton Strachan	Sr. Asst. Commissioner of Police, RBPF	Nassau	August 15, 1996
Errol Strong	Deputy Commissioner of Police, JCF	Kingston	August 13, 1996
Sean Terry	Political Officer, U.S. Embassy, Barbados	Bridgetown	July 15, 1994
Lt. Col. Trevor A. Thomas	Commander, ABDF	St. John's	August 19, 1996
G. R. Thorne	Comptroller of Customs, Grenada	St. George's	July 12, 1994
Lt. Comdr. Michal D. Tosatto	U.S. Coast Guard Liaison Officer, Bahamas	Nassau	August 16, 1996
Brig. Allan Usher	National Security Coordinator, Belize	Miami telephone	March and July, 1995
Sherrilyn Wallace	Director, National Drug Council, Bahamas	Nassau	December 22, 1994
Lennox Watson	Acting Deputy Commissioner of Prisons, Trinidad	Port of Spain	July 7, 1994
Tim Wren	Executive Director, CFATF	telephone telephone	July 11, 1995 October 26, 1996
Capt. Paul Zukunft	Commanding Officer, USCG cutter *Harriet Lane*	Caribbean Sea	May 17–19, 1996

NOTES:
1. Interviews where anonymity was requested are unlisted.
2. The titles listed are those held at the time of the interviews. Several of the people interviewed now have new positions.

*Rank at the time of this interview was Major.

Names Index

Subject Index